DENATURALIZING

Alienation from Nature from Rousseau to the Frankfurt School and Beyond

Denaturalizing Ecological Politics is an attempt to excavate from modern political thought a means of rescuing human ecology – humans' relationship with their environment – from the ideological trap of naturalism. In this work Andrew Biro develops a political theory of nature that takes seriously both the reality of the ecological crises generated by industrial and postindustrial society, and the antifoundationalist critiques of 'nature' developed in postmodern social theory.

The book opens with a discussion of the deep ecologists, who argue for a view of nature as prior to the social, and who see nature as a guide for, or absolute limit to, human action. Following is a look at the structuralist and poststructuralist social theorists, who claim that our understanding of nature is solely an effect of the social – an ideological reinforcement of social structures. In the remaining chapters the author's readings of Rousseau, Marx, Adorno, and Marcuse provide the starting point for a 'denaturalized' rethinking of ecological politics. Through a close examination of primary texts and relevant secondary sources focused on the concept of 'alienation from nature,' Biro argues that an adequate understanding of human ecology must see human beings not as biologically separate from the rest of nature, but as historically differentiated through the self-conscious transformation of the natural environment. He maintains that only after the complexities of the intertwining of nature and the social are fully grasped can we begin to disentangle the social relations and processes that are necessary for a liberatory human ecology from those that serve to reinforce relations of domination.

ANDREW BIRO is an assistant professor and Canada Research Chair in the Department of Political Science at Acadia University.

ANDREW BIRO

Denaturalizing Ecological Politics

Alienation from Nature from Rousseau to the Frankfurt School and Beyond

UNIVERSITY OF TORONTO PRESS
Toronto Buffalo London

Toronto Buffalo London
Printed in Canada

ISBN 0-8020-8022-7 (cloth)
ISBN 0-8020-3794-1 (paper)

Printed on acid-free paper

Library and Archives Canada Cataloguing in Publication

Biro, Andrew, 1969–
Denaturalizing ecological politics : alienation from nature from Rousseau to the Frankfurt School and beyond / Andrew Biro.

Includes bibliographical references and index.
ISBN 0-8020-8022-7 (bound). ISBN 0-8020-3794-1 (pbk.)

1. Political ecology. 2. Nature – Political aspects. 3. Human ecology – Political aspects. 4. Alienation (Philosophy) I. Title.

GE40.B57 2005 403.2′01 C2004-907410-5

This book has been published with the help of a grant from the Canadian Federation for the Humanities and Social Sciences, through the Aid to Scholarly Publications Programme, using funds provided by the Social Sciences and Humanities Research Council of Canada.

University of Toronto Press acknowledges the financial assistance to its publishing program of the Canada Council and the Ontario Arts Council.

University of Toronto Press acknowledges the financial support for its publishing activities of the Government of Canada through the Book Publishing Industry Development Program (BPIDP).

For Lisa,

for everything

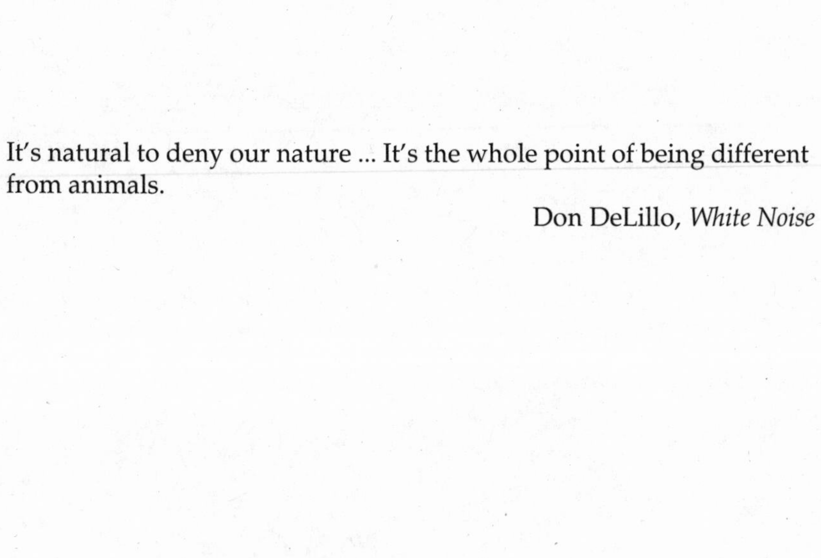

It's natural to deny our nature ... It's the whole point of being different from animals.

Don DeLillo, *White Noise*

Contents

Acknowledgments

This book began as a PhD dissertation at York University. Important revisions were done while I was a postdoctoral fellow at the University of Toronto, and now, at last, the book is being finished at Acadia University. Along the way, a number of friends and family members commented on what seemed to them the 'lonely' nature of academic work, and of textual analysis in particular. But like all forms of labour, the writing of a book has a strong social component, and this one could not have been completed without the friendship and support of many people. I want to acknowledge them here.

My dissertation supervisor, Asher Horowitz, steered me through the intellectual challenges of the project itself, as well as through the challenges of completing graduate school and beginning an academic career. Thanks are also due to Gord Laxer and Stephen Clarkson, who enabled and supervised my stint at the University of Toronto. At various stages, a number of people offered sympathetic critiques of portions of the manuscript, or on all of it. They included Asher Horowitz, Rob Albritton, Shannon Bell, Roger Keil, Nick Xenos, Shane Gunster, and Catherine Kellogg. Greg Pyrcz offered helpful suggestions on the Rousseau chapter, and also helped in many ways to ease the transition from Toronto to Nova Scotia. Steven Hayward read more than I thought right to impose, consistently made insightful comments, and was a source of support in many other ways besides. Two anonymous reviewers solicited by the press provided constructive and supportive feedback, and Matthew Kudelka's editorial assistance helped refine and clarify the prose. Stephen Kotowych and Virgil Duff of University of Toronto Press provided, I am sure, more help than I can ever know in getting the book published.

Intellectual and emotional support in various forms came from a great many people, many of whom I met while at York in the late 1990s. They made that time and place – and the Department of Political Science in particular – the source of an excellent education in political science and politics.These people included: Greg Albo, Julian Ammirante, Judy Barton, Davina Bhandar, Marlea Clarke, Regina Cochrane, Barbara Falk, Peter Fargey, Fred Fletcher, Katrin Froese, Samir Gandesha, Derek Hrynyshyn, Peter Ives, Pam Leach, Roddy Loeppky, Michelle Mawhinney, Steve Newman, Peter Nyers, Leo Panitch, Jason Potts, Marlene Quesenberry, Chris Roberts, Stephanie Ross, John Saul, Yasmine Shamsie, David Shugarman, and Keith Stewart. My doctoral research was also supported by a fellowship from the Social Sciences and Humanities Council of Canada. At Acadia I now find myself in a supportive and engaging intellectual community, one that has helped me get through the final stages of revising and polishing the manuscript. Thanks on that score are due to Paul Abela, Edith Callaghan, Graham Daborn, David Duke, Antonio Franceschet, Susan Franceschet, Greg Pyrcz, Bruce Matthews, John Roff, and Ian Stewart, and also to the Canada Research Chairs program, which allowed me to come to Acadia.

Teaching courses in contemporary political thought at York in 1998, and in critical political theory at Acadia in 2004, not only nicely bookended the writing process, but also helped clarify my thinking about some of the issues discussed herein. Along with the good students in those courses, I have also been fortunate to have a number of excellent teachers. Some of them, at York, are mentioned above. Others – Joe Carens, Gad Horowitz, and Alkis Kontos, as well as Richard Barry and Terry Maley – introduced me to the field of political theory and encouraged my study of it. Larry Peters deserves credit for being the first to teach me to think about learning to read and write as a lifelong project. A number of other people helped in ways too numerous to detail, but no less important: Lang Baker, Steve Bull, Drew Evans, Dave Goutor, Ronni Hannon, Arnd Juergensen, Lou Kaczmarek, Gabrielle Kemeny, Tom Kemeny, Mike Lakatos, Jean Paul Laurin, Michael Ma, Dave McGuffin, Kelly McLeod, Lara Mills, Chris O'Brien, Dave Pearce, Ed Yeh, and especially Alex Cobb.

Finally, many members of my extended family – grandparents, cousins, uncles and aunts, in-laws – provided love, support, and humour, without which this project surely would not have been completed. My sister Susie, even when she was on the other side of the world, was always there for me, and the encouragement and support of my parents, George and Eva, for as long as I can remember, has been absolutely unstinting. And the depth of generosity, patience, and love that I have received from my partner, Lisa Speigel, to whom this book is dedicated, continues to astonish me. Since I began writing this book, our two children, Kaela and Nathan, have come into our lives, while my grandfather, Emery Gero, has departed. Although these changes happened only in the later stages of writing this book, each has become retroactively – but in a way that is no less real – an important part of the inspiration for it.

Portions of chapters 1 and 2 appeared as 'Towards a Denaturalized Ecological Politics' in the Winter 2002 issue of *Polity*.

DENATURALIZING ECOLOGICAL POLITICS

INTRODUCTION

Nature or 'Nature'? Ecological Politics and the Postmodern Condition

In an often cited phrase, Raymond Williams begins a definition of 'nature' by stating that it 'is perhaps the most complex word in the English language' (Williams 1976, 184). And as a host of recent writers have made clear, it has become especially troublesome of late. On the one hand, recent social and political theory has worked very hard to insist that claims about 'nature' are necessarily mediated by culturally specific prejudices: that when we talk about 'nature,' we are really only talking about our particular society's ideas about nature. In this sense, appeals to 'nature' can be seen as inherently socially conservative; and if this is indeed the case, then any sort of radical or even progressive politics that is worthy of the name must be willing to cast a highly skeptical eye on any claim that invokes 'nature' as the basis of its authority. When we are confronted with claims that, for example, women's nature makes them ill suited to certain professions, or that people of African descent are naturally less intelligent than Europeans, it is not difficult for us to see the appeal of this sort of scepticism.

But things look rather different when we are confronted with, for example, business lobby groups' claims that economic growth should not be curtailed to protect the natural environment – that in other words, there are no natural limits that might act as a brake on economic expansion. In other words, when we leave the terrain of, say, gender or 'race' for that of environmental issues, progressive politics seems to demand that we take precisely the opposite tack. Here the impulse is to argue that there are indeed certain natural limits and that we cannot culturally construct a new definition of nature as a way of averting ecological catastrophe. Contemporary progressive politics thus seems to demand both a defence of nature and a thorough-going critique of 'nature.'

Since the mid-1990s, a number of works have tackled head-on this problematic dichotomy. In *Postmodernism and the Environmental Crisis*, for example, Arran Gare sees the opposition as stemming from a disjunction between the 'two cultures' of literature and science, and argues that 'to address properly either the issues raised by the postmodernist condition or the environmental crisis, this disjunction will have to be overcome' (Gare 1995, 2). In an effort to overcome this opposition, Gare introduces a 'new grand narrative' grounded in the philosophy of process.

Similarly, Kate Soper in *What Is Nature?* ultimately defends a 'realist' conception of nature, which she describes as one that 'achiev[es] some reconciliation of these two perspectives' (1995, 8). In her book, Soper moves through a series of deconstructions of the two poles – which she terms 'nature endorsing' and 'nature skeptical' – and demonstrates how each pole ultimately relies on the other. Although she rightly cautions against reading broad political labels too quickly from what are ultimately epistemological arguments – and urges us to avoid the 'presumption ... that these [labels] reflect some simple antithesis between a "green" and a "postmodernist" politics' (4) – such labels are difficult to avoid. In spite of certain similarities and complementarities,

> to focus on this difference is to be made aware of the extent of tension between these seemingly complementary forms of resistance to Western modernity. For while the ecologists tend to invoke nature as a domain of instrinsic value, truth or authenticity and are relatively unconcerned with questions of representation and conceptuality, postmodernist cultural theory and criticism looks with suspicion on any appeal to the idea [of nature] as an attempt to 'eternize' what in reality is merely conventional, and has invited us to view the order of nature as entirely linguistically constructed. (6)

Soper's realist perspective points to the fact that all claims about nature are political – which is not to deny nature's extra-discursive existence. Following her vein, we arrive at the finding that the 'value' of nature and the naturality of particular forms of behaviour cannot be deduced solely from natural scientific inquiry; furthermore, there are natural 'structures, processes and causal powers that are constantly operative within the physical world,' as well as a 'nature to whose laws we are always subject, even as we harness them to human purposes, and whose processes we can neither escape nor destroy' (155–6).

In *Uneven Development*, Neil Smith – like Gare and Soper – shows how both 'scientific' and 'romantic' conceptions posit nature as simultaneously 'external' to human culture *and* 'universal' (and hence applicable to human affairs) (1990, 3–16). Smith, like Soper and Gare, contends that the path through this binary opposition involves positing a third understanding of nature. Ultimately, however, Smith's Marxian understanding of nature takes the side of the social production of 'nature': 'nature is nothing if not social ... What must be done is to show the concrete relationship by which nature is invested with this social priority' (30). Finally, approaching the dichotomy from a slightly different perspective – arguing against what he terms 'derivative' and 'dualist' accounts of the relationship between nature and politics – John M. Meyer (2001) calls for a 'constitutive' understanding of nature: for nature as a category that is necessarily politically delineated.

Ultimately, all four of these authors share a great deal. They differ in certain ways, but those differences are mainly of shading and emphasis. All four already offer something like what I will be arguing for here, namely, a 'denaturalized ecological politics.' The distinguishing feature of what I will offer relates not so much to the content of my conclusions, as to the form in which I wil be presenting my argument. Of course, form and content are inevitably linked – a point I will take up at length in due course – so to say that only the form is different while the content remains the same would be somewhat disingenuous. My point here is that the form this book takes will be dictated by its content – that is, by the particular inflection I want to give to these ongoing debates about the status of nature within progressive theorizations of politics.

Ideas of nature are of course not only highly complex and contradictory, but also deeply embedded, both individually and culturally, and they affect virtually every aspect of our lives. They are in fact the very definition of ideological. We do not simply choose a conception of nature the way we might choose a new car, by weighing the pros and cons of this or that option. Nor, assuming that we can take on a new conception of nature (something that clearly at some level must be possible), is the process like trading an old model for a new one, or, to choose a more environmentally friendly example, selling one's car in favour of taking public transit. The choice is not a simple binary one ('yesterday I believed nature was like a machine, today I believe it is a provident Goddess'), but neither is it entirely an individual one. The terms that Raymond Williams applies to this problematic when discussing culture and hegemony – the relevance of these terms here may be already apparent – are 'dominant, residual, and emergent' (1977, 121–8). So instead of beginning by stating the conception of human-nature relations that I will argue is necessary to avoid both socially rationalized domination and ecological catastrophe, I will begin simply by stating that this book will arrive at that conception eventually. And I will reach it through a genealogical tracing that will allow us to see such a conception as an emergent one – without, of course, suggesting that its eventual dominance is guaranteed. A historical account of past ideas of nature will be indispensable for understanding my conception; furthermore, once we see how those ideas are embedded in historical trajectories, that they are not simply free floating, we will be able to embrace a certain amount of hope that a new conception will be adopted, even though the end points of those trajectories are by no means certain.

To begin this genealogical tracing, then, let us return to our original dilemma: can we claim that appeals to nature are always in fact appeals to culturally specific *ideas* of nature, and yet still maintain an ecologically grounded defence of nature? We can observe first that this is not an eternal question. In fact, its emergence can be dated fairly precisely: both the modern environmental movement and radical critiques of 'nature' in social scientific theory began to emerge around the 1960s. From an environmentalist's perspective, the decade is bracketed by the publication of Rachel Carson's *Silent Spring* in 1962 and the first 'Earth Day,' held on 22 April 1970. This decade is also often marked as the starting point of postmodern theory, or at least its immediate French structuralist and post-structuralist antecedents: Roland Barthes's *Mythologies* (1957), Michel Foucault's *Madness and Civilization* (1967), Jacques Derrida's *Margins of Philosophy* (1967), and Jean Baudrillard's influential collection of essays, *For a Critique of the Political Economy of the Sign* (1972). In France, of course, these texts constitute the intellectual bookends for *les evenements* of May and June 1968. More globally, postmodern theory is associated with the rise of the 'new social movements' (including, of course, contemporary environmentalism itself), which carried the bulk of the progressive political impulses that remained after the rise and fall of the New Left. In other words, at almost precisely the same time as the defence of nature was becoming articulated as a radical and global social movement, radical social theory was working to unmask the ways in which 'nature,' in all its guises and all its forms, was an ideological construct.

This is not merely a perverse coincidence. It does not simply demonstrate how concrete forms of political action can perpetuate precisely the ideological structures that theory finds at the root of the problem; nor does it simply demonstrate how putatively radical academic inquiry leads to relativism and political paralysis, depending on one's perspective. The truth of the matter is quite different: Fredric Jameson's analysis of this privileged decade helps us understand that these apparently contradictory social forces emerged as the product of a deeper historical logic (Jameson 1988). For Jameson, the 1960s were not only (as it is commonly perceived) a time of profound *crisis* for capitalism, but also, simultaneously, a time when capitalism underwent a dynamic expansion. Drawing on Ernest Mandel's periodization, Jameson notes that in that decade, a number of events converged so as to mark those years as the birth stages of 'late capitalism.' Two developments were key. The first was decolonization in the Third World, accompanied by the Green Revolution, which is increasingly tying Third World agricultural production to networks of commodity exchange. The second was the rise in the First World of what Guy Debord (1995) has called the 'society of the spectacle' – a highly mediatized culture, accompanied by the detachment of signs from their referents (and of signifiers from signifieds) in such a way that 'culture' now simultaneously embraces everything and has lost its autonomy from other levels, thus vitiating its potentially critical character. 'Late capitalism,' for Jameson, 'can therefore be described as the moment when the last vestiges of Nature which survived onto classical capitalism have been eliminated: namely the Third World and the unconscious. The 60s will then have been the momentous transformational period when this systematic restructuring takes place on a global scale' (1988, 207).

In this essay, Jameson noted a shift in the 'hot spots' of resistance to capitalism, from the industrial working class to an array of social movements. Yet in the same essay, he never quite perceived resistance to capitalism as a *defence of nature*. For Jameson the social movements of the 1960s, from Third World national liberation movements to the hippies to feminism, were all expressions of the contradictions of late capitalism. Yet surprisingly absent from his list was the environmental movement itself.

He rectified this absence in a later essay, in which he offered environmentalism a more central place. In 'The Antinomies of Postmodernity,' he notes the 'host of remarkable and dramatic "revivals" of nature,' which include identity politics based on naturalized senses of identity, to be sure, but also 'the passionate ... revival' of 'ecological Nature' (Jameson 1994, 46). Making the observation that we have already seen others make, he points out that these 'revivals' of nature occur at precisely the moments when the concept of nature is problematized by antifoundationalist and anti-essentialist philosophy. Late capitalism's colonization of 'Nature' in all of its guises (the Third World, the unconscious, the body, and so on) spins out two apparently contradictory responses: an insistence on the importance and value of nature as something external to the increasingly totalizing matrix of social relations; and at the same time an insistence that all understandings of 'nature' are always already products of the social.

But if the critique of 'nature' seems to be an ideological reflection of capitalist longings, wherein all that is solidly natural melts into the air of socially constituted exchange-value, Jameson nevertheless insists that the *defence* of nature is equally problematic. He claims to want to retain the importance of certain ecological truths – in particular the growing awareness of the ecological destruction perpetrated by capitalism – yet he also insists that the defence of nature is far from being identical with an emancipatory political program. Noting that ecology often calls for the 'repression' or moderation of human desires, Jameson states: 'It is important to identify this repressive dimension of the contemporary ecological ethic, about which it does not particularly matter whether it is voluntary and self-administered or not (or perhaps one should suggest that it is far worse if it *is* voluntary and self-administered), in order to grasp the kinship between a politics most of us feel to be positive and ideologically desirable and one we may feel rather differently about, namely contemporary authoritarianism' (1994, 48).

Jameson's analysis of late capitalism thus brings us back to the familiar antinomical binary: either nature is something to be passionately defended against capitalist predations, or 'nature' can always be revealed as an ideological mask for oppressive social relations. But it cannot, at least as the problem is so formulated, be both at once. The deconstruction of 'nature' can point to conservative or even reactionary tendencies in certain environmental political programs, and the ecological defence of nature can point to the moral relativism of postmodern social theory, in an apparently seamless cycle of mutual critique.

What seems to be required, and what this book will point toward, is a way of talking about nature that avoids both uncritical endorsement and paralysing scepticism – in other words, something that will allow us to talk about both nature and 'nature' at once. What is attempted here obviously requires that we not champion one pole at the expense of the other, but it also eschews any effort at dialectical sublation that would consume both perspectives in order to generate a greater whole. I will argue that this attempt to arrive at an emancipatory ecological politics must take particular care with regard to its recourse – rhetorical or otherwise – to 'nature' (a point quite rightly made by a number of the authors already cited); and furthermore, that the debates over the politics of nature/'nature' need to be reframed or supplemented by including a new category: nature viewed, as it were, from the other side of the glass – alienation from nature.

The first two chapters will point out the truth value of what Soper calls the nature-endorsing and the nature-sceptical positions. At the same time, these chapters will point to the political shortcomings and logical contradictions of these positions. Much of mainstream and even radical environmentalism – the subject of the first chapter – rightly draws attention to human embeddedness in natural processes and the ecological devastation that is so often wrought in the name of 'development.' But arguments for a more 'natural' way of organizing society (for example, critiques of anthropocentrism, and arguments for a more positive valuation of 'natural' objects and processes) obscure the ways in which our understandings of what is 'natural' are always culturally conditioned. At the other extreme, postmodern social theory, considered in chapter 2, aims – and rightly so – to point out the ways in which all political categories, including 'nature,' are ideologically charged. But the conclusions to be drawn from this (remember here Lyotard's famous injunction to express scepticism toward totalizing narratives) may lead us to moral relativism and political quiescence, or at the very least to an emphasis on the purely local that neglects analysis of the global drivers of ecological crises.

What is required is a way of talking about nature that is sensitive to the truth value of both of these positions, but that does not succumb to their logical or political shortcomings. The rest of the book is mainly an attempt to excavate such a position by developing the category of 'alienation from nature' in the works of Jean-Jacques Rousseau, Karl Marx, Theodor Adorno, and Herbert Marcuse. If the formulation of an ecological politics adequate for the postmodern era were simply a matter of dropping this felicitous phrase into political arguments, then going back to the eighteenth century might indeed seem an unnecessary philosophical diversion. But the phrase lacks the sort of magical aura that would allow it to instantaneously transform the landscape of political arguments. Rather, the phrase itself must be understood as a form of shorthand, an allegorical figure, partly captured by the idea of thinking about human society as simultaneously embedded in, and apart from, natural processes.

As well, this understanding of the phrase as an allegory suggests that the excavation of such a way of thinking cannot simply be a matter of 'clocking the phrase' – that is, tracing its appearances through various canonical texts. Each of chapters 3 to 6 discusses how the political theories of the respective authors suggest what the phrase might stand for. More specifically – and to return to the point about the importance of the form of presentation – I will develop the authors' theories both by negotiating the primary texts and by restaging selected interpretive debates in the secondary literature. This might strike some as extensive detours into debates over divergent interpretations of the political theorists; actually, it is at least in part a means of organizing the theorists' overarching arguments. But also, and more important, the persistent recourse to contemporary interpretive debates will help us retain a certain volatility or tension within those theoretical structures (as well, of course, as an implicit argument for the theorists' continued relevance). In other words, within the form of the argument, or its methodology, lies a claim that certain strategies of reading can better allow us to see historical texts and their contemporary interpretations as intertwined aspects of evolving theoretical totalities.

This metatheoretical claim that sees political theories as volatile or evolving is especially important here, because I will be arguing that each of the authors, read in conjunction with particular interpretations, develops a way of thinking about 'alienation from nature' in a manner that allows for certain important distinctions to be made, without succumbing to either side of the antinomical binary discussed earlier. Thus, the sometimes complementary, sometimes contradictory, interpretations of each theorist that I elaborate will serve to highlight both the difficulties of maintaining the tensions of such a finely balanced argument, and its character as an ongoing project rather than an achieved product.

The need to make such distinctions perhaps also helps explain the seemingly curious choice of figures to be discussed in a book on ecological political theory or understandings of 'nature' in modern Western political thought. No doubt, others could have been chosen: Locke, Kant, Burke, Hegel, Mill, Nietzsche, Heidegger, and others. All have important things to say about 'nature' – about its culturally constructed character or the perils of the modern way of relating to it. What each of the four figures who form the central focus of the discussion here can do, however, as we shall see, is provide at least the beginnings of a way of thinking that allows us to think about both of these problems of 'nature' at once. The book's concluding chapter – which discusses selected trends and figures in contemporary environmental political theory – is thus an attempt to see the usefulness of such an understanding of alienation from nature for contemporary debates. It is an attempt, like the book as a whole, to argue for the relevance of a denaturalized ecological politics.

CHAPTER 1

Ecocentrism and the Defence of Nature

> This myth of the human 'condition' rests on a very old mystification, which always consists in placing Nature at the bottom of History ... Progressive humanism, on the contrary, must always remember to reverse the terms of this very old imposture, constantly to scour nature, its 'laws' and its 'limits' in order to discover History there, and at last to establish Nature itself as historical.
>
> Barthes 1973, 101

It should be noted at the outset that not all 'environmentalist' thought points to the need to thoroughly transform contemporary society. Indeed, given that support for 'environmental' issues is currently embraced by a large proportion of the population, at least some varieties of 'environmentalism' must sit quite comfortably with social conservatism. As Timothy Luke observed in the 1990s: 'Many major corporations now feel moved to proclaim how much "every day is Earth Day" in their shop, what a meaningful relationship they have with nature, or why their manufactures are produced with constant care for the planet's biosphere' (1997, 116). On the other hand, the scope of ecological change on a broad variety of fronts – including atmospheric pollution, climate change, ozone depletion, and species extinction – should serve as a warning that reformist proposals may not be enough to avert catastrophe. As well, the difficulty of implementing even fairly moderate changes, such as the Kyoto Protocol for the reduction of greenhouse gases – within existing political and economic frameworks suggests that radical changes in the ways in which we interact with the natural environment will require radical changes to social structures. If we recall

Jameson's characterization of capitalism as a system wherein 'nature' is increasingly penetrated and colonized by the social, such that *everything* must eventually become a resource for the necessarily ceaseless expansion of capital, then it becomes increasingly clear that an ecologically benign version of capitalism is an impossibility (Kovel 2002). What is required, to use Arne Naess's highly influential terms, is a 'deep' rather than a 'shallow' form of ecological thought and practice (Naess 1973).

At the same time, it is important not to overstate the extent to which a recognition that capitalism is ecologically destructive translates into a diagnosis of capitalist relations as the root of ecological problems. Given the ecological devastation that has been perpetratd by avowedly anti-capitalist societies in the twentieth century, it is hardly surprising that there is little agreement among environmentalists – even among 'radical' environmentalists – as to whether capitalism or something else constitutes the 'ultimately determining instance' of ecological crises. For many, the problem lies not so much in the economic structures of society, but rather in an unwarranted privileging of human beings over the rest of nature (anthropocentrism). There are two moments to this critique of anthropocentrism, each of which I will consider in turn. The first is the philosophical critique of anthropocentrism, whereby ontological claims are used to argue against the unwarranted privileging of human beings in moral arguments. The second is the axiological approach, which argues that a higher value should be accorded to nature.

Questioning Anthropocentrism

A common caricature of radical environmentalists suggests that they are in full revolt against modernity – against modern science and technology in particular. For example one of the slogans of the ecocentric group Earth First! is 'Back to the Pleistocene!' (Thiele 1999, 227). Such a caricature is confounded, however, by the ways that deep ecologists so often marshal scientific evidence (often gathered through highly technologically advanced means) in support of their claims that we are indeed facing a profound ecological crisis. As Andrew Ross has noted, 'ecology [is] exceptional among social and political movements in its overriding appeal to science for proof of the justice of ecological claims' (1991, 194). This dialectic is at work in broader ways as well: Although in many ways hardly radical, the World Commission on Environment and Development (1987) notes that a revolution in environmental awareness occurred when 'we saw our planet from space for the first time.' In other words, this revolutionary change, which the authors argue may have 'a greater impact on thought than did the Copernican revolution,' (1) was made possible by the Cold War and the military-industrial complex. Thus, notwithstanding some radical environmentalists' efforts to thoroughly critique modernity and to celebrate primitivism, anti-anthropocentrism remains in some respects fundamentally in keeping with the trajectory of modern science. There is a sense in which this ontological claim – which points to the arbitrariness of any distinction between humans and non-humans – is a perfectly logical extension of the decentring of human beings from the 'Great Chain of Being' (by Darwinian evolutionary biology) and from Judeo-Christian cosmology (by Galilean astronomy) (Evernden 1992, 88–103).

For many, the practice of a 'deep' ecology rests precisely on this refusal to privilege human interests over the interests of non-humans when calculating moral responsibilities and freedoms. According to Naess's own definition, deep ecology is ecocentric and thus requires the development of 'an awareness of the equal right (of all things) *to live and blossom*' (Naess 1973, 100; emphasis in original). This moral-political claim is itself based on the ontological claim that the positing of a strict antithesis between humanity and the rest of nature is – as C.S. Lewis's classic essay on the meanings of 'nature' suggests – 'philosophically scandalous' (1990, 46); and on the related epistemological claim that ecological science provides us with an understanding of the world that supports this view. One of this view's more sophisticated exponents is Robyn Eckersley, who provides a comprehensive summary of the ecocentric position from the perspective of ecological science, which emphasizes the dynamic interdependence of species and environment:

> According to this picture of reality, the world is an intrinsically dynamic, interconnected web of relations in which there are no absolutely discrete entities and no absolute dividing lines between the living and the nonliving, the animate and the inanimate, or the human and the nonhuman. This model of reality undermines anthropocentrism insofar as whatever faculty we choose to underscore our own uniqueness or specialness as the basis of our moral superiority (e.g. rationality, language, or our tool-making capability), we will inevitably find either that there are some humans who do *not* possess such a faculty or that there are some nonhumans who

> *do*. Nonanthropocentric ethical theorists have used this absence of any rigid, absolute dividing line between humans and nonhumans to point out the logical inconsistency of conventional anthropocentric ethical and political theory that purports to justify the exclusive moral considerability of humans on the basis of our separateness from, say, the rest of the animal world. (Eckersley 1992, 49-50; emphases in original)

In Eckersley's formulation, the problematic nature of anthropocentrism is revealed by the fact that 'whatever faculty we choose to underscore our own uniqueness or specialness as the basis of our moral superiority ... we will inevitably find either that there are some humans who do *not* possess such a faculty or that there are some nonhumans who *do*.' Eckersley's argument here seems solidly grounded, in that we can no doubt think of counter-examples to invalidate any conceivable definition of 'human nature' – animals that learn to use tools or language, humans who are in a 'vegetative' state, and so on. But a closer examination reveals this ground to be less solid than Eckersley seems to think. Or, perhaps a bit more accurately, it is not so much a (natural) ground as a (built) foundation.

For Eckersley's claim to be valid – indeed, for it even to be comprehensible – we must already understand human nature as a contestable concept. The background against which her claim (that 'we will inevitably find either that there are some humans who do *not* possess such a faculty or that there are some nonhumans who *do*') can even be understood, let alone assented to, is a pre-established understanding of where the human–nonhuman divide lies. If, for example, the use of language were *universally* accepted as the defining characteristic of humanity, then we would not be able to 'find' humans without language (regardless of any other similarities with us, such beings would be, by definition, nonhumans) or nonhumans with language (again, regardless of any other differences, these would have to be considered human).

That the circularity of this argument goes unnoticed suggests that there is more at stake than simply analytical rigorousness. For ecocentrists claim that the more accurate picture of nature that an ecological perspective provides, is one that is not susceptible to the critique that it is just another social construction, or ideological view of 'nature.' And this becomes especially troublesome when this scientific view of nature is used to arrive at conclusions in the social realm.

For example, Holmes Rolston III (1986) suggests that ecological science carries within it an ethical imperative. Ecology teaches us that 'the human vascular system includes arteries, veins, rivers, oceans and air currents. Cleaning a dump is not different in kind from filling a tooth' (23). This appeal to an expanded consciousness, or a 'transpersonal ecology,' is not at all uncommon among ecocentrists (Eckersley cites transpersonal ecology as 'a general theoretical articulation of ecocentrism' [1992, 70]). Among the problems with such a view, however, is the fact that it remains too voluntarist to serve as a political imperative. It is not difficult to think of circumstances in which people might not bother getting a tooth filled (especially if the tooth is not causing too much immediate physical discomfort), either because they simply have more pressing problems, or out of some more deep-seated self-destructive pathology. So at least as important as the transpersonal ecologists' goal of 'realiz[ing] as expansive a sense of self as possible' (Fox 1995, 249) might be the need to recognize the material causes that allow some of us to ignore the discomfort of environmental blight more easily than others (because dumps are not randomly distributed across the physical landscape), and to seek the sources of such destructive (or self-destructive) pathologies.

Eckersley herself, however, seems more careful than the transpersonal ecologists; she avoids the claim that knowledge about nature is entirely non-ideological. Thus, she maintains that 'the authority of nature (as known by ecology) is no substitute for ethical argument' (1992, 59). But although she does state that knowledge of nature cannot provide the *positive* justification for a particular model of social relations, she also suggests that such knowledge can be used negatively, to demonstrate the falsity of the assumptions that underlie particular political views. According to Eckersley, contemporary scientific insights that confirm the ecological model of reality *can* serve to undermine the atomistic assumptions of liberal individualism. Liberal individualism is properly seen as an 'ideological' view, insofar as it can be seen to rely on an outdated Newtonian model of reality. Notwithstanding her denials, Eckersley is thus ultimately incapable of keeping ethical or political and supposedly 'value-neutral' scientific arguments apart:

> Many ecocentric theorists are keenly interested in the history and philosophy of science and are fond of pointing out the reciprocal interplay between dominant images of nature ... and dominant images of society. This mutual reinforcement is reflected in the resonance between medieval Christian cosmology and the medieval political order (both of which emphasized a hierarchy of being) and between the Newtonian worldview

> and the rise of modern liberal democracy (both of which emphasized atomism). Ecocentric theorists are now drawing attention to what Fox has referred to as the 'structural similarity' between the ecological model of internal relatedness and the picture of reality that has emerged in modern biology and physics, although it is *too early* to say what the societal implications of these developments might be. (Eckersley 1992, 51–2; emphasis added)

The positing of this 'structural similarity' between conceptions of nature and of society undermines the claim (made by Eckersley herself a few pages later) that 'ecological science cannot perform the task of normative justification in respect of an ecocentric political theory' (1992, 59). In fact, science or, more broadly, any understanding of nature – serves precisely this function and has done so for quite some time. The problem, as Eckersley confesses in the extended quotation above, is rather the Hegelian one of the owl of Minerva flying only at dusk: it is simply 'too early' to tell which political arrangements the contemporary views of nature can or will be mobilized to support.

For ecocentrists, the fact that there are no 'absolute dividing lines' in the (natural) world, or, in other words, that any such dividing lines are inventions – that they are the product of culture or language – suggests that such lines are ethically indefensible, or at least highly suspect. For example, Fox (1995) notes that 'anthropocentric assumptions – assumptions that magnify our sense of self-importance in the larger scheme of things – are obviously self-serving assumptions' (13–14). But the fact that definitions have no basis in nature does not mean that decisions in ethical matters and the 'rigid distinctions' that come with them can be done away with. Or, to put it another way, the decision to try *not* to draw distinctions between the human and the non-human is itself a choice, and may even have self-serving implications of its own. Even if we acknowledge, as Leslie Paul Thiele suggests, that notions of biocentric equality serve only a 'mythic' function, and are not to be construed literally – something that is necessary to avoid the conundrums that would be associated with trying to afford egalitarian treatment to pathogenic viruses (Thiele 1995, 178–9) – the ecocentrism/anthropocentrism paradigm may still be considered problematic insofar as its particular definition of what constitutes an ecological 'problem' may exclude 'social' issues.

Emphasis on nature's seamless interconnections may obscure the all too real (even if socially constructed) dividing lines that demarcate inequalities between human beings in terms of levels of consumption and control over resources. In other words, the 'ecological' view of nature, in obscuring certain 'social' issues, serves an *ideological* function. This is not to suggest that the understanding of nature as a seamless, interconnected web does not contain some truth, nor is it to suggest that it is absolutely no better than the neo-Darwinian view that sees nature only as an agglomeration of individuals locked in mortal combat over scarce resources. Rather, it is to suggest that even such a seemingly politically progressive view of nature works to naturalize certain problematics and issues, and hence to remove them from the ambit of political inquiry.

For example, Ramachandra Guha notes that in India, the ideology of 'wilderness preservation' – defined by deep ecologists Bill Devall and George Sessions (1985) as a 'vital need' (8) – 'has resulted in a direct transfer of resources from the poor to the rich.' Guha concludes that it is not unreasonable to argue that 'invoking the bogy of anthropocentrism is at best irrelevant and at worst a dangerous obfuscation' (1989, 74–5). Nor is this simply a case of an inappropriate application of Devall and Sessions's views. More generally, Devall and Sessions (1985) argue from a deep ecological (and antianthropocentric) perspective against even the 'moral extensionism' of animal rights (or, for that matter, a utilitarian calculus that includes 'thinking like a mountain'). They claim that insofar as these privilege characteristics such as sentience, this form of thinking remains rooted in anthropocentric discourse and undermines the goal of 'ecological egalitarianism in principle' (54–5).

But what would it mean to purge ourselves of even the 'anthropocentrist' assumption that the moral privileging of sentience is a characteristic that should be factored into our decision making? Devall and Sessions argue (1985) that deep ecology calls on us 'to reawaken something very old, to reawaken our understanding of Earth wisdom.' In spite of the aforementioned affinities between ecocentrism and complex modern science, they argue that the 'way out' of ecological crises 'may be simpler than many people realize' (ix). In terms of social and political organization, the 'simplicity' that is involved in shedding off anthropocentrist assumptions would mean a return to hunter-gatherer societies, for which they claim humans are 'genetically' designed (172–3). Ecological impact should be deliberately minimized – except in cases where it is a matter of rectifying human-induced ecosystem distress – on the principle that 'the best management [of nature] is, in principle, the least management.' (152). But the claim that an immersion in our 'natural' state, or a return to a way of living for which we are 'genetically' programmed, is one that appeals to the authority of modern science as a means to avoid the dilemmas of political action and responsibility.

The view held by Devall and Sessions rests on Stanley Diamond's assertion that 'primitive society may be regarded as a system in equilibrium' (quoted in Devall and Sessions 1985, 21). Similarly symptomatic of this belief that nature – rather than political deliberation – provides us with the template for social organization, is their claim (following Jack Forbes) that in contrast with its contemporary condition, California was 'preserved in its natural state for 15,000 years' while it was inhabited by Native Californians (20).

Yet as Mike Davis has noted, the environmental history of California is extraordinarily dynamic. (He characterizes it as 'Walden Pond on LSD.') There, major wildfires, two-hundred-year droughts, and severe earthquakes punctuate periods of relative stability, with each of these equilibrial periods having very different 'norms' in terms of climatology and biotic diversity (Davis 1998, 14–39). Indeed, it is being increasingly recognized that climatic dynamism is 'normal' for the planet as a whole (Alley 2000). For Davis, the view of the earth as 'a conservative, steady state system without historical directionality' itself does a certain amount of ideological work, in that it finds confirmation in nature of a moderate, reformist view of history and thereby universalizes the conditions found in Britain and New England: 'In these temperate and forested lands, energy flows through the environment in a seasonal pattern that varies little from year to year. Geology is generally quiescent, and it's easy to perceive natural powers as orderly and incremental, rarely catastrophic.' In the nineteenth century, Sir Charles Lyell, a 'moderate Whig,' took this model of natural history and 'waged ceaseless philosophical warfare against the conceptions of abrupt "Earth Revolutions" favored by geologists in barricade-ridden France and Germany. Catastrophism of any sort, biblical or Jacobin, he branded as nothing more than prescientific superstition' (Davis 1998, 15–16).

In the case of Devall and Sessions, however, this model seems to be performing a rather different ideological function. Instead of working to naturalize a gradualist or reformist view of history, Devall and Sessions's claims about the 'natural state' of the California environment seem to be telling us that there is a 'natural' way in which humans can live, one in which ecological problems – and for that matter, social ones – will simply take care of themselves. This ideology is most clearly manifested in their 'inverted ethnocentrism,'[1] in their beliefs about the ecological sustainability of all indigenous non-Western social forms. As David Harvey points out, this entails 'belief in either some external spiritual guidance to ensure ecologically "right" outcomes, or an extraordinary omniscience in indigenous or pre-capitalistic judgments and practices in a dynamic field of action that is usually plagued by all manner of unintended consequences' (1996, 188–9). The belief that *all* indigenous peoples *consistently* managed to achieve 'ecologically right outcomes' clearly is not borne out by the historical evidence. Yet according to this ideology, when the needs of indigenous peoples do appear to conflict with the imperatives of deep ecological correctness such as biodiversity, the conflict is blamed on the deleterious impact of Western culture and technology.[2] As with natural history, local cultures are presented as being frozen in time.

In other words, Devall and Sessions's defence of primitivism is one which suggests that 'primitive' life, perhaps because it is 'natural,' is always and everywhere the same. But just as the environmental history of California shows that over the course of time, a great variety of conditions might fit the bill as 'natural,' so too we must acknowledge that 'primitive' social life is dynamic and that it encompasses a tremendous diversity of forms. Devall and Sessions hold a view that, as Andrew Ross points out, has long since been discredited in anthropology, but that continues to exercise a hold on the popular imagination – on the imagination of First World environmentalism in particular. Calls for the preservation of traditional culture, Ross (1994) notes, 'often celebrate the perennial wisdom of nature, and assume that it taught its best precepts in the presence of a stable social order, without a history, without a politics, and without any internal challenges to its hierarchical rule. Change, according to this perspective, only came from the outside, and it was all destructive' (71–2).

This ideological problem is rooted in what Carl Boggs (1997) succinctly describes as 'a highly reified conception of nature that imagines ecology to be a phenomenon quite apart from social structures and processes.' Thus, if anti-anthropocentrism is to be maintained consistently, 'theoretical critique and political intervention [are] impossible' (771).

(Re)Valuing Nature

The previous section focused on the ontological issue of developing a truer representation of what nature is 'really' like. Another tactic employed by ecocentrists has been to develop an axiological argument that challenges the dominant anthropocentric assumptions about 'value,' especially those found in mainstream economics. Conventional modes of accounting, for example, treat environmental costs as 'externalities,' do not properly discount costs to future generations when dealing with finite resources, and – perhaps what is most important – value the natural world strictly in instrumental terms. A first attempt at reform has involved rendering the instrumental terms of conventional economics somewhat less crude, by noting, for example, that a forest has a value not only insofar as it provides lumber, but also insofar as it might provide enjoyment to backpackers or birdwatchers, or relaxation for stressed urbanites, not to mention ecosystem services vital for humans as well as other ecosystem inhabitants.

But the approach of 'environmental economics' – as important as it is for pointing to the ecological destructiveness of industrial and post-industrial capitalism – may only provide a more expansive definition of the usefulness of nature. In other words, environmental economics remains anthropocentric, or a 'shallow' rather than a 'deep' form of ecology, to the extent that it continues to see nature in instrumental terms:

> The difficulty with this [economistic] argument is that it still is based on a definition of preservation within a short-term, narrowly conceived human economy. If some mineral were discovered in a Nature reserve in Brazil, for example, which was used by tourists from the United States (spending their money to see wildlife in habitat) but the mineral would yield X times more money on the world market if extracted than tourism does, then the economically rational action would be to extract the mineral even if it disrupted the habitat of wildlife and drastically reduced the income derived from tourists. (Devall and Sessions 1985, 117)

In more generalized terms, William Leiss (1974) notes the implications of treating 'environmental quality [as] merely one desirable commodity among others': 'The trap has been laid, and to subsume the matter of environmental quality under the all-embracing economic calculus is to fall victim to it' (ix). What seems to be required, then is not so much tinkering with the rules of accounting, but rather a revolutionary change in the category of value itself. As we shall see, however, we cannot avoid the ideological problems found in the previous section, even if we eschew the posing of ontological questions in favour of a more positive axiological project: a radical rethinking of what we consider 'valuable,' and why.

Such a comprehensive rethinking of the concept of value is attempted by Robert E. Goodin. Goodin (1992) differentiates his green (or 'natural attribute based') theory of value from both the consumer-based theory of value of neoclassical economics and the producer-based (or labour) theory of value found in Locke, Ricardo, and Marx (23–4). He explains this difference by alluding to his theory's non-anthropocentrism: 'It differs from a producer based theory of value in so far as it insists that those value-imparting properties are natural, rather than being somehow artefacts of human activities. And it differs from a consumer based theory of value in so far as it insists that those value-imparting qualities inhere in the objects themselves, rather than in any mental states (actual or hypothetical, now or later) of those who partake of those objects' (25). According to this understanding, value is not human-centred; rather, it inheres in the objects themselves. To be fair, Goodin does add: 'I do not want – or need – to contend that the particular theory of value I am investigating here is correct utterly to the exclusion of all others. I shall merely be insisting that it has a legitimate place, alongside others perhaps, in any larger mixed theory of value' (26). However, he does not maintain his humility throughout his argument, perhaps because he does not articulate what such a 'larger mixed theory of value' might look like – that is, he does not explain how such a metatheory of value might evaluate competing claims based on different notions of value.

If value inheres in natural objects themselves, and is a function, moreover, of their naturalness, it follows, for Goodin, that the transformation of those objects by human labour to render them more useful to human beings constitutes not an increase but rather a decrease in value: 'What is crucial in making things valuable, on the green theory of value, is the fact that they have a history of having been created by natural processes rather than by artificial human ones' (27). But this distinction does not really solve the problem of what constitutes 'value' – it simply moves it one step back. What, ultimately, makes natural processes more valuable than human ones?

Goodin attempts to answer this question by shifting to the aesthetic realm,[3] where he observes that 'fakes, forgeries, replicas, reproductions and restorations ... are less valuable – not just contingently but necessarily less valuable – than the original which they replicate' (29). If we were to discover that the *Mona Lisa* that hangs in the Louvre were in fact not painted by Leonardo da Vinci, Goodin suggests, 'It would have lost the value it once had for us as a manifestation of Leonardo's genius' (30). The argument that applies to the value of an object that symbolizes the creative power of a human being obviously applies *a fortiori* to the sublimely creative forces of nature itself. Indeed, it is precisely to the sublimity of nature that Goodin refers in his most concise rehearsal of the reasons for seeing 'naturalness as a source of value': '(1) People want to see some sense and pattern to their lives. (2) That requires, in turn, that their lives be set in some larger context. (3) The products of natural processes, untouched as they are by human hands, provides precisely that desired context' (37).

Interestingly, the first two of these propositions mirror the notion of 'cognitive mapping,' which Fredric Jameson borrows from Kevin Lynch's *The Image of the City*. Cognitive mapping refers, for Jameson, to the preconscious ways in which we attempt to understand ('map') our position in a social space (1991, 51–4). But there is a crucial difference between Goodin and Jameson, and we encounter it in Goodin's third point, with regard to his understanding of what provides the appropriate 'larger context.' For Jameson, although 'Nature' may have been an appropriate conceptualization of the sublime during the Romantic period, the sublime is now rather more appropriately understood as 'the whole new decentered global network of the third stage of capital' (38). In other words, Goodin asserts that the most meaningful 'larger context' in which we can situate our lives is the context of the natural world; whereas for Jameson, in an era when nature is increasingly penetrated and colonized by capital, the most meaningful larger context is the social.

If it were simply a question of which provides the larger context, then one would have to prefer Goodin's larger context to the one proposed by Jameson. But size is, of course, not all that matters. As Goodin (1992) notes, a larger context is valuable because 'such natural processes, and our relation to them, serve to fix our place in the external world. They help to "locate the self," in a deep psychological sense that matters enormously to people' (39). Indeed, the depth of importance of this value is such that 'all other sorts of satisfaction are somehow parasitic upon this sort' (42). Although Goodin seeks to avoid the 'skat[ing] dangerously near thin theological ice' that would be involved in asserting that a larger context 'give[s] meaning to our lives' (39), this is nevertheless the direction in which his own argument presses him. To be sure, and for good reasons, he avoids giving a *specific* content to that 'meaning,' yet it is difficult to see how one might fix one's place in an external universe (thereby valuing certain types of processes and actions) without providing any sort of meaning to one's life. Maps, after all, are always *for* something.

In this sense, although in some other crucial respects their arguments are quite different, for both Goodin and Jameson it is the recognition of a larger context that provides the foundation for political action. For Jameson, the argument (at least on this score) is rather straightforwardly Marxist: recognition of the larger social context (the extension and intensification of capitalist relations on a global scale) can allow for the construction of an emancipatory socialist project. For Goodin (1992) recognition of the larger natural context leads to the positive valuation of natural processes and to the concomitant devaluation of ('artificial') human ones, with the resultant political claim that it would be preferable for human beings to live as close as possible to nature. Better a small-scale English village than a 'postmodern megalopolis' like Los Angeles (51–2);[4] and preferable to either would be the mode of living of cultures that 'have managed to live in harmony with nature rather than trying to dominate nature and bend it to their will' (53). Echoing Devall and Sessions, Goodin further argues that preferable to any of these is 'preserving pristine nature,' (52) – that is, no human alteration of the environment at all. At this point, we can perhaps begin to see how Goodin's green theory of value leads us to the same ideological problems that we saw in the previous section.

Before elaborating on this point, however, we should first note that there is a way in which Jameson's historicizing hypothesis – that 'nature' was an appropriate larger context for the Romantic period, but is not in postmodernity – is, ironically, bolstered by Goodin himself. In arguing that the value of natural processes lies in their provision of a larger context, Goodin states that this is an idea whose 'most powerful restatement among recent green writers comes in Bill McKibben's *The End of Nature*' (Goodin 1992, 38). Goodin goes on to offer a brief quotation from McKibben, which is important enough to reproduce at greater length:

> We have changed the atmosphere, and thus we are changing the weather. By changing the weather, we make every spot on earth man-made and artificial. We have deprived nature of its independence, and that is fatal to its meaning. Nature's independence *is* its meaning; without it there is nothing but us.
>
> ... If in July there's a heat wave in London, it won't be a natural phenomenon. It will be a man-made phenomenon – an amplification of what

> nature intended or a total invention. Or, at the very least, it *might* be a man-made phenomenon, which amounts to the same thing.
>
> ... We live in a postnatural world ... Politics – our particular way of life, our ideas about how we should live – blows its smoke over every inch of the globe. (McKibben 1989, 58–60)

To be sure, McKibben, like Goodin, is *lamenting* the fact that we are now living in a 'postnatural' world. At the same time, however, it is important to recognize how this fact undermines the political implications of Goodin's argument. If we are in need of a larger context by which to orient our lives, that larger context seems now (in the 'postnatural' moment) to be unquestionably the social. For even if we seek to return to some form of life that is more attuned to natural rhythms and processes, these have themselves been irremediably altered by social processes. So we can better map the larger social context ('the whole new decentered global network of the third stage of capital') from a postmodern megalopolis than from a traditional English village; and furthermore, the perspective afforded by a 'global city,' with its clogged freeways, diverse manufacturing processes, and globe-spanning informational and communicational networks, may well provide us with a better grasp of what we used to think of as *natural* processes.[5]

This is not to say, however, that McKibben and Goodin are unaware of this. Indeed, as Soper (1995) notes in her discussion of Goodin's theory, the fact that there is no longer any part of the planet that is unshaped by human activity 'is precisely the force of so construing it [the end of nature], namely that it brings so clearly into view its actual disappearance' (18). Thus, Goodin's 'green theory of value,' like McKibben's lament for unaltered nature, underlines the extent to which almost all the things in our world are 'fakes, forgeries, replicas, reproductions and restorations' of nature.

But as Soper is quick to point out, Goodin's theory continues to be plagued by certain problems. For if those aspects of nature which have been altered by humans 'are less valuable – not just contingently but necessarily less valuable' (Goodin 1992, 29), then the logical conclusion – or so it would seem – is that 'it would have been better by far had the [human] species never existed' (Soper 1995, 19). Goodin attempts to defuse this objection – which he nevertheless sees as perhaps applicable to 'the deepest ecology' (Goodin 1992, 43) – by arguing that 'things can only have value *in relation to* us' and thus that 'it is necessarily the case that human beings figure essentially in deriving value from nature' (44;

emphasis in original). Of course, Goodin cannot wholly embrace anthropocentrism either, so he concludes by arguing that although value is only created in the presence of humans, 'value-imparting characteristics' still reside in natural objects (1992, 45). Goodin wants to resist the idea that 'values are all in people's heads' (1992, 45). Nevertheless, it seems to be an inescapable conclusion– especially given that Goodin is writing a book on the subject – that the decision to impart those 'value-imparting characteristics' to natural objects is itself a social (if not necessarily a conscious) one.

Soper points briefly to yet another problem in Goodin's argument, one that deserves to be pursued further. Once we arrive at the troubling conclusion that things would be better if human beings did not exist, since more of nature's creation would be left undisturbed,

> we might begin to wonder why the same argument could not apply to other living creatures, albeit they are said, unlike ourselves, to belong to nature, since they, too, make use of its resources, destroy each other, and in that sense corrupt its pristine paradise. In other words, we may ask what it is exactly that makes a human interaction with 'nature' intrinsically devaluing, where that of other species is deemed to be unproblematic – of the order of nature itself ... We may begin to wonder what it is exactly that renders even the most primitive of human dwellings an 'artificial' excrescence, but allows the bee-hive or the ant-heap to count as nature ... Or to put the point in more political terms: we may wish to suspect that this is an approach to the 'value' of nature that is too inclined to abstract from the impact on the environment of the different historical modes of 'human' interaction with it, and thus to mislocate the source of the problem – which arguably resides not in any inherently 'devaluing' aspect of human activity, but in the specific forms it has taken. (Soper 1995, 19)

As should be clear already, I agree with Soper's argument here, especially as it is formulated in its 'more political terms.' At the same time, there is a sense in which her point might be read as unfair to Goodin specifically, if not to deep ecology in general. Goodin, after all, does concede that humans are a part of nature and that there is likely no part of nature that is 'literally untouched by human hands.' Furthermore, he admits that the idea of nature untouched by human hands (along with the radical distinction between the 'artificial' and the 'natural') is no more than a 'first approximation' (Goodin 1992, 37n38 and 45–54).

However, the way in which he attempts to refine this 'first approximation' is instructive, especially as it allows us to flesh out the critique that Soper begins to develop in the passage cited above.

Goodin, we may recall, does not simply say that 'the most primitive of human dwellings [is] an artificial excrescence' and leave it at that. At the very least, it is not as troubling an artificial excrescence as a highrise apartment building. Let us recall his claim that traditional English villages represent a 'clearly' preferable mode of living in comparison with postmodern megalopolises (1992, 52). But on what grounds? If human beings are a part of nature, and what we do is by extension natural, then we cannot claim that English village life is any less natural than life in a postmodern city, because city building must be conceded to be natural. As David Harvey (1996) succinctly puts it, 'there is nothing *unnatural* about New York City' (186; emphasis in original).[6] The crucial difference between the premodern village and the postmodern city does not lie in the ecological impact of various forms of habitat construction, all of which are at once both 'artificial' and (because humans are a part of nature) 'natural.' The crucial difference, we should recall, lies in the mode of life that the social form engenders (the capacity to provide the 'context' within which inhabitants are able to situate their lives). Tucked away in a footnote, Goodin acknowledges that 'the difference really does, I think, have to be cast in terms of "forms of society" as a whole. It is (oddly enough, perhaps) at that macrosociological level that we can best talk about living in harmony with nature' (1992, 52n76).

But it is precisely at that macrosociological level that Goodin's analysis is weakest. For even if he does in some sense acknowledge the importance of understanding (as Soper puts it) 'different historical modes of human interaction with' the external environment, when it comes to providing some assessment of these different forms of society, Goodin tends to rely on vague generalizations about premodern societies (including both pre-Contact non-European societies and 'earlier periods of our [sic] own cultures') (53). Although his reference to 'the original inhabitants, both in Australia and the Americas' (54) is somewhat more specific than 'primitive' social forms *tout court*, it nevertheless encompasses a tremendous range, not only geographically and historically, but also in terms of social forms and modes of interacting with nature.

Even if we accept Goodin's assumptions – that it is possible for human beings to 'live in harmony with nature,' and furthermore, that it would be possible to agree on at least the vague outline of what such a form of life might look like – the weakness in his argument remains his failure to specify the 'macrosociological' characteristics of those cultures – that is, those characteristics which determine their mode of interacting with the natural environment. The problem, for Goodin as much as for Devall and Sessions and for anyone else subscribing to inverted ethnocentrism, lies in the treatment of 'respect for nature' in an overly abstract or idealist manner. If 'living in harmony with nature' is indeed a category that is determined at the 'macrosociological' level, then surely what is needed is a comparison of the nature of *social* relations in societies that do or do not live in harmony with nature.

Yet as Goodin's admission of the 'oddness' of his claim suggests, the analysis of social forms does not seem to be in keeping with the tenets of the 'green theory of value' that he is proposing. He claims that value resides in the products of natural processes, not in those of artificial (or, in other words, social) processes, and that the latter are always mere knock-offs of the former. This suggests that for him, distinctions between one social form and another are at best of secondary importance, far below the distinction between the natural and the social. The 'green theory of value' serves a similar ideological function to the critiques of anthropocentrism discussed in the previous section (as well as to McKibben's identification of 'politics' with 'pollution'). Like the ontological approach of Eckersley, Goodin's axiological approach similarly deflects attention from considerations of social relations.

Historicizing Nature

In his essay 'Ideas of Nature,' Raymond Williams observes that 'out of the ways in which we have interacted with the physical world we have made not only human nature and an altered natural order; we have also made societies.' He goes on to argue: 'If we talk only of singular Man and singular Nature we can compose a general history, but at the cost of excluding the real and altering social relations' (1980, 84). We might summarize the foregoing by saying that ecocentrism lends itself to what Williams calls 'general history.' This preference for 'general history' – which can properly be characterized as ideological – reflects an inability or unwillingness to see the ways in which the defence of nature is always also a defence of 'nature,' or in other words a defence of a particular, culturally given understanding of nature. As such, ecocentric ontological and axiological commitments may lead to a variety of logically and/or politically dubious positions. If ecocentrism is to avoid a nihilistic apoliticism (based on the understanding that all human activity is destructive), then it too often succumbs to the inverted ethnocentrism that uncritically valorizes 'primitive' modes of social organization, based on their presumed closeness to nature. Although the latter may lead to some logical contradictions, the political implications of such a general history are perhaps even more disturbing: a willingness to accept (and in a few cases even an eagerness for) the reactionary authoritarianism that often accompanies attempts to legislate social organization on the basis of what is deemed to be 'natural.'

As the quotation from Roland Barthes at the beginning of this chapter suggests, the ideological misrecognitions that constrain much of ecocentric thought might be rectified by a more thoroughly historicized understanding of 'nature.' This historicization of nature, moreover, would function at multiple levels. First, an understanding of the historically constructed character of 'human nature' would help reveal the implicit assumptions in Eckersley's critique of anthropocentrism. We saw earlier how Eckersley's critique rests on a prediscursive, 'common-sense' understanding of where the human-non-human divide lies. But this 'common sense' is historically constructed: although today we might agree that, for example, the aboriginal inhabitants of Australia and the Americas are fully human beings, this has by no means been universally (or transhistorically) accepted. Indeed, European colonial expansion (not to mention the slave trade) was predicated on a racializing ideology that constructed non-Europeans as, in some important senses, *sub*humans (Gould 1994). We can, furthermore, trace this trend back to the beginnings of written Western philosophy. For Aristotle, man was by nature a *zoon politikon* (Aristotle 1958, 5) – a definition that condemned to the status of not fully human both barbarian non-Greeks (who did not live in a polis) and Greek women and slaves, who did not participate in political life. Now, of course, women and non-Greeks are recognized as fully human – as beings endowed with 'universal human rights.' This change, however, has come about because of a political (in the broadest sense) process, rather than a value-free attempt to find the human–non-human dividing line in nature. In this sense, Aristotle was correct: 'human' beings can be understood as those beings who engage in what must be seen as a political (and hence historical) process: the attempt to make sense of what it means to be human.

There is, however, another sense in which historical thinking serves as an important category in these debates. It is not simply that our understanding of what it means to be human changes as a result of historical forces. It is also the case, I will be arguing, that this *historicity constitutes the dividing line* between the human and the non-human. *Contra* Eckersley, I would argue that there is an 'absolute dividing line' between the human and the non-human. But I would like to make this case without resorting to biological or genetic differences between humans and non-humans. Rather, the absolute dividing line, I would suggest, is historical, not biological.

The historical event that constitutes the dividing line between the human and the non-human is human beings' *self-conscious* transformation of their natural environment. It is, in other words, the fact of humans' alienation from nature. When Soper asks why bees building a hive counts as 'natural' among 'nature-endorsing' theorists, whereas humans building a house does not, one suspects that this is the answer that nature-endorsing theorists would give: non-humans transform their environment only in accordance with instinct, whereas humans possess the capacity to deny their instincts – that is, to break from the dictates of nature. This capacity for instinctual denial allows for a diversity of forms of human life – in other words, culture.

For those who draw political conclusions from ecocentric premises, however, this alienation from nature (in its multiple senses: construction of a built environment to replace or supplement the natural environment, denial of instincts, seeing ourselves as uniquely endowed and hence morally superior to other species) is the source of our present ecological crisis and is also, for many, an important source of many of our 'social' problems. From such a perspective, 'alienation from nature' is simply a problem rather than a complex, multifaceted, and essentially human condition, and any attempt to undo the mediations that separate us both from external nature and from our internal (instinctual) nature is to be welcomed as an attempt to get 'back to nature' in every sense of the term.

But alienation from nature, or the mediations between ourselves and our natural environment (from agriculture to city building to computer modelling of global climatic trends) is not simply a static and inescapable mixed blessing. It is also a dynamic condition that changes forms as it evolves. It is fundamentally historical. The difference between humans and non-humans is not simply the biological *capacity* of human beings to self-consciously transform their environment; rather, it is the *historical fact* of this self-conscious human labour. This way of making the distinction is important for a number of reasons. First, it allows the historical fact of human alienation from nature to be more easily divorced from the thesis that human beings are separate from the rest of nature. When we suggest that humans differ from other animals in the fact that they have self-consciously transformed the natural environment, we need not argue that human beings are therefore separate from nature (and that therefore the human transformation of nature is 'unnatural'). Even though we 'go against nature' by repressing our instinctual urges and transforming our natural environment, it is 'natural' for us to do so. In so doing, we do not transcend nature, but remain natural beings.

Second, an emphasis on biological capacities might suggest either that change is impossible, or alternatively, that it is achievable through a one-time genetic modification. We should reject the claim that human beings' apparent propensity to be despoilers (as opposed to modifiers) of their natural environment is in any sense encoded in our genes (that it is part of an irresistable 'human nature'). Change is possible, as is suggested by the fact that different societies have had differing modes of interacting with nature. But this also suggests that the nature of our alienation is determined at the level of what Goodin calls 'macrosociological' categories at least at much as at biological levels. Moreover, this postlapsarian moment – the story of the human race after the fact of alienation from nature – should not be thought of as an undifferentiated whole. Our alienation continues to evolve in both nature and form as we continue to transform our natural environment.

This leads to a third reason for emphasizing historical rather than biological categories. Human alienation from nature is an ongoing process that transforms not only the external environment but ourselves as well. The shift from medieval villages to postmodern cities entails not only a massive transformation of the external environment, but also a transformation of our internal natures as well. The type of person who can thrive (or even survive) in a postmodern city is very different from the type of person who can thrive in a medieval village. And just as neither social form can be understood as a more or less 'natural' mode of living (as even Goodin admits), neither are the inhabitants of one or the other living according to a transhistorical 'human nature.' In both cases, what human beings need to do in order to survive (or what is seen as 'natural' human behaviour) is overdetermined by macrosociological or historical as well as biological factors. What all this means, finally, is that if the problem is alienation from nature, the solution cannot be a simple return to a prealienated existence (getting 'back to nature'); rather it can only be grasped through a thorough understanding of the ways in which our nature is, at least in part, determined by our history. At the same time, however, this emphasis on the historical risks being overstated, especially if it is taken to suggest that there is nothing to nature but its social construction. It is to this view that we turn next.

CHAPTER 2

Postmodernism: The Critique of 'Nature'

> When I visited the University of Colorado at Boulder last spring, some of the younger humanities faculty told me that postmodernism was proving to be a tough sell out there; nature, however mediated by human interventions, was simply too *present* to be dismissed as a social construction.
>
> Lears 1997, 145; emphasis in original

In *Postmodernism and the Environmental Crisis* – in fact, in the first sentence of the book's opening chapter – Arran Gare observes: 'The Modern-Day Dictionary of Received Ideas says of "postmodernism": "This word has no meaning. Use it as often as possible." With a few notable exceptions, cultural theorists have been following this advice" (1995, 4). This simulacric definition of the postmodern (the internal quotation is attributed not to any original text titled *The Modern-Day Dictionary of Received Ideas*, but to a journal article, citing a newspaper review) provides a useful point of departure, and not only for the way in which it seems to confirm suspicions that academic theorizations of the contemporary social world – or indeed, contemporary academic discourses in general – are only so much hot air. It is a good starting point for discussion because it is (or rather, can be read as) an indictment of theorizations of postmodernity, and at the same time an excellent example of just how such theorizations are correct.

In the first instance, the statement is suffused with cynicism and a distrust of the elitism inherent in the hierarchical structure of institutionalized (and especially 'higher') education. This cynicism is symptomatic of what Gare rightly refers to as 'the most widely accepted characterization of the postmodern condition ... that offered by [Jean-François]

Lyotard. It is "the incredulity towards metanarratives"' (1995, 4; see also Lyotard 1984, xxiv). The 'grand narratives' offered by intellectuals are to be regarded with immediate suspicion. This postmodern cynicism, however, is not to be confused with the anti-intellectualism of earlier eras, insofar as the former does not posit a singular 'commonsensical' alternative that supposely is more grounded in the lived reality of everyday experience and hence closer to the 'truth.' Rather – and here we are moving toward the way in which the quotation is exemplary of the postmodern condition – 'truth' is understood to be always relative, that is, the result of competing and constantly shifting discursive power formations. And insofar as truth remains discursive, the question of whether those discourses are adequate to the object itself must remain bracketed.

The lack of a referent is thus not seen as a drawback to this 'definition' of postmodernism – the statement that the term has no meaning is immediately followed by this injunction: 'Use it as often as possible.' Indeed, Gare himself follows this advice: 'postmodernity' is found in the title of his book; furthermore, that term (or variations of it) is found in three of its five chapter titles, and according to the book's index, it appears in the book's text more often than any other. Gare's injunction – 'This word has no meaning. Use it as often as possible' – is thus not only a sly reference to the jargon- and neologism-ridden character of postmodern discourse, but also a recognition of the (postmodern) insight that language itself is always a site of political contestation and struggle. Thus Gare concludes his opening paragraph: 'To define the postmodern is not just to define a term. It is to characterize the present age and to assess how we should respond to it' (1995, 4).

We might conclude from all this that the postmodern condition entails giving up the search for a permanent ground to definitions, including (perhaps even especially) the search for what Jean Baudrillard (1981) calls 'the great referent Nature' (1981, 202). But this does not necessarily entail forgoing struggles to 'save' the 'environment' or 'nature.' On the contrary: if we recognize that the understanding of 'nature' as that which is radically external to 'culture' or human influence is no longer tenable, this can be taken as an injunction to explicitly politicize 'environmental' issues, precisely *because* these are always already political anyway. Even something as seemingly benign as restoration ecology reveals 'persistent patterns of metaphor that see vegetative politics in terms of aggression, invasion, colonization, war, defense, containment' (Rodman 1993, 152). 'Nature' – that is to say, our *conceptualization* of nature – is a part of culture and therefore should be subjected to political analysis. As Jan E. Dizard (1993) puts it: 'Nature – that which appears in some substantial way separate from and a priori to human existence – just might be the original Rorschach' (112). With our increasing ability to manipulate our lived environment – from splitting atoms to splicing genes – how our lives are organized is increasingly based on social, economic, or political rather than 'natural' factors. Thus William Cronon (1995) in his editorial introduction to *Uncommon Ground* – one of the earliest and most prominent attempts to reconcile social constructivism and environmentalism – expresses the hope that social constructivism will not prove threatening to environmentalism (as many argue) but instead will contribute to an 'environmentalism ... renewed in its mission of protecting the natural world by helping people live more responsibly in it' (26).

Of course, the leap from the discursive or social construction of 'nature' to a politicized environmentalism is not one that all postmodernists endorse.[1] It should be noted that the argument that 'nature' is culturally constructed is generally used (as we shall see below) to illustrate the social character of the regulation of sexuality. The argument, in other words, is most often deployed to reveal the culturally constructed character of human nature rather than the external environment. But the argument can be equally applied in contending that ecological 'natural limits,' just like conceptions of the 'natural' in human sexuality, are in fact reflections of the constellation of social relations: it can be argued that the 'unnaturalness' of the human population exceeding the Earth's 'carrying capacity' is as much a product of a particular culture as the 'unnaturalness' of homosexuality or miscegenation.

For this reason, many who accept the postmodernist position that all representations of nature are first and foremost politically interested truth-claims, are *opposed* to the sorts of claims to transhistorical 'truth' (whether scientific or the 'wisdom of the Earth') made by those who seek to re-orient social organization in response to ecological crises. So-called 'natural limits' of all kinds are not simply natural, but are culturally specific discursive constructions. Notwithstanding the attempts of a few theorists to assert a postmodern environmentalism, postmodernism is generally understood to be diametrically opposed to the 'nature-endorsing' tenets of ecocentrism of the sort that we explored in the previous chapter. Perhaps the best example of what Soper terms 'nature-scepticism' and its depoliticizing tendencies is to be found in the philosophy of Jean Baudrillard.

Jean Baudrillard and the End of the Real

The 'linguistic turn' in the social sciences – variously associated with 'structuralism,' 'post-structuralism,' 'postmodernism,' or sometimes simply 'contemporary French theory' – is predicated on the claim that most if not all objects of human inquiry turn out to be (as structuralist psychoanalyst Jacques Lacan said of the unconscious) 'structured like a language,' as well as on the claim that language itself refers only to itself rather than to an external world. The figure who perhaps most rigorously pursues this line of reasoning, and whose work therefore deserves some extended consideration, is the French social theorist Jean Baudrillard. As Jameson notes, the 'poststructural denunciations of the ideologies of nature and the "authentic" ... [are a] particular crusade which finds ... its full-dress ideological program in Baudrillard, in particular the Baudrillard of the critique of concepts of "need" and "use value"' (1991, 197).

Verena Andermatt Conley, who does argue for a connection between postmodern French thought and ecological awareness, claims that Baudrillard constitutes an important exception to this trend. Distinguishing between Baudrillard's earlier works (those which provide a 'critique of the concepts of "need" and "use-value,"' in Jameson's words) and his later ones, Conley argues that Baudrillard 'abandoned his earlier and incisive critiques of capitalism, which was interpreted to be a system of signs that overtake commodities in order to celebrate the procession of simulacra.' The result of this perceived break in Baudrillard's work is that 'a cultural criticism that had strong ecological affinities got lost in the shuffle of simulacra' (1997, 27). Without disputing the point that Baudrillard's work is problematic in terms of its ecological (and political) implications, it is important to note that Conley's approach to making this case is misguided. Instead of seeing a break between Baudrillard's earlier works and his later ones, in which he suddenly casts aside potentially incisive ecological critiques in favour of a celebration of neoliberal capitalism, we might find it more useful to understand Baudrillard's work as having a fair amount of continuity between its 'earlier' and 'later' phases. Establishing such a continuity will allow us to see the problems with any suggestions that Baudrillard is simply an apologist for contemporary capitalism, or that his earlier work can be rescued to ground an adequate ecological politics. And in making the latter point, we shall see that Baudrillard is less exceptional than Conley supposes with regard to the fit between contemporary French theory (or postmodernism) and ecological politics.

The first part of this task, then, involves examining Baudrillard's 'earlier and incisive critiques of contemporary capitalism.' These critiques – most of them located in *For a Critique of the Political Economy of the Sign*, a collection of essays written in the late 1960s and early 1970s – involve an attempt to extend the site of Marx's critique of capitalism from production to consumption. Baudrillard is reacting here to the rise of 'consumer society': to the extent that people in advanced capitalist economies have identified themselves in class terms, they have increasingly done so on the basis of what they consume, rather than on their position in the production process. This trend takes shape in at least three specific ways. First, class position in the production processes of an information- or service-based economy is increasingly difficult to locate: given the increasingly abstract character of what is 'produced,' the distinction between 'productive' and 'non-productive' labour is increasingly ill-defined (Baudrillard, 1993, 24–34). Second, 'class' refers with increasing regularity and specificity to consumption patterns (where one lives, the clothes one wears, the car one drives, the kinds of food one eats and where, and so on), rather than to positions in the processes of production. The third manifestation of this trend, which is closely linked to the second, relates to the transformation in the status of cultural objects or commodities in advanced capitalist societies. Class position is increasingly seen to be determined by what one consumes, and as a consequence, objects of consumption are increasingly taking on a signifying function. Timothy W. Luke (1991) summarizes these developments: 'With the planned programming of production, capitalism moves from the production of "useful" goods and services to the generation of semiotic codes and images' (348).

Wlad Godzich describes this shift as one from a 'regime of representation' to a 'regime of repetition,' whereby the use-value of commodities, increasingly produced by 'productive unproductive labour,' is not immediately evident and must be attributed through 'the production of demand' (Godzich, 1994, 200–4). Where products no longer 'represent' the labour that has gone into them, but are produced through the 'repetition' of a production design, the 'meaning' (or value or class-signification) of the objects produced is not established immediately, but only through mediating agencies such as the advertising industry. In other words, what is new about 'consumer society' is that the cost of producing a commodity now must include the cost of producing the symbolic meaning of (and hence the demand for) that commodity. The addition of this unprecedented cost, and struggles over whether and how it is externalized, lay the groundwork for a potential crisis of accumulation (and allow us to see more clearly why Baudrillard's model remains, in a sense, a Marxian, production-based model): 'The mode of repetition is then faced with its breakdown: it produces artifacts whose use-value cannot be easily (read: cheaply) established, and which therefore remain unsold; it then uses up surplus-value in the attempt to sell them, that is, in the attempt to make them meaningful to buyers; and thus it begins to use up capital that would have been invested in the production of commodities" (Godzich 1994, 203).

But Godzich's conclusion here – that it is the field of semiotics itself that functions as a sign that secures ideological closure for this latest regime of capitalism – is not as important to our purposes as the point that gives rise to his analysis. His analysis begins with the observation that this new relationship between objects and signs is very widely recognized as a 'crisis of meaning,' which is felt specifically as a 'crisis of the commodity' (1994, 197).

This brief excursus into Godzich's analysis allows us to better appreciate the critical insights of *For a Critique of the Political Economy of the Sign* – to see it as an intervention made at the moment when the 'crisis of the commodity' manifests itself as a 'crisis of meaning.' For Baudrilllard, the appropriate response to this is to apply Saussurean linguistics to Marx's analysis of commodities. Saussure argues that language is best understood as a *system* of signs, wherein each sign derives its significance not from being attached to a referent outside of language, but from a differential articulation internal to the system itself. If a commodity – or more precisely, commodity consumption – has a signifying function, then we should not be surprised to find that the 'system of needs' (Baudrillard, 1981) is structured like a language. In advanced capitalist economies, one's status – or even class identity – is defined by what one consumes. Drawing from Saussure's theory (and Saussure does argue that structuralism should be generalizable to all the human sciences), Baudrillard notes that the 'sign value' of the objects of consumption – Big Macs or grilled calamari; a Mercedes or a Harley Davidson – is constantly shifting because of technological or social change, or simply because of changing fashions. The sign value of commodities is thus not consistently defined by any referent external to the system of consumption, least of all the cost of production (the labour theory of value) or functional utility (use value, or a 'consumer-based theory of value,' in Goodin's terms). 'The definition of an object of consumption is entirely independent of objects themselves and *exclusively a function of the logic of significations*' (Baudrillard 1981, 67; emphasis in original).

But Baudrillard draws equally from Marx as from Saussure. From Marx, he takes the point that the real structural effect of every act of consumption is to reinscribe relations of class inequality and domination. As we have seen Godzich argue, the structure that attaches meaning to consumption is not produced cost-free, and the distribution of those costs is a result of social struggle. Thus, even though he argues that one's class position in advanced capitalist society seems to be determined by consumption rather than by production, Baudrillard nevertheless recognizes that the conspicuous consumption of sign values is a reflection of the fetishism of commodities.

Having resituated the critique of the fetishization of commodities in the sphere of consumption, however, Baudrillard is able to argue that not only is 'exchange value' fetishistic, but so also is 'use-value,' since it is based on what one 'needs' to consume. 'Needs' are themselves socially constructed and thus a product of the capitalist axiomatic; and consumption patterns, no less than production relations, are a function of an individual's alienation: 'People discover a posteriori and almost miraculously that they need what is produced and offered at the marketplace (and thus, in order that they should experience this or any particular need, the need must already exist inside people as a virtual postulation)' (1981, 71). Thus, Baudrillard concludes, to the extent that Marxism is predicated on a naturalization of 'needs' (as in 'to each according to his needs'), it remains an impediment to the development of an adequate critique of capitalism: 'Marxist analysis has contributed to the mythology (a veritable rationalist mystique) that allows the relation of the individual to objects conceived as use values to pass for a concrete and objective – in sum "natural" – relation between man's needs and the proper function of the object ... Against all this seething metaphysic of needs and use values, it must be said that abstraction, reduction, rationalization and systematization are as profound and as generalized at the level of 'needs' as at the level of commodities' (1981, 134–5). Thus, for Baudrillard, 'it was not use-value which should have been contrasted with exchange-value, but symbolic exchange which should have been contrasted with commodity exchange' (Gane 1993, x).[2]

However, Baudrillard is concerned here not only with demonstrating the ideological character of needs, but also with the more general and abstract problem of the *sign*. As a result, he wants to show that in a society in which cultural objects are increasingly understood as signs, the 'real' (the world of objects independent of a system of signs) disappears. In other words, if the system of objects is 'structured like a language,' then the question of whether there are any 'real' objects outside of or behind the sign-system must necessarily be bracketed.[3] As 'signs ... overtake commodities' (Conley 1997, 27) – and indeed, as signs overtake the referent in general – all that remains is 'the simulation system of hyperreality' (Luke 1991, 350). For our purposes, what is crucial here is to see that Baudrillard understands 'needs' for commodities not as distortions or falsifications of 'real' needs, but rather as simulacra. Thus, 'ideology only corresponds to a betrayal of reality by signs; simulation corresponds to a short-circuit of reality and its reduplication by signs. It is always the aim of ideological analysis to restore the objective process; it is always a false problem to want to restore the truth beneath the simulacrum' (Baudrillard 1983b, 48).

Conley, then, is correct to assert that for Baudrillard, 'the problem facing ecologists is by and large their inherent ingenuousness of wanting to return to a pre-existing real, a world in which physical materiality of things and rhythms of life had no names to alienate them or to install a rift between mental, symbolic, and physical activities' (1997, 32). This sentiment is also evident in *For a Critique of the Political Economy of the Sign*, which refers specifically to the ecology movement: 'The social control of air, water, etc, in the name of environmental protection shows men entering the field of social control a little more deeply themselves' (Baudrillard 1981, 203). To return to the point made by Jameson, with which our discussion of Baudrillard began, it is precisely in the works of the 'earlier' Baudrillard – 'the Baudrillard of the critique of concepts of "need" and "use value"' – that the destabilization of the category of 'nature,' with its problematization of much of what passes for progressive ecological politics, is most forcefully articulated.

When we do not try to fit Baudrillard's earlier work into traditional understandings of 'progressive' politics, it is perhaps easier to see the continuity between his earlier and later works. Here, we might also suggest that it is just as problematic to try to fit his later works into traditional understandings of 'conservative' politics. Douglas Kellner, like Conley, is critical of Baudrillard's later work, at least in part because his understanding of consumer society is too totalizing. On this reading of Baudrillard, 'consumption is solely a mode of commodification, social integration and domination ... [Baudrillard] projects the fantasy of capitalists – what we might call *the capitalist imaginary* – as the governing principle of consumer society. In other words, Baudrillard describes precisely how capitalists would like the world to be' (Kellner 1989, 28; emphasis in original). Conley puts it even more succinctly: 'Baudrillard becomes the spokesperson for a system that indeed would *like* to work as smoothly and efficiently as he claims' (Conley 1997, 29; emphasis in original).

Mike Gane provides a more nuanced reading, however – one which suggests that 'Baudrillard ... wishes to maintain the value of revolutionary criticism,' but 'the world itself, the capitalist order, has changed so fundamentally as to make the productivist critique counter-productive' (1991, 12–13). More specifically, as values are increasingly transparently produced and attached to objects by the capitalist system, rebelliousness becomes a value, subversives a target market, and revolution a commodity, as in the infamous Gap marketing campaign in which store windows were done up to look as though they had been the target of antiglobalization protests. As Jameson suggests, Baudrillard shows 'the ways in which conscious ideologies of revolt, revolution, and even negative critique are – far from merely being 'co-opted' by the system – an integral and functional part of the system's own internal strategies' (1991, 203).

Baudrillard's argument, as we have seen, short-circuits political strategies that aim at revealing a truth, reality, or nature that lies beneath the sign-system of contemporary capitalism. Insofar as it rests on the ideological (or, more properly, simulacric) category of 'needs,' the 'productivist critique' of capitalism (i.e., Marxism) is at best doomed to failure, and at worst functional to the maintenance of the very system it seeks to overthrow. But although the more traditional avenues of radical politics are closed off by this critique of the depth model, this is not to suggest that political action is impossible. Three possible Baudrillardian strategies can be discerned.

Charles Levin and Arthur Kroker (1984) have suggested that faced with Baudrillard's diagnosis, 'the relevant and perhaps only political response is that of *ironic detachment*' (15; emphasis in original). Others, meanwhile, have suggested that the appropriate Baudrillardian response is a sort of purposeless violence that precisely resists meaning – as in Nicholas Turse's provocative claim that political radicalism for American youth in the 1990s is expressed through seemingly random or 'senseless' killing, typified by Columbine killers Eric Harris and Dylan Klebold (Turse, n.d.).

Besides ironic detachment and nihilistic violence, a third possibility is that 'hyperconformity' constitutes a form – perhaps were the most viable form – of 'resistance.' (Baudrillard 1983a, 41–8). Hyperconformity is a form of action that often *seems* to take the form of a 'celebration' of advanced capitalism; however, it is not to be mistaken for complacency. It is not a suggestion that we are doing just fine, but rather the claim that 'a system is abolished only by pushing it into hyperlogic, by forcing it into an excessive practice which is equivalent to a brutal amortization. "You want us to consume – OK, let's consume always more, and anything whatsoever; for any useless and absurd purpose"' (Baudrillard 1983a, 46).

But there is also a sense in which the radicalism of Baudrillard's critique leads him into what might best be described as an apolitical empiricist descriptivism, even when the more clearly apolitical strategies such as ironic detachment and purposeless violence are eschewed. Baudrillard's insistence that the masses are in some sense working against what he calls 'the logic of socialization' precisely *by* conforming, means that, for him, entertaining the hope of transcending 'our modernity' through revolutionary politics or dialectical thinking is not only false, but in fact counterproductive and dangerous. Baudrillard's disdain for abstract, strategic theorizing is summed up in the following quotation: 'The point is not to write the sociology ... of the car, the point is to drive ... Drive ten thousand miles across America and you will know more about the country than all the institutes of sociology and political science combined' (1988, 54–5). Such a statement, even if true, participates in a power/knowledge formation of which it seems blissfully unaware: we may be able to learn a great deal about America – and, by extension, any other (post)modern society, of which America is the hyperrealization – by driving through it and conducting/experiencing what Baudrillard terms 'an anthropology of its driving behaviour' (1988, 54). This is so, however, only because America has *come to be* defined by what André Gorz has termed 'the social ideology of the motorcar' (1980, 69–77).

Baudrillard's perspective suggests that the only way out (if indeed there is a way out) is to push this logic, or this social ideology, to its limits. A look at recent history, however, might hold some lessons about the difficulty of distinguishing Baudrillardian *hyper*conformity from mere conformity. The typical behaviour of *Homo economicus* under advanced capitalism has increasingly come to resemble the Baudrillardian orgiastic consumerist frenzy. This is most visible perhaps in the exhortation to spend as usual (if not more intensely than usual) both as a means of staving off economic recession and as a form of patriotic duty to demonstrate national resolve in the face of terrorist attacks. The presentation of consumerism as a constructive and strategic response to terrorism may have started with President George W. Bush's response to the attacks of 11 September 2001, but it has since found resonance elsewhere (Stein 2002, 9).

Thus the idea that this 'brutal amortization' might by itself 'abolish' the system perhaps now seems as quaint as the notion of global proletarian revolution once seemed to Baudrillard himself. As Baudrillard's own analysis teaches us, consuming is never 'for any useless and absurd purpose'; it is always consumption in the service of establishing an identity that is, in the totalizing sign-environment of advanced capitalism, increasingly precarious.

This precariousness of individual (or even national) identity, however, does not necessarily extend to the system as a whole. For hyperconformity to pose an explosive threat at *this* level requires that the social logic be set into another, larger context. For hyperconformity in, for example, automotive consumption to pose any threat at the systemic level, the social ideology of the motorcar must be understood as itself having certain (the word now at last emerges) *natural* limits. And whether these limits are to be figured as the atmosphere's capacity to absorb carbon dioxide, or humans' psychological capacity to deal with gridlock and road rage, is perhaps less important than the fact that nature reappears here to provide a grounding for normative critique and political action.

Michel Foucault and the Problem of the Body

Not all scholars of postmodern 'nature-scepticism' are as depoliticized as Baudrillard. What other, more explicitly political postmodern theorists do share with Baudrillard is a problem that emerges from the postmodern critique of the depth model. In the case of Michel Foucault, for example, the critique of the depth model does not lead to a perceived apoliticism, as it does in Baudrillard. Rather, with Foucault, who personally never shied away from political commitments, the problem is this: How are we to interpret his normatively grounded political commitments in light of his philosophical antiessentialism, and vice versa?

As with Baudrillard, the radicalism of Foucault's anti-essentialist position appears unassailable. One observer summarizes Foucault's position as follows: 'There never was anything true, any true self or true needs, behind the truth, the self, and the needs constituted by power' (G. Horowitz, 1987, 63). In short, for Foucault there is not, and there never was, any such thing as human nature. Unlike Baudrillard, however, Foucault's critique of essentialism serves a definite and clear political purpose: to establish 'a new politics of truth' by 'detaching the power of truth from the forms of hegemony, social, economic, and cultural, within which it operates at the present time' (Foucault 1980, 133).

Foucault's critique of 'human nature' is most clearly staked out in the first volume of *The History of Sexuality*. As the title suggests, in this work Foucault argues for a historicization of what has traditionally been considered a transhistorical, essential part of human nature – sexuality, or the sexual drive: 'Historical meaning becomes a dimension of *wirkliche Historie* [historical sense] to the extent that it places within a process of development everything considered immortal in man ... We believe in the dull constancy of instinctual life and that it continues to exert its force indiscriminately in the present as it did in the past. But a knowledge of history easily dislocates this unity' (Foucault 1984a, 87). What is at stake in this project, however, is much greater than simply a historicization of sexuality, since the historicization of sexuality for Foucault ultimately necessitates a radical rethinking of our understanding of power as something that is not purely repressive, but rather is productive – constitutive of our very subjectivity. In an interview late in his life, Foucault claimed that his primary academic concern had always been the role of power and discourse in the constitution of subjectivity: 'In fact, that has always been my problem, even if I have expressed in different terms the framework of this thought. I have tried to discover how the human subject entered into *games of truth*, whether they be games of truth which take on the form of science or which refer to a scientific model, or games of truth like those that can be found in institutions or practices of control.' (Foucault, 1989, 1; emphasis in original). In this sense, a historicization of sexuality 'can only be considered a privileged [example], since power seemed in this instance, more than anywhere else, to function as prohibition' (Foucault 1990, 90).

Thus, although the focus of this section will be on that crucial tension which marks some of Foucault's key texts, it is important to note the consistency that runs through Foucault's work – a consistency that underpins those contradictory moments or impulses which will be highlighted here. As Nancy Fraser has noted, *The History of Sexuality* (one of Foucault's later works) is similar to his earlier work in that it rejects foundationalist or essentialist categories as a possible basis for emancipation. What is more, Foucault argues that the use of such categories as 'grounds' for emancipatory politics is positively a hindrance. The very categories that are purported to be instruments of emancipation are in fact strategies of power whose use merely serves to reinforce subjection. 'In a fashion that parallels his treatment of "Man" and the subject, then, Foucault rejects "sex-desire" as a normative category on two analytically distinct but functionally interrelated counts: (1) it is foundationalistic, and (2) it is an instrument of domination' (Fraser 1989, 60).

Foucault's case against foundationalism is in some respects made most strongly in *Discipline and Punish*. In this book, he argues that the rise of the modern penal system marked a transformation from a medieval system of exceptional and spectacular punishment, to a modern system of subtle coercion primarily by means of constant observation. Moreover, the modern penal system is modular, and its theories and tactics are applied throughout a network of social institutions, which Foucault terms 'the carceral archipelago' (Foucault 1979, 297). Power, in this system, is not a matter of prohibiting certain forms of behaviour through occasional public and highly visible – in a word, spectacular – punishments intended as deterrents. Rather, power is understood as operating more effectively through the imposition of a subtle, totalizing disciplinary apparatus. Such an apparatus disciplines 'docile bodies'[4] through 'hierarchical observation' and 'normalizing judgement,' in order to produce subjects who, in most cases, police themselves. In other words, power does not operate by repressing or elevating certain aspects of human nature that exist as a biological 'foundation' on which the social is erected. Instead, subjectivity is constituted through and through by power relations.

The constitution of a self-policing subject, Foucault argues, is achieved through a number of technologies, all of which operate under the 'panoptic' principle. In the eighteenth century, Jeremy Bentham posited the panopticon as an ideal prison. In a panopticon, individuals are placed in cells with opaque side walls but transparent fronts, arranged in a circle around a central tower. The cells are backlit so that observers in the tower can see into the cells, but not vice versa. The circular arrangement of the cells ensures that prisoners are unable to communicate with one another. Under this ideal schema, the prisoner 'is seen, but he does not see; he is the object of information, never a subject in communication' (Foucault 1979, 200). The only relation that the prisoner has, therefore, is with the observer in the central tower, although, since the prisoner cannot see into the tower, he can never be sure if or when he is being observed. 'A real subjection is born mechanically from a fictitious relation ... He who is subjected to a field of visibility, and who knows it, assumes responsibility for the constraints of power; he makes them play spontaneously upon himself; he inscribes in himself the power relation in which he simultaneously plays both roles; he becomes the principle of his own subjection' (202–3).

Foucault's argument for a reconceptualization of power as productive thus hinges on the structuralist psychoanalysis of Jacques Lacan – in particular, on Lacan's emphasis on the centrality of 'the gaze.' (Fraser notes (1989) that for Foucault, 'the gaze' is the paradigmatic example of modern power, in that it is 'synoptic and individualizing' (22).) For Lacan, it is 'the scopic field,' or the field that is produced by the gaze, in both its possibility and its impossibility (both the possibility of seeing and the impossibility of seeing all, or the possibility and impossibility of truly seeing oneself), on which subjectivity is constructed: 'In the scopic relation, the object on which depends the phantasy from which the subject is suspended in an essential vacillation is the gaze' (Lacan 1981, 83). 'The gaze,' Lacan makes clear, is not to be understood simply as the capacity one has for seeing, but rather as the fact that one *is seen*, that one is a part of the 'scopic field' of the Other. Moreover, 'the Other' is defined by Lacan as the 'symbolic order,' and thus cannot be specified as a particular person. It is not that one is seen, for example, by one's parents or one's peers, or any other identifiable individual. Instead, what is most important is that one thinks of (or sees) oneself being seen. 'The gaze I encounter ... is, not a seen gaze, but a gaze *imagined by me* in the field of the Other' (84; emphasis added).

By now, it is perhaps apparent why this is important for Foucault and for his understanding of power as something that can operate without violent coercion. 'The exercise of discipline presupposes a mechanism that coerces by means of observation' (Foucault 1979, 170). Here, he is alluding to the imposition of a scopic matrix. Although such a matrix would seem to rely on technological inventions like the telescope, and on the innovations of 'minor techniques of multiple and intersecting observations,' (171), in fact one of its most important instruments for 'seeing' lies within the subject being observed: 'Solitude assures a sort of self-regulation of the penalty and makes possible a spontaneous individualization of the punishment: the more the convict is capable of reflecting, the more capable he was of committing his crime; but, also, the more lively his remorse, the more painful his solitude; on the other hand, when he has profoundly repented and made amends without the least dissimulation, solitude will no longer weigh upon him' (237).

But to the extent that for Foucault disciplinary mechanisms operate through the individual's reflection-induced remorse (to the extent, in other words, that people change because they feel badly about their acts or the person they have become, rather than because are *told* to feel badly about it), Foucault is perhaps not quite the radical antiessentialist that some make him out to be. Perhaps it is the case that essentialism reappears in the guise of the desire to confess and repent, what 'Freud and all his followers, on the right and on the left [including, presumably, Lacan], have found beneath the actually existing sexual forms[:] the generalized prediscusive prepersonal bodily pleasure potential of the it – and beneath that, the prepersonal, prediscursive childhood need for love' (G. Horowitz 1987, 71). But as Horowitz also makes clear, such a reading is difficult to sustain. In *The History of Sexuality*, vol. 1, 'Foucault does not suggest, even for a moment, that there is something – pleasure-multiplicity – prior to or beyond the specific forms of our sexuality that we are to search for, discover, liberate, and live up to. He is not a closet essentialist' (68).

The second point that Fraser notes is common to all of Foucault's work, is his argument that foundationalist categories, although posited as means for achieving liberation, in fact operate in the service of domination. Once again, it is in *Discipline and Punish* that this view finds its clearest expression. In that book, Foucault notes that the rise of disciplinary institutions (or the 'accumulation of [subjected] men') is closely tied to the rise of capitalism – the accumulation of capital (1979, 220–1). The purpose of the network of disciplinary institutions – including but of course not limited to prisons – is 'the constitution of a power relation ... a schema of individual submission and of adjustment to a *production* apparatus' (243; emphasis added). In other words, the institutions of a disciplinary society function to create the sorts of subjects required by capitalism.

Yet Foucault also notices that such a project, as Bentham's example serves to show, is utopic. The contradictions inherent in capitalism's economic logic – not least of which is the necessity for capital to maintain a reserve of 'unemployed' workers – ensure that it is impossible to turn every single member of society into a model worker/citizen. So we must look to these fundamental contradictions, Foucault argues, if we are to understand why, in the 150-year-long existence of the prison system, there has been no reduction in criminality. Thus, the real purpose of the penal system (which, Foucault argues, includes the prison reform movements) is to 'handle' rather than eliminate or even reduce illegalities – to channel potentially subversive acts (crimes against property in response to its unequal distribution) into politically less dangerous forms:

> For the observation that the prison fails to eliminate crime, one should perhaps substitute the hypothesis that prison has succeeded extremely well in producing delinquency, a specific type, a politically and economically less dangerous – and, on occasion, usable – form of illegality; in producing delinquents, in an apparently marginal, but in fact centrally supervised milieu; in producing the delinquent as a pathologized subject.... Now this process that constitutes delinquency as an object of knowledge is one with the political operation that dissociates illegalities and isolates delinquency from them. (Foucault 1979, 277)[5]

Once again, Foucault's analysis here of 'delinquency' and the penal system is exemplary rather than exceptional. The form of the critique outlined in *Discipline and Punish* is mirrored in, for example, *The History of Sexuality*. In the latter work, Foucault argues against the 'repressive hypothesis' – the dominant metadiscourse of sex in the modern Western world – which asserts that sex is something that is and has been repressed in our 'Victorian' culture: 'A censorship of sex? There was installed rather an apparatus for producing an ever greater quantity of discourse about sex ... Toward the beginning of the eighteenth century, there emerged a political, economic, and technical incitement to talk about sex' (Foucault 1990, 23). And although psychoanalysis may have been progressive to the extent that it posited a 'ground[ing of] sexuality in the law' against the fascist goal of totally administered sexuality, for Foucault psychoanalysis remains trapped in the old (repressive) model of power, and as such, 'is in the last analysis a historical "retro-version"' (150).

For Foucault, the repressive hypothesis is false not only because of the manifest explosion of discourses around sexuality since what he terms the classical age, but also, and more important, because it posits a prediscursive 'sex' that can be liberated from social repression, when in fact sex is 'a complex idea that was formed inside the deployment of sexuality' (1990, 152). More generally, 'the biological and the historical are not consecutive to one another ... but are bound together in an increasingly complex fashion in accordance with the development of modern technologies of power that take life as their objective' (152). Thus the liberatory impulse that the repressive hypothesis engenders – that we ought to minimize sexual repression – turns out to perform precisely the same function as the prison reform movement in another context: it holds out a false promise of liberation that works to ensure domination by deflecting attention away from the true nature of power: 'Finally, the notion of sex brought about a fundamental reversal; it made it possible to invert the representation of the relationships of power to sexuality, causing the latter to appear, not in its essential and positive relation to power, but as being rooted in a specific and irreducible urgency which power tries as best it can to dominate; *thus the idea of "sex" makes it possible to evade what gives "power" its power; it enables one to conceive of power solely as law and taboo*' (155; emphasis added).

But although Foucault rejects 'sex' as a feasible point from which to launch a criticism of power he does not lapse into apolitical 'fatal' theorizing as Baudrillard does. He seems not to dismiss the possibility of finding such a point; in fact, he asserts its existence: 'The rallying point against the deployment of sexuality ought not to be sex-desire, but bodies and pleasures' (1990, 157).

But this immediately raises a question: What is this call to rally around 'bodies and pleasures,' or this 'turn toward a new metaphysics – one of bodies' (Fraser 1989, 59), if not a return to just the sort of essentialism that Foucault rejects? Has Foucault not shown us in *Discipline and Punish* precisely how even 'bodies and pleasures' are not given, but are constructed by power? In an essay on Nietzsche, Foucault describes the body as 'the inscribed surface of events ... [Genealogy's] task is to expose a body totally imprinted by history and the process of history's destruction of the body' (1984a, 83). There would seem to be three possible responses to this apparent paradox.

First, one might take Foucault at his apparent word in the conclusion of *The History of Sexuality*: that he is positing the existence of 'bodies and pleasures' as something that is – in some sense at least – prior to or outside of power. At the end of the introductory chapter of *Discipline and Punish,* he discusses what brought his attention to the prison as a 'political technology of the body': recent prison revolts, which seemed paradoxical in that they were revolts not only against the conditions in old, decrepit prisons, but also against the conditions in the most modern, comfortable prisons. 'In fact, they were [in both cases] revolts, *at the level of the body,* against the very body of the prison. What was at issue was not whether the prison environment was too harsh or too aseptic, too primitive or too efficient, but its very materiality as an instrument and vector of power' (Foucault 1979, 30; emphasis added).

In this same vein, Michel de Certeau (1984) discusses the social production of 'bodies' explicitly in the context of *Discipline and Punish*: 'Where does the disciplinary apparatus end that displaces and corrects, adds or removes things from these bodies, malleable under the instrumentation of so many laws? To tell the truth, they become bodies only by conforming to these codes. Where and when is there ever anything bodily that is not written, remade, cultured, identified by the different tools which are part of a social symbolic code? Perhaps at the extreme limit of these tireless inscriptions, or perforating them with lapses, there remains only the cry' (147). What de Certeau seems here to be arguing is that bodies are never encountered prior to power, but at the same time, in spite of this fact, there is nevertheless something ('the cry') that is outside of or opposed to power.

Such a reading of Foucault, however, remains problematic, for reasons that were suggested earlier in the discussion of antiessentialism. If this view is accepted, Horowitz notes, then 'Foucault gives up here the insistence that is crucial to his whole argument about power and subjectivity, that it is false and dangerous to search for any extradiscursive truth' (G. Horowitz 1987, 68). Horowitz then provides another possible response to the paradox posed earlier: 'Bodies and pleasure' is simply Foucault's way of specifying for the sexual sphere the nature of the resistance to power that is always and everywhere the concomitant of power. If there were no "deployment of sexuality" (power) there would be no "bodies and pleasure" (resistance) ... Saying yes to sex is saying no to power insofar as one is saying yes to polymorphous sexuality – bodies, pleasures – and not to any norm or standard of liberated, healthy, or politically correct sex' (68–9).

Such a reading emphasizes Foucault's antiessentialism as well as the Nietzscheanism that is involved in Foucault's deconstruction of the metaphysical subject. What Foucault shares with Nietzsche is an intellectual project that seeks to reveal that 'we are constructed de novo in the here and now of discursive practices, not in our nonexistent depths. We are simply beings who oppress ourselves with a delusion of depth' (G. Horowitz 1987, 70). Foucault, in other words, agrees with Nietzsche's assertion in 'The Genealogy of Morals' that 'there is no "being" behind the doing, acting, becoming; the "doer" has simply been added to the deed by the imagination – the doing is everything' (Nietzsche 1956, 178–9). For Foucault, 'one has to dispense with the constituent subject, to get rid of the subject itself, that's to say, to arrive at an analysis which can account for the constitution of the subject within a historical framework' (1980, 117).

The problem with this understanding of Foucauldian analysis, as Horowitz and others are quick to point out, is that it does not provide a ground from which to launch the sort of normative critique in which Foucault wants to engage. Notwithstanding their profound methodological similarities, Foucault does not share Nietzsche's politics. Nietzsche seeks to liberate the aristocratic few from the stultifying grip of conventional morality; in contrast, there is little doubt that although Foucault is equally critical of conventional morality, his political sympathies are informed by a much more egalitarian sensibility. Nietzsche seeks to liberate the 'will to power'; Foucault is more concerned with what we might term the 'will to resistance.' The problem is that his philosophy seeks to undercut precisely any normative grounding for such an impulse. If, as Foucault suggests, 'knowledge is not made for understanding; it is made for cutting' (Foucault 1984a, 88), how are we to decide where or what to cut? Nietzsche seeks to naturalize relations of power and impulses to dominate; Foucault, without disputing the naturality or inevitability of power, seems to want to make a normative case against domination – why else should we attend to the call of 'bodies and pleasures'? What, after all, is wrong with being constructed to believe in and pursue a liberatory possibility that does not exist?

This conundrum is what Fraser is referring to in her claim that one of the most problematic aspects of Foucault's work is that it strives to be 'politically engaged' while remaining 'normatively neutral' (Fraser 1989, 19). Fraser says there can be little doubt that *Discipline and Punish* is highly critical of modern power and advocates resistance to it; but, she adds, this criticism seems to be based on precisely the liberal humanist values the book is seeking to undermine: 'If one asks what exactly is wrong with that [carceral] society, Kantian notions leap immediately to mind' (30). She then provides a third position on this paradox in Foucault's work.

Fraser begins by suggesting that Foucault's use of the term 'bodies' is somewhat misleading:

> In fact, Foucault does not identify any positive characteristics of bodies 'as they really are in themselves' apart from the ways in which they are historically 'invested.' Nor does he derive any universal normative political ideals from his putative suprahistoical corporeality. On the contrary, he calls his project the study of the history of the political technology of the body [which] is a history of the politically and historically invested body. [Hence, the body] prior to power ... can never be encountered and has no identifiable properties whatsoever. (60–1)

Fraser thus clearly rejects the idea that for Foucault, there is anything comprehensible outside of discourse or power, since 'claims couched in the language of the pleasures of our bodies are no more intrinsically immune from co-optation and abuse than are claims made in any other vocabulary' (63). Of course, this leaves her reading of Foucault open to the sort of objection outlined above: If there is nothing that is not already implicated in power and constructed by power relations, what grounds can there be for resisting power?

According to Fraser, Foucault 'should' respond to these objections by claiming that he is arguing for a 'new metaphysics of bodies' – but only at a 'pragmatic' rather than an 'ontological' level. Thus, the central question shifts from one of metaphysics to one of political tactics. Fraser asks: 'Is "body language" really more efficacious than "rights language" or "desires language" or "needs-and-interests language"?' (61). In other words: 'Can we sum up our objections more efficaciously by saying that panoptical practices and the like produce an offensive economy of bodies and pleasures or by saying that they fail to respect the rights that express our sense of how persons ought to be treated?' (63). Fraser 'suspects' that it is the latter option that is more likely to be politically efficacious; this in turn 'suggest[s] the possibility of the sort of immanent critique that consists in condemning the institutions of a culture for their failure to realize its own widely accepted ideals' (64).

But this suspected answer reveals its own problems. Fraser acknowledges that 'there is something disturbingly conservative in [the rights] approach' (64). This approach, like the 'closet essentialist' reading, which sees Foucault's position as an argument merely for 'some slack in the sexual order' (G. Horowitz 1987, 69), ends up turning Foucault into a reformist rather than a radical thinker, and cannot be convincingly squared with his critique of humanist rights-based discourses.

The problem with seeing Foucault as a reformist seems to lie with Fraser's assumption that the two discourses (bodies and pleasures on one hand, and rights on the other) aim at the same thing. But her own characterization of rights-based language, as one 'that consists in condemning the institutions of a culture for their failure to realize its own *widely accepted ideals*' (Fraser 1989, 64; emphasis added), should alert us to the fact that there are important differences between the two. For although *Discipline and Punish* can be read as an indictment of a society that fails to live up to its own stated ideal of individual autonomy, this is surely not Foucault's main point. Even (or perhaps especially) 'widely accepted ideals' are themselves a result of struggles and relations of power. Rights-based discourses may be more efficacious in terms of resisting certain particular political practices, but they sidestep the questions – the radical questions – that Foucault's antiessentialism seeks to raise: How did we come to think of ourselves as subjects with rights? On the basis of what exclusions did 'our ideals' become 'widely accepted'? Rights-based discourse, with its injunction that we must all be liberated from repressive restrictions on our rights, is in this sense no different from the 'repressive hypothesis' of sexuality, or the demand for more sanitary prison conditions, which Foucault is precisely seeking to critique. 'Rights,' fully as much as 'the soul,' are 'the effect and instrument of a political anatomy.' Rights, too, can be construed as 'the prison of the body' (1979, 30).

We seem here to have arrived at an impasse: the political commitments of a radical antiessentialism, it seems, can only be either an antipolitics that risks being mistaken for aristocratic conservatism, as in the case of Baudrillard, or a putative radicalism that, like Foucault, risks being coopted by liberal or social democratic reformism. In the case of Foucault, none of the posited resolutions to the problem of grounding a critique in radically antiessentialist discourse quite manage to hold the normative and the antiessentialist poles of his work together. This impasse is a serious one if we hope to discern an environmental politics that does not end up reproducing undesirable (and unnecessary) naturalized social oppression.

One possibility at this point is to stop trying to ground social criticism in any kind of transcendent value system. Such an approach is the preferred position for many postmodernists, given the Lyotardian injunction that postmodernism involves dispensing with totalizing narratives. It would also seem to be the one preferred by Foucault himself, who argued for the need for 'specific,' rather than 'universal' intellectuals engaged in local struggles (Foucault 1980, 126–33), and who expressed irritation at charges of inconsistency in his work as early as the late 1960s.[6] At best, it seems, we are left with what Éric Darier argues: that such a position allows us to see that in spite of an 'irreconcilable conflict' between Foucauldian antiessentialism and 'the frequent recourse by many environmental theorists to a naturalistic position in the last instance,' there is a potential common ground 'when it comes to practical political tactics and to understanding the construction/deconstruction of subjectivities' (Darier 1999, 27).

Environmental issues, however, are global rather than strictly local in scope; and as we saw in the previous chapter, ecological crises are likely to require changes in the self-conception and self-fashioning of vast numbers of people, in ways that run quite contrary to the dominant mode(s) of the self produced by and in the interests of the dominant institutions of industrial and postindustrial capitalist society. To the extent that, for example, ecological concerns will require us to counter consumerist ideology and the tremendous social power of the multibillion-dollar advertising industry, a normative grounding of ecological criticism would seem to be indispensible, or at the very least strategically crucial. Although it is lacking in ecological overtones, this is nevertheless the thrust of Jameson's critique of Foucault: 'Since he did not believe in "desire," he was not equipped to measure the "seductions" of the market itself' (Jameson 1991, 203).

Immediately following this observation about Foucault, Jameson goes on to discuss a structurally similar problematic in contemporary American cultural criticism. Jameson's primary target here is Walter Benn Michaels's *The Gold Standard and the Logic of Naturalism*. Michaels's argument, as Jameson presents it, is that a critique of consumer society is impossible within American cultural criticism, because America is a consumer society, and everyone who writes from within it is implicated in it: 'Although transcending your origins in order to evaluate them has been the opening move in cultural criticism at least since Jeremiah, it is surely a mistake to take this move at face value: not so much because you can't really transcend your culture but because, if you could, you wouldn't have any terms of evaluation left – except, perhaps, theological ones' (Michaels, quoted in Jameson 1991, 204).

Or, as Jameson puts it, illuminating more clearly the parallels between Michaels's argument and French structuralism: 'This takes us all the way to the dilemma of getting out of the total system (which Michaels reinvents here): however it is conceived – whether the market and capitalism, or the American character and exceptional experience (American culture) – the power with which the system is theorized outsmarts the local act of judging or resisting it from within, revealing that to have been yet another feature of the system itself, whether ruse or incest taboo, programmed into it in advance' (1991, 204).[7]

Foucault's theorizations, like those of Baudrillard, are symptomatic of what Jameson terms postmodernism's 'depthlessness,' or its 'critique of... the depth model' (1991, 5 and 12). Regarding the latter, Jameson notes, the first volume of *The History of Sexuality* stands as a 'programmatic and symptomatic' text (1991, 12). We might also note in passing that this structural incapacity of 'depthless' postmodern theorizations to generate politically efficacious radical criticism bears a certain resemblance to the distinction drawn between 'deep' and 'shallow' ecological movements. Asserting a 'deep' ecological position seems to be a rhetorical attempt to forestall the incorporation or cooptation of environmental criticism, by appealing to a simplistic – and utimately untenable – ontology.

Gilles Deleuze characterizes this collapsing of surface and depth as a conflation of inside and outside. Foucault's radical antiessentialism means that 'instead of moving from an apparent exteriority to an essential "nucleus of interiority" we must conjure up the illusory interiority in order to restore words and things to their constitutive exteriority.' The result is that 'nothing in Foucault is really closed off' (Deleuze 1988, 43).

'Nature,' Inside and Out

The discovery of this structural similarity between the arguments of Baudrillard and those of Foucault allows us now to deal with the possible nagging objection that neither Baudrillard nor Foucault can be unequivocally labelled 'postmodernist,' and that the philosophical positions of both are 'structuralist' rather than 'post-structuralist.' We can defuse this objection, however, by showing that the same problem – a radical epistemological position, manifested as a conflation of interiority and exteriority, that is incapable of grounding radical political commitments – is encountered in the more decidedly *post*-structuralist elaborations of Foucault's theoretical apparatus. In other words, for those who suspect that Baudrillard and Foucault suffer from these problems because they are perhaps not postmodern enough, we shall see that the problems arise even in the work of their more explicitly postmodern followers.

Perhaps the best example of this is Judith Butler's *Gender Trouble*, in which the valorization of drag and parodic representation as a means of destabilizing ossified structures of sex/gender formation rests similarly on a confusion of inside and outside. Drag simultaneously features a man on the inside and a woman on the outside (a man's body wearing women's clothing), *and* a woman on the inside and a man on the outside (a woman 'trapped in a man's body') (Butler 1990, 137–8). For Butler, this perfectly captures the impossibility of figuring the sex/gender division as one of inside (sex) and outside (gender), since ('scientific') determinations of sex are always already imbricated with socially constructed notions of gender (106–10).

The tension we saw in Foucault's work between the two poles of normative critique and radical antiessentialism is most evident in the opening pages of Butler's subsequent book, *Bodies That Matter*. Here, Butler attempts to clarify her ideas in *Gender Trouble*, while also answering what she claims was the most persistent objection to her earlier book: 'What about the materiality of the body?' (1993, ix). In this context, she rethinks the oppositional value of drag: 'Drag tends to be the allegorization of heterosexuality and its constitutive melancholia ... At its best, then, drag *can be read for* the way in which hyperbolic norms are dissimulated as the heterosexual mundane' (1993, 237; emphasis added). But here she further concedes 'that there is no necessary relation between drag and subversion, and that drag may well be used in the service of both the denaturalization and reidealization of hyperbolic heterosexual gender norms. At best, it seems, drag is a site of a certain ambivalence' (1993, 125). This 'ambivalence' is strongly reinforced by her discussion of Jennie Livingston's documentary film about the New York African-American/Latino drag 'balls' of the 1980s, *Paris Is Burning* (1993, 128–37) – in particular, by her discussion of the film's disquieting conclusion, during which previously subversive acts ('vogueing') become thoroughly commodified texts appropriated by the fashion industry and Madonna, and during which the failure to conform to gender norms is seen to result – for at least one of the film's subjects – in violent death.

Yet, even in *Bodies That Matter*, Butler remains committed to the usefulness of 'queering' as a political strategy. The problem, which is another manifestation of the postmodern rejection of surface/depth, essence/appearance distinctions, is that queering depends for its subversive success on the imperfect nature of the citation of the performative utterance. But if such citations are, as Butler suggests, *constitutively* imperfect, then there is no way for us to discern which citations or utterances are 'a turn *against* this constitutive historicity [of the discursive term]' (1993, 227; emphasis in original), and which of them simply reinforce hegemonic understandings. In other words, Butler provides no way of answering the question she poses in the introductory paragraph of the book's conclusion: 'When and how does a term like "queer" become subject to an affirmative resignification for some when a term like "nigger," despite some recent efforts at reclamation, appears only capable of reinscribing its pain?' (223).

The postmodern critique of 'nature' thus comes to resemble a ride on a Möbius strip: inside and outside, the natural and the social, like depth and surface or essence and appearance, are ultimately indistinguishable. For this reason, normative criticism, and the political action that follows from it – both of which rest on the possibility of an 'outside' acting as a foundation on which the critic can at least imaginatively position herself – become susceptible to radical interrogation that may well be unanswerable. Once we are faced with the realization that all truth claims are politically interested, there seems no compelling reason for us to choose Foucault's (or Butler's) democratic sensibility over Nietzsche's aristocratic valorization of the will to power, other than by referring to discourses (such as democratic humanism) that can themselves be revealed no more than effects of power.

This is not to suggest, however, that the postmodern critique of 'nature' lacks its own moment of truth. Once the antiessentialist genie is out of the bottle, it cannot easily be stuffed back in:

> Popular concern about the environment often implicitly appeals to a kind of naïve realism for its intellectual foundation, more or less assuming that we can pretty easily recognize nature when we see it and thereby make uncomplicated choices between natural things, which are good, and unnatural things, which are bad. Much of the moral authority that has made environmentalism so compelling as a popular movement flows from its appeal to nature as a stable external source of nonhuman values against which human actions can be judged without much ambiguity. If it now turns out that the nature to which we appeal as the source of our own values has in fact been contaminated or even invented by those values, this would seem to have serious implications for the moral and political authority people ascribe to their own environmental concerns. (Cronon 1995, 25–6)

In other words, no matter how comforting such a naive realism may be, we cannot believe in it simply because it is a safer bet (as Pascal said of the afterlife). The contingency of the foundations of social life is not merely imagined, and 'postmodernism' is not the only word that 'has no meaning.'

Thus, if the problem of depthlessness is to be avoided, or if we are to be able to meaningfully say that human ecology is faced with some 'real' problems, it would seem that we need to understand the material world as at least *relatively* autonomous from linguistic representations of it. On the other hand, as we saw in this chapter, we also need to understand that the natural world is only accessible to us in linguistically and socially mediated form. Our understandings of nature are always ideological, in the Althusserian sense of being a 'subject's *Imaginary* relationship to his or her *Real* conditions of existence' (quoted in Jameson 1991, 51). In other words, we need a way of understanding ourselves as both beings who are within (or a part of) nature, and as beings who are outside of or separate from (capable of denying, transforming, and re-presenting) nature.

The remainder of this book is devoted to the excavation of such an understanding. The understanding of human beings as 'alienated from nature,' or perhaps more precisely as beings who *alienate themselves* from nature, is one that might form the basis for preserving the moments of truth in both the ecological defence of nature and the postmodern critique of 'nature.' At its most basic level, 'alienation from nature' can be understood as the ongoing process whereby human beings self-consciously transform their natural environment. In what follows, I attempt to refine and expand on this concept by examining how it has been deployed by a number of thinkers, for whom it functions as an important aspect of their thought.

CHAPTER 3

Jean-Jacques Rousseau: Modernity and the Historicization of Alienation

The concept 'origin' ought to be stripped of its static mischief.

Adorno (1973, 155)

The distinction between nature and convention is a theme that runs back to the beginnings of Western philosophy. The choice of Jean-Jacques Rousseau as the historical starting point for this particular analysis might therefore seem an arbitrary or even misguided one. One could certainly find thinkers predating Rousseau who at least on the surface address ecological issues more explicitly. But as the two previous chapters have sought to show, what seems to be required is a way of thinking about the human relationship with nature that does not force us into choosing nature at the expense of convention or vice versa. Rousseau *is* perhaps best known for his romantic intervention against those who saw convention as unmitigated progress over nature (Hobbes and Locke in the social contract tradition of political theory, the Enlightenment *philosophes* in moral philosophy). But even if Rousseau's romanticism can in this sense provide inspiration for contemporary deep ecologists, his importance for contemporary ecological politics, I will argue, lies elsewhere, in his treatment of 'alienation from nature' as a historical category – or, in other words, in his role as a progenitor of a denaturalized ecological politics.

In spite of Rousseau's harshly critical attitude toward our alienated existence, it is not the case – as his contemporary, Voltaire, suggested – that Rousseau's ideal was to have human beings return to the forests to walk on all fours. For Rousseau, if the state of nature functions as a regulative ideal, it is one to which not even an *attempt* at an unmediated return can be made. 'A real return to nature,' according to Rousseau, would entail 'the destruction of the [human] species.' (A. Horowitz 1987, 33). Instead of arguing for a return to what he presents in the *Discourse on the Origins of Inequality* (hereafter the *Second Discourse*) as human beings' natural state (the 'state of nature'), Rousseau attempts – in his later works in particular – to articulate solutions to the problem of alienation from nature while maintaining human beings in a social (or postnatural) state. It is with this eighteenth-century thinker, therefore, that the beginnings of a solution to the antinomy outlined in the previous two chapters can be found. Or more precisely, we should say that the beginnings of a solution are to be found in the interstices of various recent interpretations of Rousseau – the 'Rousseaus for our times,' to alter slightly the title of a special issue of *Daedalus* published in 1978, on the two-hundredth anniversary of Rousseau's death. Rousseau himself clearly and from his earliest writings notes that alienation from nature is a chief source of human misery. That he wrestled with the problem in a number of ways throughout his works suggests that he considered it a soluble problem. But as we shall see, his explicit solutions are unconvincing, and this has left his interpreters with the task of finding a solution either by attempting to rationalize Rousseau's theoretical methodology, or by reading Rousseau's texts against the historical or psychological limits of the author, or by speculatively reconstructing arguments implied in the texts. More specifically, the problem that will guide our reading of Rousseau and his interpreters will be to connect Rousseau's various and at times contradictory works in a way that is plausible and that also highlights 'alienation from nature' as a central problematic, if not for Rousseau himself, then at least for our contemporary reappropriation of his works. Before turning to these posited solutions, however, we should first understand how Rousseau sees the problem of the human relationship with nature, and why a return to nature is impossible.

The *Second Discourse*: The Natural History of Alienation

Rousseau deals most clearly with the problem of alienation from nature in the *Second Discourse*. This essay begins with a quotation from Aristotle's *Politics*: 'Not in depraved things but in things well-oriented to nature, are we to consider what is natural' (Rousseau 1987, 23). This quotation offers a précis of the critiques of earlier social-contract theorists – a précis that Rousseau elaborates in the rest of the essay. For

Rousseau, theorists such as Hobbes and Locke posited a 'state of nature' from which human society developed, but they did so without taking into account the effects of society on human character and development: 'They spoke about savage man, and it was civil man that they depicted' (38). In particular, Rousseau is critical of the naturalization, or hypostatization, of what C.B. Macpherson famously calls 'possessive individualism' (Macpherson 1962) For Rousseau, vanity (*amour-propre*), which causes the desire for differentiation of social status, and which leads to social inequality, is a result of the particular trajectory of human *social* development and is not something found in 'natural man.'

But it is not simply the development of vanity that marks the difference between 'natural' and 'social' humans. In the state of nature, 'man' is independent and strong, and 'all his needs are satisfied' (Rousseau 1987, 40). In constrast, social living renders people dependent on one another and often unable 'to satisfy a multitude of passions which are the product of society' (53). In sum: 'In becoming habituated to the ways of society ... he becomes weak, fearful, and servile; his soft and effeminate lifestyle completes the enervation of both his strength and his courage' (43).

Although nature exerts a strong normative pull on Rousseau's understanding of the human condition, and even though Rousseau here sets aside the issue of human physiological development (1987, 40), he seems on the verge of suggesting that human nature itself is historical. But for Rousseau it is not simply a matter of contrasting life in the state of nature with social existence in general. In this sense, Rousseau's romantic critiques of modernity are quite different from the contemporary ecocentric critiques of modernity that we considered in chapter 1. As we shall see later, for Rousseau the 'state of nature' is irrecoverable. Yet the question for Rousseau remains this: How might human development have been (and yet be) different? In a passage that seems a remarkable prefiguration of Foucault's antiessentialism, Rousseau states in 'Considerations on the Government of Poland and on its Projected Reformation': 'When reading ancient history, one believes oneself transported into another universe and among other beings. What have Frenchmen, Englishmen, Russians, in common with the Romans and the Greeks? Almost nothing but their shape' (Rousseau 1997a, 179).

Yet for precisely this reason, Rousseau's decision to quote Aristotle for the essay's epigraph might seem a curious one. The main argument of the *Second Discourse*, after all, is that the 'origins of inequality' are almost entirely social, and that 'natural' inequalities are insignificant relative to the inequalities engendered by society. Shane Phelan describes Rousseau's telling of the founding of society as 'a parody of earlier contract theory; in his story, the contract is a sham' (Phelan 1993, 48). Aristotle, in contrast, is one of the great defenders of the *naturality* of inequality. For Rousseau, the fact that human beings in society are fundamentally different from humans in the state of nature – that 'the difference between the savage man and the domesticated man should be still greater than that between the savage animal and the domesticated animal' (Rousseau 1987, 43) – suggests that it is impossible for human beings in society to achieve a real understanding of 'human nature.' The harder we try to refine our techniques for understanding our human nature, the more distant we become from the natural human state: 'Thus, in a sense, it is by dint of studying man that we have rendered ourselves incapable of knowing him' (33). This historical and non-progressive view of human development (a story of increasing alienation) holds the key to understanding Rousseau's curiously approving citation of a great defender of inequality – from a society with which his has 'almost nothing' in common, no less – to begin the essay.

According to Rousseau, Aristotle is just like Hobbes and Locke in that he defends inequality based on an insufficiently historical understanding of human nature, according to Rousseau. In the *Social Contract*, Rousseau mentions Aristotle's defence of slavery and states that 'Aristotle was right, but he took the effect for the cause' (142). According to Rousseau, our 'depraved' or unnatural existence extends back to the beginnings of society, or the moment when we left solitary existence in the state of nature. It would be wrong, therefore, to judge the naturality or rightness of inequality on the study of human life beyond any point after we *became*, in Aristotle's words, a 'political animal.'

But the 'political' nature of human beings' existence outside of the state of nature is tied in with myriad other aspects of our alienated existence. In Part Two of the *Second Discourse*, Rousseau suggests that political relations arose gradually but ineluctably as a result of inequality: political authority flows from the notion of property rights (1987, 76–7), which themselves constitute the basis of civil society. Rousseau begins Part Two by declaring that 'the first man who, having enclosed a plot of land, took it into his head to say *this is mine*, and found people simple enough to believe him, was the true founder of civil society' (60; emphasis in original). But Rousseau is quick to point out that this apparent 'foundation' is in fact far from the bottom: 'But it is quite likely that by then things had reached the point where they could no longer continue as they were. For this idea of property, depending on many prior ideas which could only have arisen successively, was not formed all at once in the human mind. It was necessary to make great progress, to acquire much industry and enlightenment, and to transmit and augment them from one age to another, before arriving at this final stage in the state of nature' (60).

When we peel back the historical layers, or go back to before the 'final stage' of life in the state of nature, we discover that reason itself lies at the root of inequality: 'Reason engenders egocentrism [*amour-propre*], and reflection strengthens it' (Rousseau 1987, 54). More specifically, we could say that one idea required for the development of inequality is comparative thinking, – that is, the idea of difference itself. Thus, Rousseau notes of 'man' in the state of nature, that 'while as yet hardly knowing how to distinguish the ranks, and contemplating himself in the first rank by virtue of his species, he prepared himself from afar to lay claim to it in virtue of his individuality' (61). In other words, underpinning political or economic inequality is the *idea* of inequality, which also must be invented. Thus, Rousseau opens his essay by reminding us with the words of Aristotle that we cannot discover natural characteristics in beings that are in a 'depraved' condition, and then returns to just these terms to remind us that 'the man who meditates is a depraved animal' (42).[1]

But at the same time, as Ernst Cassirer points out, Rousseau in his *Confessions* emphasizes that the critiques of reason developed both in the *Second Discourse* and, even earlier and more emphatically, in the *Discourse on the Sciences and the Arts* were not 'designed to throw mankind back into its original barbarism' (Cassirer 1954, 54). Cassirer goes on to cite Rousseau – here referring to himself in the third person – directly:

> But human nature does not turn back. Once man has left it, he can never return to the time of innocence and equality. It was on this principle that he [i.e., Rousseau] particularly insisted. [...] He has been obstinately accused of wishing to destroy the sciences and the arts [...] and to plunge humanity back into its original barbarism. Quite the contrary: he always insisted on the preservation of existing institutions, maintaining that their destruction would leave the vices in existence and remove only the means to their cure, putting plunder in the place of corruption. (quoted in Cassirer 1954, 54; bracketed ellipses added by Cassirer's translator)

An insistence on this point allows for the construction of a tight relationship between the *Second Discourse* and the later writings such as the *Social Contract* and *Emile*. According to this view of Rousseau's work, the earlier writings provide the diagnosis of the problem ('alienation from nature'), and the later writings attempt to prescribe a solution. Given the historicized understanding of the problem Rousseau develops, however, it should be apparent that the 'prescription' must be positive, or forward-looking, rather than a regression: 'This is the question to which the *Contrat social* addresses itself. The return to the simplicity and happiness of the state of nature is barred to us, but the path of *freedom* lies open; it can and must be taken' (Cassirer 1954, 54; emphasis in original).

The *Social Contract*: The Impossibility of a Political Solution

It is a testimony to the monumental impact Cassirer's study had on the field of Rousseau studies to say that it is now widely (although, as we shall see, not universally) accepted that the *Second Discourse* explains how inequality and alienation have come about, and that the *Social Contract* is Rousseau's attempt to provide a political solution to these problems. The *Social Contract*, Rousseau says, is an attempt to 'render legitimate' (Rousseau 1987, 141) the bonds of social obligation, which impinge on the freedom human beings enjoyed in their natural state (as described in the *Second Discourse*).

The relationship between the *Second Discourse* and the *Social Contract* is even more striking when one considers the so-called 'Geneva Manuscripts,' which constituted an early draft of the *Social Contract*. For example, in the *Second Discourse*, as we saw earlier, Rousseau claims that the need for political institutions arises out of inequality, which itself can be traced back to the conceptualization of difference. This use of humanity's capacity to reason, however, is itself the result of the dynamic nature of humanity's interaction with its environment: 'In proportion as the human race spread, difficulties multiplied with the men. Differences in soils, climates and seasons could force them to inculcate changes in their lifestyles' (1987, 61). The *Social Contract* restricts its discussion of the 'first societies' (Book 1, chapter 2) almost exclusively to 'the only natural [society], that of the family' (142); yet the same chapter in the 'Geneva Manuscripts' begins not by claiming that families constitute a sort of natural protosociety, but rather – more along the lines of the *Second Discourse* – that 'the need for political institutions arises' only when natural man's 'state changes and his needs increase' (Rousseau 1997b, 153)

The same chapter in the 'Geneva Manuscripts' also contains a critique of existing political institutions (which the *Social Contract* does not). This critique is strikingly similar in formulation to the conclusion of the *Second Discourse*, which explains the establishment of political society. In the *Second Discourse*, Rousseau declares that the establishment of political society – or what we might term the actually existing social contracts – 'gave new fetters to the weak and new forces to the rich, irretrievably destroyed natural liberty, established forever the law of property and of inequality, changed adroit usurpation into an irrevocable right, and for the profit of a few ambitious men henceforth subjected the entire human race to labor, servitude and misery' (1987, 70).

The 'Geneva Manuscripts' finds Rousseau similarly decrying the false promise of actually existing social contracts: 'The general society which our mutual needs might engender thus offers no effective help to man become miserable, or rather it provides new forces only to the one who already has too many, while the weak, lost, stifled, crushed in the multitude, finds no refuge to which he might flee, no support in his weakness, and in the end he perishes a victim of this deceptive union from which he expected happiness' (1997b, 154).

As many commentators have noted, however, Rousseau's attempts to replace the freedom of the state of nature with a higher, social form of freedom are not entirely successful. Even allowing that Rousseau is not suggesting a simplistic 'return to nature,' his social prescriptions for dealing with the problem of alienation from nature leave something to be desired. Rousseau contends that the form of society he describes in his *Social Contract* is one to which people would freely consent. But, as his liberal critics often note, he fills the *Social Contract* with a number of illiberal institutions, such as the Legislator[2] and the civil religion,[3] which seem designed precisely to mystify social relations and to confound the possibility of rational choice and thereby the possibility of free consent.

Rousseau, therefore, is remembered not only as a social contract theorist, one who attempted to provide a rational basis for political rule, but also as 'the thinker perhaps most commonly identified as the key source of the nationalist idea' (Plattner 1997, 184), or, from the perspective of the latter half of the twentieth century, a theorist who helped establish *irrationalism* in politics:

> A significant connection may be remarked here between the two most illiberal of Rousseau's political principles, the idea of nationality and that of the civil religion. The real case for regarding him as an enemy of liberal Europe comes back almost inevitably to these ideas, which are closely associated, because the civil religion is the religion of the state, of such a state as is upheld in Rousseau's nationalism, for the sake of which in fact it exists. Moreover nationalism as expounded in [Rousseau's *Constitution of*] *Poland* comes sometimes perilously near to being the rule of prejudice and of mass emotion. (Cobban 1964, 118)

Cobban notes that Rousseau was writing at a time when the technologies and social institutions that made the creation of national communities possible were barely beginning to be developed, so he was incapable of envisioning nationalism as anything but a 'conservative, defensive force' that would be 'necessarily strongest in small states, and weakest in large ones' (1964, 121). On the other hand, there can be little doubt that for Cobban – and indeed, for liberals more generally – the conditions of the present day do not permit us to accept Rousseau's political prescriptions. For liberals, as N.J.H. Dent suggests, although Rousseau's aim of legitimating political authority on the basis of the natural freedom of the individual is admirable, the 'compromise[s] ... [and] *ad hoc* remedies' that are to be found throughout the *Social Contract* 'show that Rousseau's theoretical proposals are misfounded' (Dent 1988, 212). From this perspective, Rousseau is right to want to 'render legitimate' the chains of political obligation, but he fails to do so, insofar as he posits myth and obscurantism as the proper basis for political society, rather than rationally informed consent. To put it another way, for reasons which will become clear later in this chapter, we might say that for liberals, freedom within a society demands that our political or social relationships be called what they are – that the language used be denominative rather than metaphorical. The problem in Rousseau, on this account, is that he fails to ground the *Social Contract* in the transparency of rational consent that is made possible by denominative language.

Before explaining the significance of the resort to metaphorical language, we should take note that it is not only Rousseau's *liberal* critics who claim that he offers a solid understanding of a political problematic (specifically, how to guarantee natural rights in the context of a society) but is unable to articulate a political solution. Many Marxists read Rousseau as a perceptive *critic* of nascent bourgeois society, but one who, because capitalism was only just emerging in his time, was unable to formulate an adequate solution to the problem he so shrewdly identified.

For Louis Althusser, for example, the logic of the *Social Contract*, and in particular what Althusser calls 'the absolute limits to posing the problem' – namely, that Rousseau forbids 'any solution which introduces an element external to that field itself' (Althusser 1982, 123)[4] – leads to a series of what he terms 'discrepancies' (*décalages*).[5] He begins with the discrepancy between Rousseau's claims that, on one hand, the alienation of liberty is 'incompatible with man's nature' (1982, 127; Rousseau 1987, 144–5), and that on the other hand, the social contract itself is predicated on 'the total alienation of each associate, together with all of his rights' (Althusser 1982, 126; Rousseau 1987, 148) As Althusser succinctly summarizes it, Rousseau seems to present the contradictory position that: 'Total alienation is the solution to the problem of total alienation.' (Althusser 1982, 127) Althusser then traces 'this Discrepancy and… its denegation, which do not arise as accidents in Rousseau's thought but *constitute* and *determine* it,' (Althusser 1982, 133; emphasis in original) through to the point where Rousseau's *Social Contract* is impelled simultaneously into two equally unsatisfactory directions: a 'flight' into 'ideology' (the civil religion and the importance of 'manners and morals') and an economic 'regression' (the institutionalization of 'petty artisanal production'). Althusser states: 'Flight forward in ideology, regression in the economy, flight forward in ideology, etc. This time the Discrepancy is inscribed in the practice proposed by Rousseau. This practice concerns not concepts, but realities (moral and religious ideology which *exists*, economic property which *exists*). The discrepancy really is in so many words the Discrepancy of theory with respect to the real and its effect: a discrepancy between two equally impossible practices' (159; emphases in original). Such is Althusser's conclusion – or very nearly so. In fact, he makes one more point after this one: that Rousseau is able to make a further shift, to the realm of literature. For Althusser, Rousseau's literary works are a consequence of his failure to achieve a political theoretical solution to the problem posed in political theoretical terms: his 'admirable "fictional triumph"' is predicated on 'the admirable "failure" of ... the *Social Contract*' (160).

A similar reading of Rousseau is offered by Lucio Colletti. For Colletti, Rousseau's genius is that he anticipated the inequality necessarily engendered by a bourgeois civil society predicated on formal equality. This, along with his politicization of the problem of evil (redefined by

Rousseau as social inequality) – 'the problem of the elimination of evil from the world comes to coincide with the problem of revolution' (Colletti 1972, 145) – marks Rousseau, for Colletti, as an important precursor of Marx. Rousseau remains committed to 'economic regression' (as Althusser terms it) as a consequence of his inability to grasp the dynamic nature of capitalist economic development – that is, his belief that 'one man's wealth arose *directly* from the impoverishment of another' (Iring Fetscher, quoted in Colletti 1972, 157; emphasis in original). But he is nevertheless able to articulate a critique of bourgeois civil society that does not call for a return to feudal hierarchy. In fact, this blindness to the nature of capitalist economic development is what allows Rousseau to be such a perceptive critic of bourgeois society. Rousseau's physiocratic contemporaries unproblematically equated overall economic growth with general enrichment; in contrast, Rousseau's belief that 'the "individual" always grew rich at the expense of his fellows' (Colletti 1972, 162) made him more sensitive to the difference between economic growth and general enrichment. And this distinction between individual self-interest and the interest of the community as a whole – a distinction, it should be recalled, that is rooted in the problem of alienation from nature – is of course what the *Social Contract* is intended to overcome.

Ever since Adam Smith, the ideology of the market has been arguing that the general good is achieved when individuals pursue their own selfish interests. According to Rousseau, however, this only exacerbates the problem that arose as a consequence of invidious comparison. What is needed – and what Rousseau proposes in the *Social Contract* – is a 'general will' that – along with the social institutions which support it – aims to preserve or recapture the freedom enjoyed in the state of nature, but to do so without allowing for the instrumentalization of other people that emerges in bourgeois society. Colletti, therefore, might agree with Allan Bloom's classic assessment that for Rousseau, 'the bourgeois stands somewhere between two respectable extremes – the good natural man and the moral citizen' (Bloom 1997, 146). Colletti says similarly that civil society 'denatures man both too much and too little' (1972, 172), but he would insist on giving Bloom's argument a materialist, or economistic, foundation – he would suggest that Bloom has stood Rousseau on his head, so to speak, and place him back on his feet. Colletti first cites Rousseau's apparently 'extravagant' claim in *Emile* that the construction of a society requires us to strip away a human being's natural experience of individualized existence and replace it with the 'transfer [of] his self into a common unity.' He then goes on to argue that

> if one thinks about it a little, the opposite assumption to Rousseau's seems much more extravagant: that a "society" can be built while private interests remain "dissociated." To create a society is to create a common interest, an association or real socialization of interests. If the common interest is restricted to the agreement or contract by which all agree that each shall follow his own private interests, society does not exist (it is only "formal"), and the socialization of man has not taken place: he has remained in the "state of nature" with the sole addition of the safeguard of the state. (Colletti 1972, 173)

As was suggested earlier, for Colletti, as for Althusser, Rousseau remains unable to articulate a convincing solution to the problem of the inadequate socialization that occurs in bourgeois society. 'It is a fact that Rousseau sees this "socialization" essentially in moral and political terms, not yet in economic ones; he sees it as giving rise to the *volonté générale* and the *loi commun*, but not to the socialization of property too.' This problem, in turn, stems – as was the case with Althusser's diagnosis – 'from an objective historical limitation inevitable in his times, i.e. from the impossibility, in the conditions of eighteenth-century France, of thinking concretely a solution of that kind' (1972, 174).

Earlier in the text, Colletti provides a clue as to what might be necessary for such a 'concrete' thinking of the solution. In an extended footnote in his discussion of Rousseau and Adam Smith, Colletti remarks that Rousseau and Smith made a similar error – one that Marx, a century later, would only begin to overcome. Both Smith and Rousseau conflate 'exchange' with the 'division of labour.' In fact, the terms are not identical: 'exchange' society is a particular form of the social division of labour; in other words, the former is a subset of the latter. The 'division of labour' is common to all forms of society ('Living in society, in fact, means living within a division of labour'). On the other hand, 'the "particular" historical form of the social division of labour which is called "exchange" *and presupposes "commodity" production* is quite a different matter.'[6] The result of the conflation of the two, in Rousseau, is that 'the critique of a "determinate" organization of society then becomes the critique of society in general' (Colletti 1972, 164n; emphasis added). In other words, in spite of the seemingly unrelievedly historicist character of Rousseau's work, he is, because of the objective historical circumstances in which he finds himself, unable to historicize sufficiently. The inability to make this distinction between 'exchange' and the 'division of labour' is, for his Marxist critics, what structures the limits to Rousseau's posited solutions to the problem of alienation from nature.

In one sense, this problem of insufficient historicization is traceable to the more abstract levels of Rousseau's argument, in his apparent conflation of the social division of labour with commodity exchange; in another sense, its symptoms are much more manifest. The frustration that both Althusser and Colletti feel with Rousseau lies in the fact that Rousseau so brilliantly diagnoses the problem of bourgeois civil society in the *Second Discourse*, but then insists on what might be called a return to petty bourgeois ideology in the *Social Contract*. This problem is most obvious in Rousseau's insistence in the very opening of the *Social Contract* – and seemingly against precisely the arguments that are brilliantly made in the *Second Discourse* – on 'taking men as they are' (Rousseau 1987, 141).

Situating the Texts: Historicity, Fiction, Language

Of course, this discrepancy is a problem only if we insist that the two texts (the *Second Discourse* and the *Social Contract*) be yoked together. For Jean Starobinski, however, this approach to Rousseau is faulty. Starobinski argues that this 'Hegelian-Marxist interpretation' of Rousseau mistakenly attempts to synthesize the *Second Discourse* and the *Social Contract* through the trope of 'revolution.'[7] (1988, 29) Starobinski contrasts the conclusion of the *Second Discourse* (where the *historicized* understanding of the state of nature concludes with the establishment of social order, seen as the establishment of 'equality in servitude'), with the *Social Contract* understood as, quite precisely, *outside* of history:

> The social pact is not an evolutionary development that follows naturally from the *Second Discourse*; it belongs, rather, to another dimension, a purely normative dimension, outside historical time ... With this new and more reasonable start, history begins not with the possessive assertion – 'This is mine!' – but with the transfer of the common will into the hands of the collectivity. Such a hypothetical society is not condemned to the inevitable historical misfortune that condemned actual humanity to fall into an irrevocable state of corruption. It is, rather, an ideal model against which corrupt society can be judged. (30)

For Starobinski, then, this Hegelian–Marxist interpretation is flawed (and similarly, so is the Kantian interpretation that provides a synthesis of Rousseau's thought through the trope of 'education,' where *Emile* rather than the *Social Contract* is the key text that unlocks the whole of Rousseau's thought [1988, 30–2]). These interpretations are challenged insofar as they see a 'need for a global interpretation of Rousseau's theoretical contribution' (31) For Starobinski, who does not quite go so far as to propose a fragmentary reading of Rousseau's texts, the key to a 'global interpretation' lies elsewhere, within the psyche of Rousseau himself (33).

But is this discrepancy or dislocation between the *Second Discourse* and the *Social Contract* so clear as Starobinski claims? Even if we grant Starobinski's argument that the *Social Contract* is 'outside historical time,' to what extent is this really different from the *Second Discourse*? To be sure, the *Second Discourse* cloaks itself in the mantle of a historical narrative, but it is crucial to recall that this is a 'historical' narrative that begins by highlighting the epistemological problems inherent in the very possibility of conceiving such a project ('it is by dint of studying man that we have rendered ourselves incapable of knowing him' [Rousseau 1987, 31]), and 'by putting aside all the facts' (38). It is a historical narrative that begins at a point (the state of nature) 'which no longer exists, *which perhaps never existed*, which probably never will exist' (34; emphasis added).

Moreover, we might in fact question Starobinski's claim that the *Social Contract* is 'outside historical time.' For Althusser and Colletti, the problem with the *Social Contract* could be understood as lying in its insistence on 'taking men as they are.' This insistence, when coupled with Rousseau's historicized view of human nature elaborated in the *Second Discourse*, suggests that the *Social Contract* is in fact operating within 'historical time.' In other words, Rousseau takes human beings 'as they are,' not because he subscribes to a transhistorical conception of human nature (in the *Second Discourse* this is what he argued was the *problem* with Hobbes, Locke, and Aristotle) but rather because he is attempting to locate the moment of the *Social Contract* historically, in what might be called the counterfactual (or fictional) present. The *Social Contract* may well be the expression of a utopian ideal that 'belongs [to] a purely normative dimension' (Starobinski 1988, 31), but as Rousseau well knew, even utopian political projects must be historically situated, because historicity is what allows this utopia to assume a concrete or at least written form.

The problem with an interpretation of Rousseau that connects the *Second Discourse* with the *Social Contract*, then, is not with the attempt to tie together a historicizing narrative with a utopian political project that operates outside of historical constraints. Rather, as Paul de Man contends, it is a problem that can only be solved by recognizing the fictionality of the state of nature (which is, in a sense, as fictional as Rousseau's social contract) and by coming to grips with 'the significance of this fiction with regard to the empirical world' (de Man 1979, 136).[8] De Man's reading thus offers a counterpoint both to Starobinski's attempt to find the key to the totality of Rousseau's thought in an analysis that emphasizes psychological interiority, and to readings of Rousseau (such as Althusser's) that subordinate the literary works to political concerns. For de Man, all of Rousseau's works – his political writings as much as his literary ones – are primarily concerned with issues of language and representation: 'Rousseau's fictional as well as his discursive writings are allegories of (non)signification or of unreadability, allegories of the deconstruction and the reintroduction of metaphorical models' (1979, 257).

At this point it would perhaps be worthwhile to elaborate on what Jameson calls de Man's 'absent metaphysics' – his overarching argument, which claims that 'this susceptibility to ideological representation is the correlative picture of his [i.e., de Man's] own rigorous picture of the functioning, or the systematic dysfunctionality, of language as such: in spite of itself and against its own will, the attention to and focus on the linguistic apparatus ends up conjuring an impossible picture of what falls outside language and what language cannot assimilate, absorb, or process. (Jameson 1991, 246).

For de Man, in other words, one of Rousseau's decisive contributions is his claim (nowhere expressed, but everywhere implied) that the impossibility of literal representation is inherent in language itself. To return at last to the liberal reading of the *Social Contract* that was discussed earlier, we can see that according to de Man's reading, Rousseau's insertion of illiberal institutions results neither from some sort of casual slip-up by the author, nor from an atavistic or pathological hostility on Rousseau's part to transparency or rational decision making. Rather, it must be seen as an *integral* part of the text, whose object is, in part, to point to the *impossibility* of purely rational political attachments, or more generally, to the impossibility of a purely denominative language.

In a passage from the *Second Discourse* that is worth quoting at length, Rousseau seems to be distinguishing between naming and conceptualization, or between the literal and metaphorical (the terms de Man uses are 'denominative' and 'figural') functions of language:

> At first each object was given a particular name, without regard to genus and species which those first founders [of language] were not in a position to distinguish; and all individual things presented themselves to their minds in isolation, as they are in the spectacle of nature. If one oak tree was called A, another was called B. (For the first idea one draws from two things is that they are not the same; and it often requires quite some time to observe what they have in common.) Thus the more limited the knowledge, the more extensive becomes the dictionary. The difficulty inherent in all this nomenclature could not be easily alleviated, for in order to group beings under various common and generic denominations, it was necessary to know their properties and their differences. Observations and definitions were necessary, that is to say, natural history and metaphysics, and far more than men of those times could have had.
>
> Moreover, general ideas can be introduced into the mind only with the aid of words, and the understanding grasps them only through sentences. (Rousseau 1987, 50)[9]

This passage, as de Man points out, *appears* to argue both for the strict separability of denominative and figural language, and also for the priority of the former over the latter (de Man 1979, 146). In this sense, it seems to support the liberal contention that purely rational and transparent political arrangements are possible. Yet the passage itself undermines this distinction. On the one hand, Rousseau is asserting that denominative language exists prior to figural language and conceptualization; that is, before figural language arises, language consists only of an expanding 'dictionary.' But on the other hand, this dictionary is one that must operate without 'sentences' of any kind, including 'definitions,' as these would require conceptualization. It would not even be enough to suggest that this dictionary would be simply a list of proper names, since even that would entail the assumption that 'an observer, so keenly aware of difference that he fails to notice the resemblance between one oak tree and another would be unable to distinguish the difference between the word *a* and the tree *A*, to the point of considering them as united in some common essence' (de Man 1979, 148).

So just as Rousseau's discussion of the interplay between nature and culture led us to conclude that it is impossible to have a fully adequate 'knowledge' (which is always already cultural) of nature, here we can see the impossibility of a purely literal language, a non-metaphorical or non-figural language, or a language that actually refers to the world of objects rather than to the language about the objects. As de Man puts it:

> To the extent that all language is conceptual, it always already speaks about language and not about things. The sheer metonymic enumeration of things that Rousseau describes in the *Discourse* ('if one oak was called *A*, another was called *B* ...') is an entirely negative moment that does not describe language as it is or used to be at its inception, but that dialectically infers literal denomination as the negation of language. Denomination could never exist by itself although it is a constitutive part of all linguistic events. All language is language about denomination, that is, a conceptual, figural, metaphorical metalanguage. (1979, 152–3)

One further example from Rousseau – on his own use of the term 'reason' – will suffice to illustrate this point:

> I have noticed again and again that it is impossible in writing a lengthy work to use the same words always in the same sense ... Definitions would be all very well if we did not use words in the making of them. In spite of this I am convinced that even in our poor language we can make our meaning clear, not by always using words in the same sense, but by taking care that every time we use a word the sense in which we use it is sufficiently indicated by the context, so that each sentence in which the word occurs acts as a sort of definition. (Rousseau 1911, 72n.)

De Man's reading of Rousseau is helpful in its attempt to overcome the bifurcation of Rousseau's 'political' works or concerns from his 'literary' (or fictional) ones. But it is perhaps also worth emphasizing not only that Rousseau's most 'political' works (such as the *Second Discourse*) centrally revolve around 'literary' concerns (such as the dialectical opposition of denominative and figurative language), but also that even his most 'literary' concerns are politically charged. Such concerns relate to issues of representation, of difference, and of the possibility of subsuming the particular into the general, and Rousseau makes the political resonances of these quite explicit in the *Second Discourse* and even more so in the *Social Contract*. Thus, de Man concludes his discussion of the *Social Contract* by noting that 'to the extent that it is necessarily misleading, language just as necessarily conveys the promise of its own truth. This is why textual allegories on this level of rhetorical complexity [of the *Social Contract*] *generate history*' (277; emphasis added).

It deserves to be added, however, that it is not only rhetorically complex textual allegories such as the *Social Contract* that generate history. Or, rather – since this is very much de Man's point – that the nature of language itself dictates that all speech acts be in some sense, rhetorically complex textual allegories. All moments of language – even the foundational moments identified by Rousseau (such as what de Man calls the moment of 'sheer metonymic enumeration' in the *Second Discourse*, but also the birth of the term 'man' in 'Essay on the Origin of Languages' [Rousseau 1966, 13; cf. de Man 1979, 149–55]) – are shown by de Man to be always already involved in complex allegorical schemas that simultaneously signify and point to the limits of signification.

At this point, we can shift focus slightly, and move from linguistic concerns to the issues of the human relationship with nature with which we are here more centrally concerned. In order to do so, we can read Rousseau's deployment of language, as de Man understands it, as itself functioning allegorically – or more precisely, synecdochally. Language is a part that stands in for the totality of social labour. In this sense – in that language both attempts to signify objects and to point to the limits of that signification (or the impossibility of a total identification of the signifier and the signified) – we can understand language itself as a moment or form of alienation from nature. The process of social labour in general constitutes an ongoing attempt to transform the natural environment, and points at the same time to the limits of that transformation. Just as language can be seen as an ongoing effort to restore the harmony that is disrupted by original sin as Rousseau understands it (inequality, invidious comparison, the idea of difference, or language), so too we can understand labour, which at the social level 'generate[s] history' – as an attempt to recover a lost unity with the natural state. But, again as with language, this attempt simultaneously (and necessarily) points to its own impossibility. If the transformation of nature in order to satisfy human needs (from landscaping and urban development to genetic engineering) is an attempt to return humanity to the plenitude of the state of nature where 'all his needs are satisfied' (Rousseau 1987, 40), this satisfaction can now only be achieved through human alienation from nature. The inability of labour to fully realize the satisfaction of needs mirrors language's inability to provide us with an unmediated grasp of the object.

This reading suggests that for Rousseau, alienation is necessary. But does this perspective necessarily entail the conclusion that, as Althusser has it, 'total alienation is the solution to the problem of total alienation' (1982, 127)? To phrase it this way is to give Rousseau perhaps too much of a Marxian spin. In order to see how Rousseau might be read otherwise (as arguing that it is not 'total alienation' that might be a solution to the problem of total alienation), we must return, one last time, to Rousseau's 'state of nature.'

From the State of Nature to Reading Crusoe: 'Basic' and 'Surplus' Alienation

What is it that separates the solitary, animal-like existence of 'savage man' in the 'state of nature' from properly human existence in society? For Rousseau, alienation from nature – the splitting of the human subject from the natural object, necessary for labour or for the conscious transformation of the environment – is the defining characteristic of human existence. The marker of this difference is human beings' ability to defy instincts: 'Nature alone does everything in the operations of an animal, whereas man contributes, as a free agent, to his own operations' (Rousseau 1987, 44). We should note that even though this *potential* to act as a free agent must have existed in 'savage man' – or else the transition from him to civil man could not have occurred – it is only the *exercise* of free agency or 'perfectibility'[10] that defines human existence proper (A. Horowitz 1987, 63). Thus William Connolly notes that for Rousseau, it is human freedom and perfectibility (two key conceptual categories in the *Second Discourse*) that 'make it possible for humanity to elevate itself to a higher state; they make it impossible for humanity to remain in the natural state indefinitely' (1988, 48).

The process of exercising this capacity, which both requires and enables the use of reason – more specifically, invidious comparison, or what de Man refers to as 'the quantitative comparison of conceptual relationships' (1979, 155) – is what leads, seemingly ineluctably, to a state of war, and then to the institutionalization of private property and finally the imposition of government, which 'irretrievably destroyed natural liberty' (Rousseau 1987, 70). Crucially, however, the development of reason, or the exercise of free agency, is itself a result of the irruption, within a bountiful natural state, of the need to consciously transform the environment or to perform labour. In a passage describing the transition from animal-like to human existence, Rousseau states: 'Such was the condition of man in his nascent stage; such was the life of an animal limited at first to pure sensations, and scarcely profiting from the gifts nature offered him, far from dreaming of extracting anything from her. But difficulties soon presented themselves to him; it was necessary to learn to overcome them (1987, 60).

Although Connolly is correct to note that freedom and perfectibility are what 'make it possible for humanity to elevate itself' out of the natural state, this is not quite the same thing as his subsequent observation that it is freedom and perfectibility that 'make it impossible to remain in the natural state indefinitely.' It would be correct to state that the historically malleable character of human needs (a consequence of human freedom and perfectibility) makes a *return* to the state of nature impossible, but returning is not the same thing as remaining. The conflation of the two is made more easily, given the convention of referring to a *state* of nature. But as de Man suggests, 'the state of nature, though fictional, is not static' (1979, 139). The rupturing moment of alienation, the splitting of subject and object, just like the foundation of private property, is not an originary moment that sets a previously static condition into motion; rather, it is a 'foundational' moment that depends on an already *evolved* set of conditions. As Rousseau himself puts it, 'it is quite likely that by then things had already reached the point where they could no longer continue as they were' (1987, 60).

But if Rousseau understands the natural 'state' to be dynamic rather than static, then it stands to reason that humanity's *alienated* 'state' might be so described as well. And it is with regard to *this* point that we look to Rousseau for a meaningful contribution to contemporary ecological politics, instead of a romantic conception of humanity's 'natural' existence. As we have seen, Rousseau does indeed claim that the life of the inhabitant of the state of nature is happier and more idyllic than that of the inhabitant of modern society. Rousseau posits the life of the former as one against which we should perhaps measure ourselves, but not as one to which we can or should aspire. It is misleading to suggest that 'natural' and 'modern' modes of existence are two states that can simply be counterposed. Rather, both moments are embedded in a historical process. And this process – the process of the conscious transformation of the natural environment – is the process of alienation itself.

But if Rousseau cannot recommend a return to a natural state, neither does he want to suggest that all moments or forms of alienation must be judged to be equal, or that (as Althusser has it) the only solution to alienation can be more alienation – that alienation must be intensified (or totalized) to allow for the possibility of bursting through to a non-alienated existence. The problem with the latter is that, to use Althusser's own terminology, it both accepts 'the absolute limits to posing the problem' *and* suggests that the solution posited is, for Rousseau, the best conceivable. In other words, in suggesting that 'total alienation is the solution to the problem of total alienation,' Althusser is taking Rousseau's insistence on taking 'men as they are' as a definitive ontological assertion, rather than as an assumption for the sake of a particular project. If we take it to be merely an assumption, however – which is not unreasonable, given the arguments advanced in the *Second Discourse* – then the 'total alienation' recommended in the *Social Contract* can be read as not '*the* solution to the problem of total alienation,' but rather as the best that can be hoped for under current conditions. Or as Asher Horowitz puts it, the *Social Contract* can be 'seen not as the solution to the problem of alienation but as one of the forms, perhaps the best form, that alienation might take under modern conditions' (1987, 211).

Thus, although Althusser seems to be suggesting that through a dialectical reversal, total alienation can lead to the end of alienation, Horowitz's reading suggests otherwise. For Horowitz, although some forms of alienation can be alleviated or attenuated, the total elimination of alienation is incompatible with human existence. Alienation – a result of freedom and perfectibility, along with the dynamism of nature itself – in some sense defines human existence.

At the same time, however, Horowitz suggests that contrary to what the pessimistic or even fatalistic conclusion of the *Second Discourse* might suggest, this is not the end of the matter. For Horowitz, Rousseau's most systematic attempt to theorize a solution to the problem of alienation comes not in the *Social Contract* – which, again, insists on a particular kind of historical rootedness ('taking men as they are') – but in *Emile*, in which Rousseau at the outset specifically excludes questions of practicality, which are always dependent on 'certain given conditions in particular places [which] may vary indefinitely' (Rousseau 1911, 2–3). With what is at the very least a difference in emphasis from the *Social Contract*, Rousseau states in *Emile*: 'Now all these particular applications are not essential to my subject, and they form no part of my scheme' (3).

The educational project of *Emile* contains Rousseau's famous repudiation of bourgeois nationalism ('He will be neither a man nor a citizen. He will be of no use to himself nor to others. He will be a man of our day, a Frenchman, an Englishman, one of the great middle class' [1911, 8]).

Rousseau proposes for his pupil an education 'for himself alone,' because 'there is neither country nor patriot,' and because the project of *Emile* is to 'consider our scholar as man in the abstract' (8–10). In contrast, in 'Considerations on the Government of Poland and on its Projected Reform' – a text whose project is of course even more circumscribed than that of the *Social Contract* – Rousseau proposes an educational system specifically designed to inculcate 'patriotic zeal' (1997a, 192). In the case of 'Poland,' wherein the student is not 'man in the abstract,' the educational process should result in a student whose 'love [of country] makes up his whole existence; he sees only his fatherland, he lives only for it; when he is alone, he is nothing' (189).

According to Horowitz, when, as in *Emile*, Rousseau is not restricted by the particularities of historical circumstances, Rousseau distinguishes 'the necessary denaturation [i.e., alienation from nature] of a cultural and social being from the unnecessary or excessive denaturation attending inequality or class-divided society' (A. Horowitz 1987, 213) This distinction loosens the tight connection of causal necessity between the transformation of nature, or 'the objectification necessary for human existence,' and tyranny over nature, or 'alienation properly so-called' (215). *Emile*, thus understood, is an attempt 'to falsify the equation between historical existence and social alienation' (214).

In the distinction between objectification and alienation, we can see a return – albeit with different terms – to Colletti's distinction between the division of labour and commodity exchange. Just as with Colletti's distinction, Horowitz is suggesting the need to distinguish a necessary aspect of all human existence (objectification) from a particular instance or form of the latter, which, although perhaps applicable to all of recorded human history, is not necessarily definitive of the human condition. The transformation of nature and the social division of labour are inescapable aspects of human life properly so-called; these have historically taken the form of alienation (or 'tyranny over nature') and commodity exchange, but they need not take these forms in the future. But according to Colletti, Rousseau confuses the two terms 'unwittingly' and 'often if not always' (Colletti 1972, 164n), whereas according to Horowitz, the conflation reflects in part the immaturity of Rousseau's earlier works, and in part the terms he sets for himself for each particular project. Thus, 'necessary' and 'excess' denaturation are conflated in the *Second Discourse*, partly because 'Rousseau had not yet squarely faced the question of whether historical-social existence as such was the irremediable root of the various forms of alienation he had begun to trace or whether alienation was a function of specific social and historical circumstances' (A. Horowitz 1987, 209). But the same conflation occurs in the *Second Discourse* because there, the problematic is presented in historical form: 'Although objectification and alienation are separable theoretically, or in principle, they have historically been inseparable' (216). Such a reading at least leaves open the possibility that a solution to the problematic is not ruled out in advance by the historical conditions of eighteenth-century France.

Similarly, for Cassirer, 'Rousseau used the word and the concept "society" in a double sense. He distinguished most sharply between the empirical and the ideal form of society – between what it *is* under present conditions and what it *can* and in future *ought* to be' (1954, 123; emphases in original). For both Cassirer and Horowitz, *Emile* marks the apotheosis of Rousseau's theorizations about the human condition, precisely because 'from the very outset, the work stands outside the conditions of social reality' (120). It is in *Emile*, at last, that Rousseau posits an alternative path for the development of natural man.

For Rousseau, as the education of Emile shows, the ideal education is a 'negative' one. The goal sounds relatively easy when described in general terms: 'Let the curb be [natural] force, not [human] authority' (Rousseau 1911, 55). But it turns out that creating an environment of 'well-regulated liberty' (56) is rather complicated under current social conditions. Cassirer points out that the system that is designed 'to lead [Emile] back to the simplicity and plainness of nature' requires a 'painstakingly constructed system of social fictions' (1954, 120). The situation is not unlike that in the *Social Contract*, where freedom is guaranteed by an illiberal Legislator and civil religion: 'Thus the fanatical love of truth, which was to guide this system of education, ends up by degenerating into a curiously complicated set of deceptions, of carefully calculated pedagogical tricks' (121).

This deception is necessary, however, because Emile must be protected from interaction with those who are highly alienated. Yet at the same time, Emile cannot receive the (non-)education of a solitary protohuman, or simply be abandoned to the forces of nature. Emile's education – and it is most decidedly an education – is not a 'return to nature' (which would be impossible) but a social project. Emile must be protected from interaction with *corrupt* society, but not from social interaction, which is a requirement of human existence: 'Human ontogenesis, like human phylogenesis as it was described in the *Second Discourse*, can only take place within an experience constructed intersubjectively in relations of social action' (A. Horowitz 1987, 222).

At this point, however, it is important to note that certain problems arise in the attempt to separate necessary from excess denaturation. As the above extract from Horowitz suggests, *Emile* seems predicated on the thesis that human ontogenesis recapitulates phylogenesis: that the development of the individual mirrors the development of the species. We should remember, however, the difficulties we had – the difficulties Rousseau himself points to – in historically situating Rousseau's account of human phylogenesis, the *Second Discourse*. In this context, we should emphasize again that what Horowitz calls necessary and excess denaturation are not historically separable, and that this applies not only to individual development but also to social development.

Thus it is somewhat misleading for Rousseau to suggest, as he sometimes seems to do, that social needs (which are in some sense the epitome of corruption) can be forestalled in Emile's development. To be clear, Rousseau never suggests that they can be done away with entirely – only that they can and should be held off until Emile has developed a strong enough sense of self to deal with them without falling into the traps of *amour-propre* and invidious comparison with one's fellows. Thus Rousseau recommends that Emile's first book should be *Robinson Crusoe*, which provides an ideal model of independent life. From Rousseau's perspective, what is most valuable about Crusoe's position is that it allows one to evaluate things without the corrupting mediation of social relations. As Peter Gay terms it, it is 'the bible of the self-reliant' (1987, xiv). Although of course he does not quite phrase it in these terms, we might say that for Rousseau, Crusoe's solitude allows him to evaluate things based solely on their use-value, rather than on their exchange-value: 'The surest way to raise him above prejudice and to base his judgments on the true relations of things, is to put him in the place of a solitary man, and to judge all things as they would be judged by such a man in relation to their own utility' (Rousseau 1911, 147).

But Rousseau seems to be suggesting that placing young Emile in the position of Crusoe is a *phase* of his education that allows for only 'necessary,' but not 'excess,' denaturation: 'Make haste, therefore, to establish him on his island while this is all he needs to make him happy; for the day is at hand, when, if he must still live on his island, he will not be content to live alone, when even the companionship of Man Friday, who is almost disregarded now, will not long suffice' (1911, 148). It is important to recall, therefore, that Emile's Robinsonade is itself predicated on certain social relations (with his teacher, for example, but also with the authors who elucidate the nature of natural existence: Daniel Defoe, and Rousseau himself) that are present even at the stage at which Emile can play at being wholly self-sufficient. Against what seems to be suggested here, we must remind ourselves that the problem is not that social relations *tout court* are added on to 'natural' individual existence, but rather that social relations are what, in some sense, define human existence, and that social relations are necessary in order to escape corrupted society.

The problem is that alienation – even 'necessary' alienation – is an ongoing process rather than something which only occurs during a particular phase of either the human individual's or the species' life. The project of Emile, therefore, is not one of finding the *moment* at which alienation becomes excessive, or even of reducing the impact of social relations down to the minimum necessary for human existence. Rather, the problem is how to discriminate between those corrupt social relations which encourage artifice and vanity, and those 'negative' social relations which in some sense mirror nature. These 'negative' relations, like Emile's relationship with his teacher, which results in a 'curiously complicated set of deceptions,' are ones that seem almost not to exist as *social* relations.

But further complications arise: given that these 'negative' social relations cannot be reciprocal, to what extent can the pedagogical project of Emile be universalized? Or more generally, to what extent can the prior fiction, on which the fiction of Emile's education is based, be universalized? To what extent, in other words, does self-reliance itself rely on the 'almost disregarded' colonized subject? In his attempt to write a tale of total self-reliance, Defoe found himself forced to provide a manservant to do the domestic labour of his independent, self-made protagonist. Even though *Emile* might be read as no less than an attempt to theorize the possibility of human existence without surplus alienation, perhaps Rousseau was similarly unable to extricate himself from ways of thinking (about women, for example, in the case of the education of Emile's female companion Sophie [Fermon 1997, 100-1 and *passim*]) that were themselves reflective of surplus alienation.

For Colletti, we may recall, Rousseau was unable to distinguish adequately between the division of labour in general and the system of commodity exchange. According to Colletti, it was Marx who was the first to begin to make this distinction. The ways in which Marx's theoretical apparatus is able to advance our understanding of the distinction between basic and surplus alienation, will be the subject of the next chapter.

CHAPTER 4

Karl Marx: Objectification and Alienation under Capitalism

> Work is necessary, as is an account of reality as practical actuality. One does not chase away the *real* emperor or pope in a single blow by exorcising or by conjuring away the mere *ghostly* form of their bodies. Marx is very firm: when one has destroyed a phantomatic body, the real body remains.
>
> Derrida (1994, 131)

If Rousseau's discussion in the *Second Discourse* showed the problems inherent in attempting to trace the origins of alienation, Marx is even more emphatic in his problematization of this type of historical narrative. In the '1844 Manuscripts,'[1] Marx points out the ideological function these narratives serve:

> We must avoid repeating the mistake of the political economist, who bases his explanations on some imaginary primordial condition. Such a primordial condition explains nothing. It simply pushes the question into the grey and nebulous distance. It assumes as facts and events what it is supposed to deduce, namely the necessary relationship between two things, between, for example, the division of labour and exchange. Similarly, theology explains the origin of evil by the fall of man, i.e. it assumes as a fact in the form of history what it should explain.
>
> We shall start out from a *present-day* economic fact.
>
> The worker becomes poorer the more wealth he produces, the more his production increases in power and extent. (Marx 1975, 323; emphasis in original)

Like Rousseau, Marx rejects the equation of economic growth with general enrichment or development. Indeed, Marx goes so far as to assert the opposite: the impoverishment of workers is a direct consequence of the expanding capitalist economy.

Under capitalism, Marx notes, 'the object that labour produces, its product, stands opposed to it as *something alien*, as a *power independent* of the producer' (1975, 324; emphasis in original). But what precisely is this 'object that labour produces,' which turns to confront the worker as an alien power? The simplest answer seems to be that the worker produces capital, which is understood by Marx as a concretion of past labour, and that the mechanism through which capital becomes an 'alien' force is the commodification of labour (where labour-power is exchanged for a wage). But the simplicity of this answer is deceiving, in that capital's alienating power works in a number of different registers.

The first of these is the argument that Marx develops at considerable length in volume 1 of *Capital*.[2] This argument emphasizes that labour has a 'double character': it is a unique commodity insofar as it can produce more than the cost of its reproduction. Under capitalism, this 'surplus-value' that can be extracted from labour (the difference between the value of what is produced and the cost of reproduction) takes the form of profit. Workers do not necessarily share in the general enrichment their labour produces, because it is the cost of reproducing labour, rather than the value of what that labour can produce, that determines wage levels. The share of social wealth that accrues to workers is not based on the productivity of labour, but on the costs of its reproduction, which are translated through the impersonal market laws of supply and demand. The commodification of labour thus mystifies the social relations of production (making unequal exchange or exploitation appear to be fair and equal); the result is that workers are disempowered.

Because capitalism as an economic system is predicated on the constant expansion of value (profit seeking), the product of labour (profits) confronts the worker in the form of a work environment that seeks to maximize the extraction of surplus-value, in part by minimizing the costs of production. One of the ways in which production costs are minimized is through an increase in what Marx calls the 'organic composition of capital.' This refers to the generalized tendency under capitalism to reduce the costs of production by substituting an increasing proportion of machine power for human labour power. This in turn tends to decrease the value of human labour power, as less of it is required for production. To the extent that there are more workers than jobs, pressures to increase wages can be resisted. In other words, the product of human labour confronts the producer as a hostile force, in that workers, by working, and by increasing social wealth, drive down the exchange-value of their labour power. An example of this would be assembly-line workers engaged in the production of robotic arms to replace human workers on assembly lines: the worker of course has no ownership stake in the robotic arm, and once her own job on the assembly line is taken over by a robotic arm, she finds that the demand for (and hence the exchange-value of) her labour power has diminished. More generally, work processes are increasingly restructured around the technical requirements of machinery, so that workers' autonomy is further restricted as their work role is increasingly defined as being an appendage of machinery. The production of capital thus tends to result in the increasing immiseration of the workers, both materially and in terms of the autonomy or richness of the experience of labour.

But neither the argument about the exploitation hidden in the wage form, nor the one about the disempowering effects of the increasing organic composition of capital, is the one that Marx develops in the '1844 Manuscripts.' In this text, he asserts: 'Labour not only produces commodities; it also produces itself and the workers as a *commodity* and it does so in the same proportion in which it produces commodities in general' (Marx 1975, 324, emphasis in original). The emphasis here is neither on workers' material impoverishment, nor on their disempowerment in the day-to-day struggle for economic survival. Rather, this passage emphasizes the point that in producing commodities, labour reproduces itself as a commodity – in other words that the production of commodities cements an understanding of the world as made up of objects (workers themselves included) best apprehended as commodities. This understanding – of human labour in commodified terms – is not natural, but historically produced. And the production of this type of consciousness is reinforced by the very material processes it sets into motion: the more workers exchange their labour for wages, the more commodities they produce, the more thoroughly commodified is their world, and the less likely it seems (the contradictions of capitalism aside) that they will be able to formulate a rupture with the logic of commodities.

In this sense, then, what confronts workers as an alien force – what they produce through their own labour – is a set of social relations, and an accompanying form of consciousness that sees the world as made up of commodities. What they produce is, in short, an ideology. Thus, Marx's famous description of 'private property as the material summarized expression of alienated labour' (1975, 334) refers not only to private property as the material objects that belong to particular economic actors, but also to the *system* of private property as a whole.

With this general background in mind, we can turn to the distinction Marx draws – alluded to in the previous chapter – between alienation and objectification. Like Rousseau, Marx takes the capacity to consciously undertake the transformation of the natural environment to be a crucial aspect of human existence: 'The practical creation of an *objective world*, the *fashioning* of inorganic nature, is proof that man is a conscious species-being' (1975, 328–9; emphases in original). At the same time, however, present-day human beings are alienated from their species-being, in that their labour is not free: labour is now 'a mere means for existence' (328). Thus although the transformation of nature is a defining aspect of the human condition, the unfree character of labour in class-divided societies – the fact that people do not fully control the products of their labour or the conditions under which they labour – is not a necessary aspect of human existence (and indeed is an obstacle to the realization of a fully human existence).

As I did with Rousseau in the previous chapter, I will argue here that this distinction between alienation and objectification must occupy a central place in any understanding of Marx's thought that sees him as recuperable for contemporary environmental politics. The interpretation of Marx I offer here will seek to bring these features to the fore, and its excavation will require a certain amount of negotiation through debates in the secondary literature. And, again as with Rousseau, such an interpretation will hinge on a connection between the author's earlier and later works. With Rousseau, the problem was how to connect the brilliant diagnostic analyses of the early work with the various 'failed' prescriptions of the later works; with Marx, in contrast, the problem lies in an apparent disjuncture between the earlier and later works in terms of both methodology and tone. But the task will not be to choose an ecologically friendly Marx by focusing exclusively on either the earlier or the later works. Rather, it will be to develop a reading of Marx that recognizes the significance of the distinction between alienation and objectification for contemporary environmental political thought, as well as the limits of this distinction as it is developed in both Marx's earlier and later works.

Marx as an Enlightenment Thinker

Marx's distinction between alienation and objectification might at first glance seem to do little to advance ecological concerns. In a critique of eco-Marxism, Val Routley concludes that 'those who work for an environmentally conscious noncapitalist society need to go beyond Marx ...

for Marx's views on nature, and associated central parts of his theory, belong to the past, and are far too close to those which lie at the root of many of our troubles' (1981, 244). Routley identifies at least two 'deep-seated conflicts between Marx's theory and environmental consciousness' (241).

For Routley, the first obstacle to reconciling Marx with environmentalism lies in Marx's unquestioning acceptance of the legacy of the Enlightenment. According to Routley (1981), this can be seen most clearly in Marx's relationship with Hegel:

> All these doctrines of Marx's regarding nature, of nature as man's body, man's creation and expression, can usefully be seen as the product of Marx's well-known transposition of God's features and role in the Hegelian system of thought onto man. If the Hegel's [sic] system of thought nature is *God's* body, His creation and necessary self-expression, that in which He recognizes Himself and, through shaping, creates and expresses Himself, in Marx's adaptation of Hegel's system all these properties now become *man's*. (239–40; emphases in original)

Marx's transformation of the Hegelian system, according to Routley, is thus typical of the Enlightenment project of 'placing man in the role previously attributed to God,' which has resulted in environmental disaster as a consequence of hubristic attempts to control natural systems that we only partially understand (240).

There are a number of problems, however, with such a reading of Marx's relationship to Hegel and the Enlightenment. The first is that in Routley's reading, Hegel appears as a sort of pre-Enlightenment figure, and that the Hegelian system only seems to become anthropocentric as it is taken over by Marx. There may be religious aspects to Hegel's system (aspects emphasized, at least to a certain extent, by Charles Taylor, on whose reading of Hegel Routley seems to rely [1981, 238]). But in fact it is Hegel's idealism, and his claim that the bureaucracy represents a 'universal' class, rather than his religiosity, that Marx most emphatically seeks to overcome. Marx opens his critique of Hegel's *Philosophy of Right* with the observation that 'for Germany, the *criticism of religion* has been essentially completed' (Marx 1975, 243; emphasis in original). And the partiality of Hegel's 'universal class' is revealed by the fact that 'This class liberates the whole of society, but only on condition that the whole of society finds itself in the same situation as this class, e.g. possesses or can easily acquire money and education' (254).

Although there certainly are significant differences between Marx and Hegel, the two are in agreement that the dialectical unfolding of history leads eventually to *human* self-consciousness. Routley's use of 'God' as the central figure of the Hegelian system thus reflects a somewhat misleading translation of *Geist*, which is most often rendered in English as 'Spirit' or 'Mind.'

All this might mean, however, is that Marx merely inherited this sort of Enlightenment anthropocentrism from Hegel instead of arriving at it on his own. The more fundamental claim – that Marx's belief (regardless of its source) in the Enlightenment project led him to place too much faith in the capacity of human beings to understand and control their transformation of the natural environment – deserves separate consideration.

Such a broad statement, which might in the end mean little more than that Marx was a product of his time, seems at least plausible. And if the fact that for Marx, 'ecological contradictions ... play little or no role in the anticipated revolution against capitalism' (Foster 1998, 185) is admitted by even one of the most committed defenders of Marx's ecological correctness, then it might seem that indeed Marx's thought is inappropriate for a time when ecological crises and contradictions are so obviously in evidence. But this would then suggest that a particular social theory is useful to contemporary ecological politics only if it identifies ecological contradictions as primary in determining social evolution. As we shall see, however, Marx's social theory is capable of providing a contribution to contemporary ecological politics, regardless of the extent to which he identies the ecological contradictions that emerge from capitalism.[3]

John Bellamy Foster acknowledges that ecological contradictions are at best of secondary importance for Marx; nevertheless, he argues for Marx's importance. Foster draws our attention to the distinction between 'Prometheanism' and an uncritical attitude toward technological development: 'If what is meant by this charge of "Prometheanism" is that Marx, in line with the Enlightenment tradition, placed considerable faith in rationality, science, technology, and human progress, and that he often celebrated the growing human mastery over natural forces, there is no denying this to be the case ... It would be a mistake, however, to conclude from this that Marx and Engels suspended all critical judgment where science, technology and the idea of progress were concerned' (1998, 181).

The 'critical judgment' enters where questions of the social uses of technology and science are raised. Thus, even if we grant Marx a typical nineteenth-century faith in the capacity of human beings to fully apprehend and control nature, this must nevertheless be tempered by his understanding of where and how scientific and technological knowledge can go awry. For Marx, capitalism allows for tremendous advances in the forces of production, but capitalist relations of production do not allow for the conscious, rational social control of those forces. Bourgeois society, Marx and Engels write in the *Communist Manifesto*, 'is like the sorcerer, who is no longer able to control the powers of the nether world whom he has called up by his spells' (Marx 1978, 478).

In an article that similarly seeks to rehabilitate Marx's ecological credentials, Charles Tolman argues (1981) that environmental problems are best understood as resulting from the disjunction (or contradiction) between highly developed and rationalized forces of production on the one hand, and irrational or mystified relations of production on the other. According to Tolman, ecological problems 'are, without doubt, a necessary outcome of certain advances in the productive forces themselves' (72) – a diagnosis with which many ecocentrists would be unlikely to disagree. But unlike most ecocentrists, Tolman concludes that 'environmental problems can be solved only by further advance in the forces of production. This means the further development of technology, but more importantly, it means the development of a better theoretical understanding of nature, production, and society so that a *real mastery of nature* can be attained' (73; emphasis added).

Of course, the notion that a 'real mastery of nature' can be achieved is precisely what is in dispute in the debates over Marx's status as an ecological thinker. Tolman is correct to point out that this 'real mastery of nature' will require not only a better understanding of nature, but also a demystification of social relations; but this does not necessarily address the ecocentric critique. It is possible that the dynamic complexity of natural processes renders a 'real mastery of nature' impossible, and that inherent uncertainties mean that strictly technological 'fixes,' no matter how sophisticated, will never be sufficient to deal with the dilemmas of human ecology (Merchant 1995, 156–7).

But Marxian inquiry takes as fundamental the specificity of what Goodin (see chapter 1) refers to as the 'macrosociological' level. This commitment to historicization can be registered at even the seemingly most abstract levels of social inquiry: questions such as whether a 'real mastery of nature' is possible cannot, from a Marxian perspective, be answered in the abstract, but only in reference to specific modes of social organization. As Alfred Schmidt notes, Marx argues in *Capital* (just as Rousseau did in the *Second Discourse*) that the development of society's productive forces brings with it an increase in human needs. Thus, Marx must claim that 'human happiness is not simply proportional to the measure of man's technical mastery of nature, but that it depends very much on the social organization of that technical mastery. The question, whether technical progress is for man's benefit or not, can only be answered in that context' (Schmidt 1971, 135). *How much* of a mastery of nature is required in order for it to be 'real' is, in other words, something of an open question – one whose answer is not necessarily the same in different social contexts.

The second point that must be made in registering the differences between Marx and ecocentric deep ecologists relates to Marx's commitment to the liberatory possibilities of the human transformation of the environment. In other words, although it may be possible to develop an understanding of Marxism that recognizes humans' embeddedness in natural processes (a point that will be developed later in the chapter), it is nevertheless important to emphasize that one of the central points around which Marx's theory revolves remains the category of human *labour*. This focus on labour informs the second of Routley's objections to the application of Marxism to ecological concerns, to which we can now turn.

The End of History? Historical Progress, Teleology, and Determinism

Central to Marx's theories is the notion that labour, the conscious transformation of the natural environment, not only is compatible with human freedom, but can be the very expression of human freedom. For ecocentrists, Marx's focus on labour reveals an anthropocentric bias insofar as his distinction between free and estranged labour seems to rest solely on the character of social relations and is therefore completely neutral regarding the relationship between human agents and the natural world. According to Routley,

> it is clear that the necessity for the domination of nature and the view of man as reaching full humanity by doing so plays a central role in Marx's theory of history and of the development of human society ... It is because of the necessity to dominate nature in order to become fully human that capitalism is seen as a necessary stage to human development ... If the necessity for nature domination is rejected, so also must be the treatment

> of human history in terms of it and the proffered explanation of the development of class society; the basis for the alleged superiority of technological society to 'primitive' non-technological societies in expressing what is truly human is not so clear either. (Routley 1981, 241)

This complex condemnation in fact raises a number of issues, and the extent to which it actually applies to Marx is debatable on several grounds. We can begin by questioning of the extent to which Marx's view of human fulfilment under socialism is necessarily predicated on 'nature domination.' The answer seems to rest on the adequacy of Routley's characterization of the Marxist theory of history, and of the Marxist understanding of human nature ('what is truly human').

According to Routley, Marx presents us with a view of human history that is not simply progressive but positively teleological. For Marx, modes of production succeed one another as the forces of production progressively increase: as feudal relations of production become a fetter to development, they are replaced by capitalism; and capitalist relations are in turn to be overthrown in a socialist revolution. Not only that, but each stage – or mode of production – is logically *necessary* for human development.

A first response to this might be to return to the quotation from the '1844 Manuscripts' with which this chapter began: Marx is beginning from the 'present-day'; and, as he also makes clear in the preface to *Capital*, his specific object of study is 'the capitalist mode of production' (1977a, 90). So he is not so much stating that capitalism is (logically) necessary for human development; more precisely, he is stating that capitalism *has* developed, and that (given that he saw human nature in terms at least as historical as Rousseau) we cannot simply abolish it and return to an earlier mode of production.[4]

But such a quick dismissal does not really do justice to Marx's arguments. For although Marx's theory of history certainly does begin with the capitalist present, rather than with 'some imaginary primordial condition,' it is also the case that Marx's normative arguments lend some credence to Routley's characterization. One has only to recall the opening pages of the *Communist Manifesto*, where Marx and Engels credit the bourgeoisie with ending nationalist narrow-mindedness, making possible world literature, and civilizing all the peoples of the world, and where they note that 'during its rule of scarce one hundred years, [the bourgeoisie] has created more massive and more colossal productive forces than have all preceding generations together' (Marx

1978, 476–7). Such a passage allows us to see that for Marx, as Jameson puts it (1991), we must 'think this development positively *and* negatively all at once' (47; emphasis in original) and see capitalism as 'historically progressive' as well as inherently and horribly exploitative.

The emphasis on the 'historically progressive' features of capitalism is a somewhat familiar line of Marxian argument. It receives perhaps its most extended exposition in relation to issues of Third World development – in particular, in the critique of dependency theory advanced by Bill Warren. Basically, Warren's thesis is that twentieth-century Marxist critiques of imperialism (such as dependency theory), which are rooted in Lenin's understanding of imperialism, have perpetuated the 'fiction' that imperialism (the 'highest stage of capitalism' in Lenin's words) should be resisted. The Leninist thesis rests on the assumption that 'socialism can be achieved almost irrespective of objective economic or cultural conditions, provided anti-imperialist fervour remains white-hot' (Warren 1980, 6). According to Warren, this view 'ignored the major analytical achievements of Marxist economics' and allowed itself to be guided 'by the political requirements of the Russian revolution' (1980, 4). In sum, Lenin's thesis – and dependency theory more generally – in its idealism, constituted a major deviation from Marx's own thought with regard to the historical role of imperialism.[5]

Marx's own writings on imperialism certainly seem to follow the logic of Warren's argument. For example, when he wrote about India, although he condemned the brutality of British imperialism, he nevertheless argued that it was ultimately a progressive historical force. In this vein, Marx argued that

> sickening as it must be to human feeling to witness those myriads of industrious patriarchal and inoffensive social organisations disorganised and dissolved into their units, thrown into a sea of woes, and their individual members losing at the same time their ancient form of civilisation and their hereditary means of subsistence, we must not forget that these idyllic village communities, inoffensive though they might appear, had always been the solid foundation of Oriental despotism, that they restrained the human mind within the smallest possible compass, making it the unresisting tool of superstition, enslaving it beneath traditional rules, depriving it of all grandeur and historical energies. (Marx 1978, 657–8)

Marx contended that the modernization of India that colonization brought about was historically progressive, not only because it liberated the human mind from superstition and what he elsewhere called the 'idiocy of rural life'[6] (1978, 477), but also because a commodity-based economy provides the material conditions for prosperity: 'Nowhere, more than in India, do we meet with social destitution in the midst of natural plenty, for want of the means of exchange.' (Marx 1978, 660) In this respect, colonization lays the necessary groundwork for socialism:

> England, it is true, in causing a social revolution in Hindostan, was actuated only by the vilest interests, and was stupid in her manner of enforcing them. But that is not the question. The question is, can mankind fulfill its destiny without a fundamental revolution in the social state of Asia? If not, whatever may have been the crimes of England she was the unconscious tool of history in bringing about that revolution. (658)

But as Mike Davis has recently shown (working very much within the framework of Marxian political economy), the introduction to nineteenth-century India (and what became the 'Third World' more generally) of various technologies and institutions of modernity – the railway, the telegraph, the cash nexus – interacted with dynamic weather conditions to create social destitution on an unprecedented scale. According to Davis, in the last quarter of the nineteenth century, some thirty to sixty million deaths were attributable to famine, and people were 'ground to bits between the teeth of three massive and implacable cogwheels of modern history' – the social impacts of climatic El Niño events, amplified by cycles of the (newly globalized) economy and the New Imperialism (2001, 7 and 12). In other words, 'social destitution in the midst of natural plenty' occurred not '*for want of* the means of exchange' but *because of* the imposition of the means of exchange – or more exactly, because of its superimposition over a matrix of massive and rigid social inequality.

Moreover, even if Warren's view of Marx seems to be supported by textual evidence from the Marxian corpus, it should also be pointed out that, as Dudley Seers has noted, Warren remains 'a very unusual Marxist'[7] (Seers 1979, 1). Seers's argument focuses on the similarities between Warren's brand of Marxism and the neoclassical economics expounded by the 'Chicago School.' These two positions are often thought of as diametrically opposed; in fact, given Marx's own grounding in classical political economy, they share some common ground (or as Jameson puts it: Marxists 'have much in common with the neoliberals, in fact virtually everything – save the essentials!' [1991, 265]). Seers lists a number of commonalities: both see human beings as driven primarily by economic (or 'material') incentives; both are optimistic, seeing history as progressive; both are 'economistic,' viewing 'progress' as best understood and measured in material terms; both develop their theories based primarily on the historical experience of Western Europe but then argue that their theories are universalizable; both view their analyses as 'scientific'; and, finally, both display 'an uncritical faith' in science and technological development (Seers 1979, 3–4).

The relevance of all this for our purposes is that the same kinds of arguments about Marxism's implication in imperialism are made about its implication in the domination of nature. For example, Roy Morrison focuses on the similarities between capitalism and socialism as 'industrialist' ideologies. In particular, Morrison critiques what he calls the 'steel triangle of industrialism,' comprising 'the synergism of hierarchy, progress and technique,' which underlies both capitalism and socialism (the latter including both 'actually existing' socialist regimes and Marx's own view of socialism which 'found in the factory the venue not only for exploitation but also for liberation'): 'Industrialism has an economics based on the maximization of production and consumption in both intensity and geographical extent; a politics based on hierarchical structures to order both production and society; a philosophy based on a concept of progress that identifies industrial change, no matter what its effects, as good; a science based on the exaltation of technique (expressed by science, technology, bureaucracy) at the service of industrial hierarchies (Morrison 1994, 133).

It should be recalled, however, that Seers's discussion of the similarities between Marxism and neoclassical economics – similarities that are strikingly similar to the ones pointed out by Morrison – was prefaced by the claim that this view of Marxism was 'very unusual.' And although much of Morrison's critique of 'industrialism' is applicable to Soviet-style command economies, it is much less clear how much is in fact applicable to the writings of Marx himself. Marx certainly favours the development (even the 'full development') of society's productive forces, but he is not simply interested in the 'maximization' of production for its own sake. As Reiner Grundmann notes, this is precisely how Marx differentiates his own views from those of the classical political economists: '"[Ricardo] is completely indifferent to the question of whether the development of the productive forces kills landed property or the workers ... Who cares, says Ricardo: The productivity of human labour has been doubled." But Marx does not say "who cares?" when workers are crushed by the factories ... Neither does Marx content himself with an increase in material wealth since this wealth assumes antagonistic forms vis-à-vis the producers' (Grundmann 1991, 143; internal quotation from Marx's *Manuscripts 1861–3*).

As well, the claim that Marx was concerned with maximizing either production or consumption seems ill-equipped to deal with the centrality of Marx's distinction between exchange-value and use-value. Marx implies that exchange-value – which is separable from use-value because the former is quantifiable – is unique to commodity-based modes of production.[8] Presumably, in a society in which people's relationship to the processes of social production and to the objects thereby produced assumed a transparent and rational (rather than mystified or fetishized) form, exchange-value and the commodity form would no longer hold sway.[9] For Marx, the problem of production for its own sake is a result not of 'industrialism' in the abstract, but of capitalism's laws of motion: the need for the constant expansion of value results in use-value being subsumed under exchange-value.

If Morrison's conclusion that Marx advocates 'industrialism' is questionable with regard to the maximization of production and consumption, what of the issues of hierarchy, progress, and technique – the three points of the 'steel triangle'? While the evidence here is more ambiguous, Morrison's claims are at least debatable. Although Marx provides little in the way of a blueprint for a socialist society, such a society must by definition involve free, conscious, and collective control over production. Whether this might nevertheless entail the hierarchical structuring of work relations is perhaps an open question, but at the very least it would necessitate a democratic (that is, non-hierarchical) ordering of society as a whole.

As well, although Marx certainly does have a conception of historical progress, it is far from clear whether he identifies this with 'industrial change, no matter what its effects,' as Morrison suggests. As with the advancement of 'technique,' technological change, by increasing the efficiency of human labour power, constitutes the precondition for 'progress.' But for Marx, 'progress' itself can be achieved only through a change in social relations. In other words, Morrison's critique of industrialism is based on technological determinist assumptions: 'For Greens, industrialism represents not merely a mode of production but a civilization that undergirds capitalism *and* socialism' (1994, 133; emphasis in original). Marxism, in contrast, is generally (although as we shall see, not universally) thought to involve a rejection of technological determinist assumptions; it sees technological development as a *result* of social relations, not as a determinant of them.

In the 'preface' to 'A Contribution to the Critique of Political Economy,' Marx states that a society's 'relations of production [are] appropriate to a given stage in the development of their material forces of production' (1975, 425), and even more emphatically that 'no social order is ever destroyed before all the productive forces for which it is sufficient have been developed' (426). Taking this statement as central to Marx's work, William Shaw, following G.A. Cohen, concludes that 'Marx considered the productive forces to be the long-run determinant of historical change' (Shaw 1978, 57; cf. Cohen 1978).

But as Grundmann points out, Marx simply does not discuss consistently the relations between technology and social forms (or between the forces of production and relations of production). At times, he notes, Marx seems to be arguing for a 'strong' technological determinism: 'To one specific technology, one social form which is determined by this technology exactly corresponds.' At other times, Marx invokes a 'weak' technological determinism: 'To a specific technology a variety of social forms may correspond, which consequently are thus not determined by technology; rather they are "allowed by" or "compatible with" that technology' (Grundmann 1991, 160). Those who claim that Marx was a strong technological determinist, or that he saw the forces of production as the true motor of history, however, must find it difficult to deal with Marx's consistent emphasis on class struggle, and his political invocations (as in the *Communist Manifesto*) for the working class to overthrow capitalist relations of production. The 'strong' version of technological determinism (and the concomitant critique of Marxism as a hopelessly 'industrialist' ideology) thus can only seem plausible if it avoids dealing with significant portions of Marx's work.

Raymond Williams provides a somewhat different approach to understanding the problem of 'determinism' in Marx (Williams is more concerned with the argument that Marx is an *economic* determinist, but the argument can be applied, *mutatis mutandis*, to readings of Marx as a technological determinist). Williams begins by noting the complexity of the word 'determine' and the fact that in most English translations of Marx's work, it does not correspond precisely to the German *bestimmen* (*bestimmen* is sometimes translated as 'definite,' and 'determine' is sometimes used to translate *konstatieren*). This 'extraordinary linguistic complexity' reflects the fact that 'determination' can be either external or internal, and that it can refer either to 'iron laws' ('strong determinism' in Grundmann's terms) or to limits that are imposed on the actions of otherwise free agents (Grundmann's 'weak determinism') (Williams 1977, 84–5). For Williams, however, the claim that Marx used determination in the sense of 'iron laws' (what Williams calls 'abstract determinism') suffers from the same problem as the 'strong' version of technological determinism advanced by both Shaw and Cohen: it omits the possibility of subjective agency, or the possibility that history can be not just understood, but changed. Williams notes that in this sense, the reading of Marx as a 'determinist' is the result of a peculiar irony:

> The strongest single reason for the development of abstract determinism is the historical experience of the large-scale capitalist economy, in which many more people than Marxists concluded that control of the process was beyond them, that it was at least in practice external to their wills and desires, and that it had therefore to be seen as governed by its own 'laws'. Thus, with bitter irony, a critical and revolutionary doctrine was changed, not only in practice but at this level of principle, into the very forms of passivity and reification against which an alternative sense of 'determination' had set out to operate. (86)

Williams advances Grundmann's distinction between strong and weak forms of determinism by further arguing that 'determination' cannot simply be seen as the limits of possibility – that agents are not completely free in choosing from determined possibilities: 'In practice determination is never only the setting of limits; it is also the exertion of pressures' (Ibid., 87). Or as Marx himself famously put it, that 'men make their own history, but ... not under circumstances chosen by themselves' (Marx 1978, 595).

It should also be noted that Williams's understanding of 'determination' leads him not exactly to a rejection of Cohen's position, but rather to an acceptance of it, albeit with a radically different understanding of 'productive forces.' Williams (1977) seems to accept the claim that the 'productive forces' are the ultimate determinant of historical change, but only on the basis of his rejection of the base–superstructure distinction (75–82). 'Productive forces,' for Williams, are defined as 'all and any of the means of the production and reproduction of real life' (91). To reduce this to industry, or technological development, or aspects of the labour process as it is generally construed (that is, wage labour), is to fall into the trap of bourgeois ideology. Again, Williams sees it as especially ironic that Marxists should define productive forces so narrowly, given that it is Marx himself who notes (in the *German Ideology*) that it is only under capitalism that 'the productive forces *appear* to be completely independent and severed from the individuals and to constitute a self-subsistent world alongside the individuals' (quoted in Williams 1977, 91; my emphasis). On the other hand, Williams notes, even Marx himself is not completely immune from this narrow (bourgeois) construal of 'productive forces,' as when he claims 'that a piano-maker is a productive worker, engaged in productive labour, but that a pianist is not, since his labour is not that which reproduces capital' (93). (And as we noted in chapter 2, the increase of this sort of 'productive unproductive labour' is especially characteristic of contemporary capitalism.) Certainly this distinction between productive and unproductive labour – which Marx seems to have appropriated rather uncritically from Adam Smith (94) – seems to lend credence to the charge that at certain moments Marx himself was subject to a certain 'Prometheanism.' And this in turn might lead to an unwarranted anthropocentric bias as well as to valorization of the domination of nature. On the other hand, it seems to be at odds with the understanding that labour produces *ideology* – an understanding that was developed at the beginning of this chapter through the brief rehearsal of Marx's arguments in the '1844 Manuscripts.' In the following two sections, the category of labour will provide the basis for a more positive elaboration of Marx's importance for ecological politics. Before turning to this, however, we should conclude our discussion of the ecocentric critique of Marx – in particular, the critique advanced by Routley, which has served a more 'negative' function – pointing to the readings of Marx that either are contradicted by the texts themselves or are simply irrelevant to the present moment.

We have seen that Marx's emphases on politics and political struggle suggest quite clearly that he subscribed, at best, to a weak version of technological determinism: that technological developments delimited certain possibilities and exerted certain pressures in terms of the relations of production, but that there was not a strict one-to-one correspondence between a mode of production's content (its level of technological development, or the forces of production) and its form (the relations of production). Yet this weak technological determinism allows us, finally, to see the grounds on which Marx actually does argue 'for the alleged superiority of technological society to "primitive" non-technological societies in expressing what is truly human' (Routley 1981, 241).

In part, at least, Marx's claim that technological society is superior rests on his conception of 'what is truly human' as the ability to *consciously* transform the natural environment in order to meet human needs. The heightened development of society's productive forces allows much more easily for the transformation of nature 'in accordance with the laws of beauty' (Marx 1975, 329). Although the advanced technology that allows for massive transformations of the natural environment is certainly by itself no guarantee of beauty, such beauty can only be secured through self-conscious and free human activity.

But there is also a sense in which Marx might regard the 'choice' that Routley presents us with – that is, between technological and non-technological societies – as a false one. As with Rousseau, for Marx technological development leads to the development of 'new needs': 'As soon as a need is satisfied, (which implies the action of satisfying, and the acquisition of an instrument), new needs are made; and this production of new needs is the first historical act' (Marx and Engels 1947, 17). Moreover – and again, as with Rousseau – Marx sees 'human nature' as something that changes over time; thus, the lure of 'primitive communism' – a state where, as in Rousseau's conception of the state of nature, 'all [people's] needs are satisfied' (Rousseau 1987, 40) – is a false promise. It is a false promise because, given what we have noted about the nature and extent of Marx's technological determinism, for Marx a 'primitive' existence is one that is by definition not rationally organized, and the activity engaged therein is, again, by definition, not self-consciously purposive. Thus in the earliest stages of human development ('tribal' and 'ancient communal' forms of ownership [9]), human beings can have only a very limited and highly mystified understanding of natural processes:

> It is consciousness of nature, which first appears to men as a completely alien, all-powerful and unassailable force, with which men's relations are purely animal and by which they are overawed like beasts; it is thus a purely animal consciousness of nature (natural religion).
>
> We see here immediately: this natural religion or animal behaviour towards nature is *determined by the form of society and vice versa*. (19; emphasis added)

In other words, from Marx's perspective, alienation from nature is to be dialectically superseded (*Aufhebung*) rather than simply annulled. Shlomo Avineri summarizes Marx's argument from the *Grundrisse*:

> In former periods, when wealth was still conceived as residing in natural objects and not in commodities that are the products of human labour, no

> alienation existed at all, since alienation can be only related to an inverted form of human activity. But the non-existence of alienation also implied the non-existence of human objectification. Therefore this period of pristine innocence was incapable of unfolding the fullness and richness of human potentialities. Consequently primitive communism cannot serve in any way as a model for fully developed communism that presupposes alienation as well as its abolition. (Avineri 1968, 103)

It is not just that we cannot go back in time to a period when needs were simpler and capitalist alienation had not yet been imposed. Even if it were possible, such a 'flight backwards' would be undesirable, since capitalism not only produces alienation, but also the possibility for its supersession. And this supersession of alienation is qualitatively different from a prealienated existence. For Marx, as William James Booth argues, the promise of communist society lies not so much in the material wealth that is to be produced, or even in the more just distribution of that wealth, but in its reconceptualization of time. In a post-capitalist society, time can be conceived of as 'the "space" (*Raum*) of human development' rather than as a measure of (exchange) value: 'A person's wealth, Marx adds [in the *1861–3 Manuscripts*], does not consist in the objects he or she accumulates, but rather in the time freely available to him or her' (Booth 1989, 210) In other words, there *is* a kernel of truth in Routley's valorization of 'non-technological' societies, in that capitalism does intensify the labour process: it makes people more 'Promethean.' People in precapitalist societies may indeed have had more rather than less free time (1989, 212; Sahlins 1972). But what Routley's point misses is 'capitalism's greatest achievement, its historical "justification," the shortening of necessary labor time' (Booth 1989, 211), and the fact that the heteronomous determination of time can result from nature (the impact of seasonal and climatological variations on agricultural communities, for example) as well as from a class structure (210).

Herein lies the source of the profound difference between Marx's view and that of Routley, notwithstanding some oddly striking similarities. The biographical footnote to Routley's article notes that 'most of Routley's time is taken up with the practical activities of a rural subsistence life style. During the warmer part of the year, she works on a forest bird breeding study. She is an active environmentalist ... She is co-author of *The Fight for the Forests* ... and author of papers on environmental subjects in most areas of philosophy' (Routley 1981, 237n). This passage, clearly a valorization of a mode of existence that does not seek the domination of nature, calls to mind Marx and Engels's description of life under communism in *German Ideology*, a life where it is possible to 'hunt in the morning, fish in the afternoon, rear cattle in the evening, criticize after dinner, just as I have a mind' (Marx and Engels 1947, 22). Routley seems to be living precisely the sort of life Marx envisioned as ideal (although from a Marxist perspective one might question the implication that human freedom can be achieved through voluntary individual withdrawal from capitalist relations).

And there is a further apparent similarity: an apparent intersection of Routley's and Marx's understandings of human freedom. Routley suggests:

> The automated paradise we are offered [by Marx] as the final freeing of man appears to rest on the view of bread labor as necessarily alienated, and hence as something to be reduced to an absolute minimum through automation ... Once the nature domination assumption is abandoned, this approach is no longer plausible or appealing, and an alternative [approach] would aim to make bread labor itself a creative and expressive activity, rather than concentrating on its minimization through the substitution of energy for labor. (Routley 1981, 242; emphasis in original)

But whether such a view in fact comprises a rejection of Marx's critique of capitalism, or whether Marx sees 'bread labor' as a potential vehicle for creative expression rather than something to be abolished through automation, is a considerably more complicated question, to which we now turn.

The 'Early Marx' and the Transformation of Labour

In Marx's '1844 Manuscripts,' which emphasized the alienation of labour under capitalism, it seems quite clear that we are in fact presented with an analysis that does precisely what Routley wants – namely, with a view that will 'aim to make bread labor itself a creative and expressive activity.' Marx's argument here rests on the distinction between objectification and alienation: 'The product of labour is labour embodied and made material in an object, it is the *objectification* of labour. The realization of labour is its objectification. In the sphere of political economy this realization of labour appears as a *loss of reality* for the worker, objectification as *loss of and bondage to the object*, and appropriation as *estrangement*, as *alienation* [*Entausserung*], (Marx 1975, 324; emphases in original).

Marx here is clearly drawing a distinction between the 'realization of labour' and the way this realization *appears* (or the form this realization takes) 'in the sphere of political economy.' But of course Marx understands his intervention as a *critique* of political economy, and as an argument that 'the sphere of political economy' (that is, the capitalist mode of production) is a sphere that is to be abolished and transcended. What remains unclear – in this passage, at least – is what this distinction between alienation and objectification might mean in more practical terms. The question of what constitutes unalienated objectification has received extensive of treatment in the literature on Marx,[10] and in most respects it will suffice to note that for Marx, as was noted earlier, 'private property [is] the material summarized expression of alienated labour' (334) and that therefore the alienation of labour can only be abolished through the abolition of private property. What deserves more specific elaboration, especially insofar as it deals directly with the topic at hand, is the question of what unalienated objectification might mean in terms of the human relationship with nature. The crucial question, on which the very possibility of a Marxian ecological politics seems to rest, is this: Does even *un*alienated objectification presuppose the domination of nature, or is Marx's ideal of free labour compatible with Routley's ideal of 'mak[ing] bread labor itself a creative and expressive activity'?

In beginning to talk about alienation, Marx notes that 'the externalization [*Entausserung* – note that this same word is rendered as 'alienation' in the quotation above] of the worker in his product means not only that his labour becomes an object, an *external* existence, but that it exists *outside him*, independently of him and alien to him, and begins to confront him as an autonomous power' (1975, 324; emphasis in original). The difference between objectification (labour becoming, or being realized in, an object) and alienation (*Entausserung*) thus seems to rest on a distinction between labour's existence as 'external' to the worker in the former case, and its existence 'outside' the worker in the latter. The distinction seems rather abstruse, yet it is one that Marx nevertheless takes great pains to emphasize. As we shall see, the key to understanding this distinction lies in the '1844 Manuscripts' presentation of the category of nature – the object of labour – itself.

Famously in the '1844 Manuscripts,' Marx asserts that 'nature is man's inorganic body' (328). This oxymoronic formulation might at first seem to shed little light on the problematic distinction noted above. How, after all, can one unclear distinction (the product of labour should be 'external to' but not 'outside' the worker) be illuminated by another (the object that is worked on is 'man's ... body' yet is 'inorganic')?

For environmentalist critics of Marx, the notion that 'nature is man's inorganic body' is often taken to be proof that Marx conceives of nature as raw material to be dominated – that nature exists only *for* human beings. John P. Clark notes that 'the same Marx who sees nature as "man's inorganic body" also describes "locomotives, railways, electric telegraphs, self-acting mules, etc." as "organs of the human brain." At best, we seem to be dealing with a highly distorted body consciousness' (Clark 1989, 243; the second internal quotation is from the *Grundrisse*). Indeed, even Donald Lee, who seeks to rescue an ecological impulse from Marx's early works, falls into this trap: 'Perhaps it is unfortunate that Marx's homocentrism is so pronounced here when he speaks of the nonhuman animal and vegetable kingdom as man's "inorganic" body.' At this point, it seems that the best Lee can muster in his defence of Marx is to damn him with faint praise, arguing that 'at least he has brought us back somewhat from the extremes of the Cartesian world view' (Lee 1980, 14).

This understanding of the 'inorganic body' metaphor is even bolstered by what is in many other respects a very careful reading of the term, provided by Jay Andrews: 'The term originally used by Marx in the *[1844] Manuscripts* is *unorganischen*, a cognate of the English "inorganic." It can safely be assumed that Martin Milligan's translation of this word is as accurate as any translation can be. That which is inorganic is inanimate; it is matter which is neither plant nor animal' (Andrews 1994, 70). But such a reading does little to illuminate the character of alienated labour in the '1844 Manuscripts'; furthermore, it does little to explain Marx's conception of nature in that work, except, perhaps, to suggest that Marx was hopelessly confused. After all, only a few sentences earlier, Marx lists some of the natural objects that human beings confront: 'plants, animals, stones, air, light, etc.' (1975, 327) Over the space of a few sentences, Marx thus seems to consign 'plants [and] animals' to the category of (as Andrews has it) 'matter which is neither plant nor animal.'

Commenting on Andrews's article, John Dings thus argues that Andrews 'has got "inorganic" wrong when he interprets it as "inanimate." The figure just doesn't work if you read it that way' (Dings 1994, 81). Dings suggests that instead of being 'inanimate ... nature is man's inorganic body' 'simply by being outside of, not incorporated with, and not (yet) serving the human – not being, in short, organic *to* the human' (ibid.; emphasis in original).

Dings's highly suggestive reading lends some internal consistency to the paragraph under discussion; also, it can be usefully applied to illuminating the otherwise obscure distinction noted earlier. Marx's notion of unalienated objectification – of labour that is 'external to' but not 'outside of' the worker – can thus be understood as one in which labour is 'realized' in an object – an object that nevertheless maintains an (organic) connection to the worker. Unalienated labour, to follow the categories Marx lays out in his discussion of alienated labour, consists of the transfomation of nature such that both the *processes* and *products* of production (whether conceived as the objects produced, or more broadly as a mode of production and its attendant ideology) remain connected to or under the direction of the producer. If nature is to be understood as 'not simply exterior to the body, [but] an extension of the human physical body' (Andrews 1994, 72), then the objects produced – as well as the processes of production – should similarly be understood as extensions of the producer rather than as 'an *alien, hostile* and powerful object which is independent of' the worker (Marx 1975, 331; emphasis in original). Given that Marx understands alienation from the product of labour and from the process of labour as two primary aspects of alienation,[11] it follows that the abolition of both would lead to the abolition of the alienation of human beings from nature, from other human beings (an atomistic, class-divided society), and from what Marx calls 'species-being.'

Marx notes that because humans are alienated from the product of labour (the 'estrange[ment of] nature from man') and from the process of labour (alienation 'from his own active function, from his vital activity'), they are alienated from their species. But this alienation from the species involves more than just the existence of the ideology of individualism (this is certainly a form of alienation, but is covered under the fourth aspect: 'the estrangement of man from man' [1975, 330]). What Marx seems to have in mind here is alienation from the very aspect of humanity that defines us as a species (or should so define us): self-consciousness with respect to our transformation of the natural environment. 'Conscious life activity,' he says, 'directly distinguishes man from animal life activity.'

But Marx then immediately adds: 'Only because of that is he a species-being' (328). This sentence should alert us to the fact that Marx is not using human 'species-being' as another way of saying human nature. It is not that human beings have a particular species-being that defines the human species, just as horses might have a species-being that defines them as a species. Rather, human species-being is unique: there are no other kinds of species-being. This distinction is an important one, because Marx will go on to argue, even more strongly than Rousseau, that 'human nature' cannot be treated as a transhistorical category, but must be understood as a product of particular modes of production. As Marx states in the sixth of the 'Theses on Feuerbach': 'The human essence is no abstraction inherent in each single individual. In its reality it is the ensemble of the social relations' (1978, 145). This extends even to human physiological characteristics, as summarized in his claim in the '1844 Manuscripts' that 'the *cultivation* of the five senses is the work of all previous history. *Sense* which is a prisoner of crude practical need has only a *restricted* sense' (1975, 353; emphases in original).

Thus for Marx, alienation from 'species-being' does not quite amount to a claim that current social arrangements require us to do things that go against human nature. 'Human nature' is historical, and it is not even the case that human beings *have* a transhistorical 'nature' or that we have a species-being. Rather, as Marx says in his first mention of the category: 'Man *is* a species-being' (1975, 327; emphasis added). The importance of the semantic distinction lies in the fact that species-being itself, as Marx first defines it, is, in a sense, alienation from nature: 'Man is a species-being ... because he practically and theoretically makes the species – both his own and those of other things – his object' (327). Species-being consists not only in the transformation of the natural environment (Marx terms this 'species-life' and notes that it applies 'both for man and for animals' [ibid.]), but also in the fact that the power of abstraction – the power to 'theoretically make the species,' the very power to think in terms of 'species' (recalling Rousseau's discussion of the origin of language, noted in the previous chapter) – is what allows humans to produce 'universally' rather than 'one-sidedly,' to produce 'according to the standards of every species and of applying to each object its inherent standard,' and finally to 'produce in accordance with the laws of beauty' (329).

If this capacity for rational abstraction is itself species-being, what then is alienation from species-being? Clearly, Marx is not suggesting that we have completely lost the power of rational abstraction, or that we have become completely immersed in our environment. This complete immersion (which describes animal existence, and perhaps 'primitive communism') would imply the *non*-existence of alienation, as was suggested in Avineri's discussion of alienation in the previous section. It should be recalled that species-being inheres not only in the power of rational abstraction, but also in the transformation of nature in accordance with the latter: it is not just a matter of 'theoretically' making the species, but of doing so practically as well. This practical transformation consists not only of a practical transformation of external nature, but also, as noted earlier, of a transformation of the human species itself.

Alienation from species-being means that our species-being confronts the producer as 'an alien, hostile force.' The capacity for rational abstraction and for the conscious transformation of the environment, turns to confront us. Under capitalism, precisely those capacities which should allow for the flourishing of human life take the form of oppressive social structures. Unalienated labour can be understood as a relationship with natural objects that involves free and creative self-expression. Under capitalism, however, 'the worker becomes a slave of his object ... The culmination of this slavery is that it is only as a *worker* that he can maintain himself as a *physical subject* and only as a *physical subject* that he is a worker' (Marx 1975, 325; emphases in original). The result of class division, in other words, is that the capacity for 'free conscious activity' – which Marx identifies as a defining characteristic of human life – 'appears only as a *means of life*' (328; emphasis in original). Our species-being is turned against us, for in order to survive in a capitalist society, we must allow our capacity for labour to be heteronomously directed. 'The result is that man (the worker) feels that he is acting freely only in his animal functions – eating, drinking and procreating, or at most in his dwelling or adornment – while in his human functions he is nothing more than animal' (327).

Clearly, for Marx, unalienated labour *is* 'a creative and expressive activity,' and there seems to be no privileging of the substitution of energy for labour through increasing automation, as Routley implies. At the same time, however, Marx seems to be suggesting that unalienated labour cannot be 'bread labour': 'Man produces even when he is free from physical need, *and truly produces only in freedom from such need*' (329; emphasis added). Free activity requires release from the constraints of 'necessity,' be it socially or naturally imposed. In rejecting any appeal to return to *pre*-class divided society Marx is even more unambiguous than Rousseau.

Yet Marx is far from suggesting that in order to transcend class-divided society, we must transcend nature itself. Indeed, a relationship with nature is essential to freedom (understood as the externalization of labour): 'The worker can create nothing without *nature*, without the *sensuous, external world*. It is the material in which his labour realizes itself' (325; emphases in original). Furthermore, the sense that we are wholly separate from nature or able to transcend nature strikes Marx as an aspect of alienation. Here, he maintains that 'estranged labour ... estranges nature from man' and that 'man *lives* from nature, i.e. nature is his *body*, and he must maintain a continuing dialogue with it if he is not to die. To say that man's physical and mental life is linked to nature simply means that nature is linked to itself, for man is a part of nature' (328; emphases in original).

In a post-capitalist society, then, human needs would be met through labour, and such labour would be performed not only voluntarily but also (it would seem) enthusiastically, insofar as this labour would be experienced as creative and expressive activity. This suggests that for Marx, the opposition between necessity and freedom, or between labour and leisure, is not transhistorical. In other words, the abolition of capitalism would not only free us *from* (alienated) labour, but also free us *to* (freely) labour. In this sense, labour can be understood as belonging (potentially) to the realm of freedom, rather than simply being a part of the realm of necessity. The division between freedom and necessity, which constitutes part of the experience of living in a class-divided society (performing necessary tasks impinges on one's freedom), is historically specific to class-divided societies, even though it is often understood as a timeless aspect of human existence. This fracturing of experience – into a realm of freedom or leisure on the one hand, and a realm of necessity or work on the other – is thus ideological. As Bertell Ollman observes, this sort of abstraction or hypostatization that occurs in ideology is very closely tied to alienation itself: 'Alienated man is an abstraction because he has lost touch with all human specificity ... What occurs in the real world is reflected in people's minds: essential elements of what it means to be a man are grasped as independent and, in some cases, all powerful entities, whose links with him appear other than what they really are. The whole has broken up into numerous parts whose interrelation in the whole can no longer be ascertained. This is the essence of alienation (Ollman, 1971, 134–5).

Ollman then goes on to remark that 'if alienation is the splintering of human nature into a number of misbegotten parts, we would expect communism to be presented as a kind of reunification. And this is just what we find' (135). Quoting from the '1844 Manuscripts,' Ollman concludes that communism, for Marx, is 'the positive transcendence of all estrangement – that is to say, the return of man from religion, family, state, etc., to his human, i.e. social mode of existence' (quoted in Ollman 1971, 135–6).

But for reasons that will become clear in a moment, it is crucial to recall that this 'positive transcendence of all estrangement' cannot be a simple abolition of all estrangement, even though Marx sometimes seems to be making the latter argument. Certainly one could argue that the forms of estrangement mentioned in the previous quotation ('religion, family, state') are to be abolished under communism. Marx contends that religion is 'the spontaneous activity of the human imagination, the human brain and the human heart [that] detaches itself from the individual and reappears as the alien activity of a god or of a devil' (Marx 1975, 326). Marriage, for Marx, is 'a form of exclusive private property' (346). Under communism, according to Marx, the state should 'wither away,' insofar as the state is, like religion, a mystified expression of human powers. Religion, like the bourgeoisie, must be 'made impossible.'[12] But although the 'positive transcendence' of capitalism might entail the eradication of the conditions of possibility for some forms of alienation (private property, religion, the state), there is at least one form of alienation that would not be abolished, but instead would be positively realized.

Social alienation can be overcome insofar as the aspects of human beings' social life can be reconciled with one another. The 'kind of reunification' that Ollman suggests would transpire can be understood perhaps most clearly by examining the fracturing of social experience (alienation) described in 'On the Jewish Question.' In that essay, Marx describes how capitalism allows for partial freedoms by splintering social life into separate spheres. Social life in precapitalist societies was understood in more organic or holistic terms, the 'political emancipation' that occured with the rise of the bourgeois state involved the separation of public and private spheres and the 'displacement' of private concerns (such as religion and economic relationships) from the ambit of the state to that of 'civil society' (1975, 221–2). As a consequence, citizens of a capitalist society may be provided with equal rights and autonomy within the political sphere (the state), but for Marx this only serves to mask the inequality and heteronomy that continue to exist in the fundamental realm of material production (civil society or the economic sphere). What Marx in this essay terms 'true human emancipation,' then, can only occur once this artificial separation of the state from civil society (of politics from economics, of the citizen from the worker, and so on) has been overcome.

But the possibilities for overcoming this separation seem less clear in the human relationship with nature. It is possible to imagine, if only in vague outline, a form of social organization in which the artificial separations between social spheres necessitated by the alienation that attends capitalist production have been overcome. For example, it is at least possible to imagine what it might mean to subordinate economic production to laws freely and consciously produced through a collective political decision-making process, rather than to the 'laws' of the market. But overcoming the separation of humans from nature – 'the realized naturalism of man and the realized humanism of nature' (Marx 1975, 350) – and what this might mean in practical terms, is something rather more difficult. From a Marxian perspective, it is especially difficult because it cannot involve returning human beings to any sort of natural immanence, as some deep ecologists might want to suggest. We cannot 'return to nature,' because for Marx any understandings of 'nature' will always be conditioned by the particular society in which actual human beings live. As was noted earlier, for Marx, 'man is a species-being ... because he practically and theoretically makes the species – both his own and those of other things – his object' (327). The dashes in his sentence are telling: it is not only that human beings practically and theoretically make nature their object, but (as we saw with Rousseau's discussion of language, and as we shall see again in the discussion of Adorno in the next chapter) it is also that the abstractive power of human consciousness is a productive form of power. 'Species' do not exist in nature. They are the practical and theoretical construction of human beings. Marx's understanding of species-being, then, is both (perhaps most important) a manifestation of a separation between the natural and the social, and something that is to be realized through the abolition of alienation. Unalienated labour is indeed difficult to envision, if it is to be both the expression of our capacity for abstraction and an overcoming of the separation of the human subject from the natural object.

Marx does not address this conundrum; and as we shall see, he shifts the terms of his analysis in his later work, perhaps in part to avoid these sorts of problems. But with this shift away from the terrain of 'species-being,' and away from the idea that the production of necessities might be compatible with freedom, the claim that – to return to Routley's formulation one last time – 'bread labor' might be made 'a creative and expressive activity' also seems to disappear. Instead, the focus in Marx's later work shifts toward the 'minimization' of socially necessary labour, to the point that attempts to rescue an ecological impulse from the humanist themes of Marx's early works in particular, can be countered with the claim that 'humanist eco-Marxism ... is also no longer *Marxist*' (Eckersley 1992, 87; see also Tolman 1981, 63).

The 'Later Marx' and the Reduction of Labour

It is Althusser, of course, who provides the clearest case against such a humanist reading of Marx, arguing that the logic of the '1844 Manuscripts' 'is still philosophical, and when I say philosophical I am using it in the same sense that to which Marx later linked an absolute condemnation' (Althusser 1977, 158). But we need not even accept the Althusserian claim that there is a radical break in Marx's thought between earlier works such as the '1844 Manuscripts' and later works such as *Capital*, in order to grant a difference between Marx's earlier and later works on the subject of alienation. Schmidt (1971), for example, while insisting 'that the work of Marx does not fall into two unrelated parts' (128), suggests that 'the critical comments on the "true socialists" in the *German Ideology* and the *Communist Manifesto* can just as well be understood as a piece of self-criticism, and when Marx poked fun in the *Manifesto* at formulations such as "alienation" and "realization of the human essence," he was also attacking his own use of them in the Paris [1844] Manuscripts' (129).

Even though Schmidt rejects the Althusserian idea of a categorical break in Marx's work, the claim that the *Communist Manifesto* and *German Ideology* can be read as 'self-criticism' suggests that in some ways, the later work should be seen as a repudiation of at least some of the concepts and methods of the earlier work. Schmidt also argues that 'the attitude of the mature Marx has in it nothing of the exuberance and unlimited optimism to be found in the idea of a future society presented in the Paris Manuscripts' (1971, 139).

Moishe Postone, however, provides a different reading, arguing that Marx in his later works does not abandon the 'exuberance' that is associated with the abolition of alienation. Rather, for Postone, it is the arguments of the more "mature" Marx (in particular the notion of the 'double character of labor in capitalism' – that labour is a commodity that can produce more value than it costs to reproduce) that can be used to more adequately ground the concept of alienation. For Postone, 'people in capitalism constitute their social relations and their history by means of labor. Although they are controlled by what they have constituted, they "make" these relations and this history in a different and more emphatic sense than people 'make' precapitalist relations (which Marx characterizes as spontaneously arisen and quasi-natural [*naturwuschig*])' (Postone 1993, 165).

For Postone – and contrary to the view suggested at the beginning of this chapter – the argument that the 'alien hostile force' that workers under capitalism produce can be understood as the social *system* that dominates them, rather than simply as the 'dead labour' that is accumulated in capitalist factories and machinery, is in fact advanced most strongly Marx's later works – in *Capital* in particular. In this text, it is the analysis of the fetish character of commodities that shows most clearly how, under capitalism, unlike in precapitalist modes of production, 'social compulsion is effected abstractly' rather than through 'direct compulsion' (Postone 1993, 160). In other words, the specificity of labour under capitalism is that it produces commodities (or 'exchange-values'), which function as a system that mediates social production. Thus, for Postone, it was Marx's analysis of the commodity form in *Capital* that at last allowed him to grasp successfully 'the "rational core" of Hegel's position – in this case that objectification *is* alienation' (ibid., emphasis in original). Thus, for Postone, finally, the separation Marx calls for in his early critique of Hegel, between objectification and alienation, is only fully explicable by the *later* works' emphasis on the specificity of commodity exchange:

> It is well known that, in his early writings, Marx maintains that labor objectifying itself in products need not be alienating, and criticizes Hegel for not having distinguished between alienation and objectification. Yet how one conceptualizes the relation of alienation and objectification depends on how one understands labor. If one proceeds from a transhistorical notion of 'labor,' the difference between objectification and alienation must be grounded by factors external to the objectifying activity ... In Marx's later writings, however, alienation is rooted in the double character of commodity-determined labor, and as such, is intrinsic to the character of labor itself ... Labor in capitalism gives rise to a social structure that dominates it. This form of self-generated reflexive domination is alienation.

> [The analysis of Marx's mature works] shows that objectification is indeed alienation – if what labor objectifies are social relations. This identity, however, is historically determinate: it is a function of the specific nature of labor under capitalism. (1993, 159–60)

Postone's argument thus seeks to recuperate in Marx's later works the exuberance that is associated with his early works. He creates this sense of almost seamless continuity by emphasizing the analysis of the specific character of labour under capitalism developed in the later works, and by reading this as a response to the problematic of alienation/objectification broached in the earlier works.

For Schmidt, in contrast, there seems little question that at least for the more mature Marx, although the abolition of capitalism may mean a qualitative transformation of some aspects or types of labour, it will not mean the complete abolition of toil. Although there is discussion in the '1844 Manuscripts' about the qualitative transformation of labour, such that it becomes identified with human freedom and self-realization, the later works are more preoccupied with the *reduction* of labour time.

Of course, this is not to suggest that Marx completely abandons the notion that labour will be different in a post-capitalist society. Rather, Schmidt argues, it is Marx's materialism, and his rejection of Hegel's totalizing idealistic dialectic, that leads him to conclude that only *some* forms of socially necessary labour are made necessary by class divisions. Schmidt first points out that for both Hegel and Marx, over time, 'greater and greater areas of nature come under human control. In Marx, however, and this distinguishes him from the idealist Hegel, the material of nature is never totally incorporated in the modes of its theoretico-practical appropriation' (Schmidt 1971, 136). For Marx, therefore, the fact that 'the metabolism between man and nature is independent of any historical form' (ibid.), and that 'mankind must always engage in metabolic interaction with nature, whatever the historical conditions' (138), suggests that even a classless society will be marked by a distinction between a realm of human freedom and a realm of (nature-imposed) necessity. Schmidt concludes, citing vol. 3 of *Capital*: 'In a more rational society, the realm of necessity will be mastered and its role will decline in relation to that of the cultural sphere. Despite this, Marx insisted that the arrangement of the human situation he was aiming at would by no means put an end to the distinction between one area of life which was determined by "external expedience," and another area in which "the development of man's powers ... would count as an aim for itself"' (140).

There are, however, several points to be emphasized about this call for the reduction (but also continuation) of necessary labour. The first, perhaps obvious point, is that even though Marx spends a great deal of time discussing the length of the working day in the first volume of *Capital*, and that he clearly sees the struggle to reduce the length of the working day as a just one, he is never simply arguing for a reduction of work time. Even though Marx sees 'a person's wealth ... in the time freely available to him or her' (Booth 1989, 210), and even though 'time determines the measure of freedom available beyond the necessary material practice' (Schmidt 1971, 149), questions of the length of the working day are subsidiary to the question of the social organization of production. Marx does not dispute the importance of struggling for a shortened work day; that said, the analysis of the first volume of *Capital* aims to show that any victories in this struggle remain fragile as long as social production is geared toward the expansion of exchange-value. That the development of humans' productive capacities will lead to the freeing of time can only be *assured* through the achievement of transparency in the realm of material production, if 'men's social being becomes rational in itself' (141).

There is a second and perhaps more important qualification to be made: Schmidt recognizes that the alienating character of labour is determined by the social relations of production rather than by its being a necessity imposed by nature.[13] 'It appears clearly from the *Grundrisse* that [in a post-capitalist society] the surviving, humanized realm of necessity can just as well become a sphere of man's self-realization as the realm of freedom which depends on it' (143). We can see here the similarities with Postone, who also acknowledges that 'there can, however, be a form of freedom within this sphere [of necessity] as well,' although this of course depends on the transcendence of capitalism, or 'the transformation of the structure of social production and the abolition of the abstract form of domination rooted in commodity-determined labor' (Postone 1993, 381).

As Schmidt also points out, however, the transformation of labour in the realm of necessity into 'a sphere of man's self-realization' is by no means automatic: 'The *practice* of a more rational society would have to show that, in essence, labour is richer than its alienated forms would allow us to suppose' (Schmidt 1971, 143; emphasis in original). For this practice to overcome the stark division between free activity and labour, or for labour to be compatible with human development, labour would have to lose not only the alienating characteristics imposed on it by the social organization of production, but also the drudgery that might be imposed by the natural material or processes. This can occur only if labour is understood not so much as the direct production of goods, but rather as the administration of processes of production:

> [Marx] had in mind the *total automation* of industry, which would change the worker's role more and more into that of a technical 'overseer and regulator.' This however implies *a qualitatively different* relationship between the active subject and the object: 'It is no longer the modified natural object which is inserted by the labourer between the object and himself as an instrument, but the natural process, transformed by him into an industrial process, which is inserted as an instrument between himself and inorganic nature, over which he has gained control. He stands beside the process of production, instead of being its main agent. In this metamorphosis, it is neither the direct labour, done by the man himself, nor the time he takes over it, but rather the appropriation of his own general productive powers, his understanding of nature, and his mastery of the latter through the agency of his existence as a member of society – in one phrase, the development of the social individual – which now appears as the great foundation-stone of production and wealth.' (Schmidt 1971, 147; emphases in original, internal quotations from Marx's *Grundrisse*)

Certainly this description is rather far removed from the more idyllic and well-known description of labour under socialism to be found in *German Ideology*, cited earlier. As Ali Rattansi has noted, this is consistent with what is at the very least a shift in emphasis between Marx's earlier and later works. *German Ideology* seems to suggest that the division of labour can be abolished: as labour is transformed into unalienated creative activity, and as the domination of nature is replaced by its 'humanization,' people can hunt in the morning, raise cattle in the afternoon, and so on. In contrast, in Marx's later works, the primacy given to industrial production processes ensures both that routine tasks necessary for the material reproduction of human life can be done by machines, and that some specialization of labour will continue to be necessary. Instead of seeking to abolish the division of labour *tout court*, as the passage from *German Ideology* suggests, Marx turns 'to an interest in overcoming the separation between intellectual and manual tasks' (Rattansi 1982, 175). It is necessary to overcome this separation in order to realize human freedom, which, as Schmidt's citation of the *Grundrisse* (above) shows, is closely associated with the scientific mastery of nature. Thus, there seems little question that for the mature Marx, at least, the realization of human freedom is predicated on the sort of detachment from nature that makes scientific knowledge possible.

As the discussion of ecocentrism in chapter 1 suggested, however, this sort of detachment or alienation is not something to be rejected out of hand as having strictly pernicious consequences. Postone (1993) argues that Marx's understanding of the transhistorical necessity for some form of labour is 'a recognition of the boundedness of humanity as a mediate part of nature. It suggests that a situation of historical freedom would also allow for a consciously regulated process of interaction with nature, a relationship with nature that should not be understood in terms of a romanticized "harmony" that expresses the subjection of humanity to the blind forces of nature, or the 'freedom' that entails the blind subjugation of nature' (383).

On the other hand, this also means that for Marx, in the third volume of *Capital*, 'the realm of freedom really begins only where labour determined by necessity and external expediency ends; it lies by its very nature beyond the sphere of material production proper' (Marx 1981, 958–9). The necessity of a metabolic interaction with nature continues to function as a limit to the extent to which the transformation of nature can be an effective form of creative expression, even under conditions of socialized production. Unlike in the '1844 Manuscripts,' labour here does not become an expression of freedom, but rather remains its necessary basis.

To sum up, for Marx, as we have seen, labour under capitalism produces the social relations and the ideology that determine (that set limits to and exert pressure on) the character of individuals' lives. What seems curious about this analysis – and Postone, by virtue of his overall argument about the specificity of labour under capitalism, must emphasize this point – is that for Marx it is an argument specifically, and exclusively, about the capitalist mode of production: 'People *in capitalism* constitute their social relations and their history by means of labor ... They "make" these relations in a different and more emphatic sense than people "make" precapitalist relations (which Marx characterizes as spontaneously arisen and quasi-natural)' (Postone 1993, 165; emphasis added). It is only labour under capitalism that produces fully *social* relations, because it is only under capitalism that labour is conceived abstractly. Although socialism would bring a transparency to social relations of production, production relations have only become truly socialized (albeit in mystified form) under capitalism. Similarly, according to Postone, it is the abstract conceptualization of labour – *alienation* – 'that allows for – and perhaps induces – social reflection on, and an analysis of, society as a whole' (1993, 165).

The usefulness of Marx's theories for contemporary ecological politics lies in their focus on specific forms of social organization as determinants in identifying problems in human ecology. The category of alienation is a crucial one in this regard, and Marx's contribution here lies especially in the fact that he separates alienation from nature on the one hand from alienation from social processes on the other. This distinction, which often is formulated as a distinction between *objectification* and *alienation*, forms at least the beginnings of a distinction between what we will come to term 'basic' and 'surplus' forms of alienation when we set out to distinguish those forms of alienation which are necessary for human survival and freedom, from those which reinforce social structures rooted in domination.

At the same time, as we have just seen, there is a sense in which, according to the logic of Marx's arguments, the more 'basic' form of alienation emerges fully only under capitalism. In other words, Marx presumes a sharp distinction between capitalist society (where domination is effected abstractly and can only be naturalized through *ideological* structures that are the product of human labour) and precapitalist society (where domination is through 'direct compulsion' and is 'quasi-natural'). Social domination is thus only denaturalized, or rendered 'surplus,' by the realization of 'basic' alienation – that is, by the advances in the 'mastery of nature' that occur under capitalism.

Where Marx's theorizations stop, however, is at the point of considering whether domination might inhere not only in the 'surplus' forms of alienation that would be abolished once social relations are demystified, or whether it might also inhere in objectification, the alienation that makes 'the rational mastery of nature' possible. In other words, Marx's characterization of precapitalist societies as ones in which domination is 'quasi-natural' might be symptomatic of his arguing for a more radical separation between the two forms of alienation than is in fact warranted. The possibility that the separation of social relations from relations with nature might itself be a form of mystification – that the 'mastery of nature' might itself be an ideological mask for social domination – is one that we will consider in the next chapter. In so doing, we will also raise the question of whether the historical disentanglement of enlightenment from mythologization – as in Marx's distinction between capitalist and precapitalist societies – can be so easily effected.

CHAPTER 5

Theodor W. Adorno: From Udeis *to Utopia*

As we have seen, Marx built his contribution to the concept of alienation on his noticing Hegel's failure to distinguish between objectification and alienation. By the end of the last chapter, however, we had noted that such a distinction raises some problems of its own. In particular, it seems to presuppose a particularity about capitalist society and the way in which capitalist social relations are constructed and reinforced: it is not only that labour's 'abstract' character under capitalism allows for ideological critique to point to the ways in which seemingly 'natural' relations are in fact socially constructed, but also that this abstract form of labour apparently means that capitalism actually represents the first time that relations have been socially constructed rather than naturally given. The rationalization of social relations through the imposition of the logic of exchange-value does more than allow for demystification – it also simultaneously constructs the very illusion that is to be demystified. The implication seems to be that, notwithstanding Marx's claims about the existence of 'primitive communism,' social domination in premodern societies is natural. Although such an argument may not demand teleological claims, or purport to have discovered an inevitable logic to history, it is perhaps not difficult to see, given such a framework, how seductive such narratives of progress can be.

In the work of Theodor Adorno, we are presented with a powerful antidote to such claims. In many important respects, Adorno remains committed to a Marxist project,[1] but he also sets out to disturb the distinction between capitalist and precapitalist social forms discussed earlier. In so doing, he also works to dispute the easy distinction between social domination and 'the rational mastery of nature,' or between objectification and alienation.

The Dialectic of Enlightenment, or, the Story of *Udeis*

Everyone wants to be Cary Grant. Even *I* want to be Cary Grant.
Cary Grant (quoted in Xenos 1989, 96; emphasis in original)

The sharp distinction between the precapitalist past and the capitalist present is perhaps most clearly and forcefully questioned in *Dialectic of Enlightenment*, which Adorno wrote collaboratively with Max Horkheimer while the two were living in Los Angeles, California, during the Second World War. This book is perhaps best understood through its central argument: the double-edged claim that 'myth is already enlightenment; and enlightenment reverts to mythology' (Horkheimer and Adorno 1987, xvi). The claim being advanced here will perhaps be better understood if we recall the context in which it was written: the authors were Jewish intellectuals, steeped in bourgeois European high culture, who had just escaped the horrors of Nazi Germany. In exile in America, they found themselves immersed in the banal cultural products of Hollywood. This wartime context rightly encourages us to focus our attention on the ways the text can be understood as an attempt to come to terms with the horrifying barbarism that was emerging during those years from the very heart of European civilization. Fascism must be understood in some way as a consequence of the same culture that produced Beethoven and Goethe and their audience. Yet America's 'democratic' mass culture – which seems to be a rejection of elite culture – is understood by the authors as little more than an *apologia* for the fracturing of life under advanced capitalism, and shares disturbing similarities of technique (not to mention content) with fascist propaganda (Horkheimer and Adorno 1987, 120–67, Adorno 1967, 1994, 1998).

The claim that 'enlightenment reverts to mythology' is a claim about the limits of the demystifying, rationalizing project of enlightenment. To borrow Max Weber's terms, it is a claim that the 'disenchantment of the world' has led us directly into the 'iron cage.' Instead of leading to greater freedom, the progress of reason has paradoxically delivered us into the hands of the totally administered society. Enlightenment was supposed to provide 'man's release from his self-incurred tutelage' (Kant 1988, 462), to release us from dependence on and subjection to the vicissitudes of nature; but according to Horkheimer and Adorno, reason has in fact left us under the thrall of a social logic, a 'second nature' as uncontrollable as the first. Enlightenment provides only the 'cold rays' under which 'the seed of the new barbarism grows to fruition' (32). Thus, *Dialectic of Enlightenment* suggests that enlightenment's best proponents are not theorists of universal equality and freedom like Kant, but those who honestly explore the implication of reason in domination, such as Nietzsche and de Sade: 'Whereas the optimistic writers merely disavowed and denied in order to protect the indissoluble union of reason and crime, civil society and domination, the dark chroniclers mercilessly declared the shocking truth' (118).

Enlightenment, or a project of rational scepticism, runs the risk of lapsing into an unquestioning acceptance of the world as it construes it to be: enlightenment is founded on the distinction between the thing and its concept (a point to which we shall return), but too often it is blind to the fact that the representations of reality that it constructs (language, mathematics, scientific models, and so on), and which are then used so successfully to manipulate nature, are mere representations rather than reality itself. Thought that does not reflect on this distinction lapses into reification: 'Enlightenment *must consider itself*, if men are not be wholly betrayed' (xv; emphasis in original).

The claim that 'enlightenment reverts to mythology' – and the attendant problem of the reification that seems inherent in representational thinking – will require further elaboration. For the moment, however, the following formulation may suffice: radical skepticism or demythologization leads to the erasure of qualitative difference and the mathematization of nature, as everything is instrumentalized by being placed within a matrix of exchange (or 'barter')[2] relations. This triumph of instrumental rationality reaches its apotheosis in the domination of nature and what members of the Frankfurt School often refer to as the 'liquidation of the individual.' The psychological repression of individuality in mass society is thus homologous to the internment and expulsion or execution of those social groups which fail to 'fit in' to myths of national purity under fascism.[3] In other words, finally, 'the capacity of representation is the vehicle of progress and regression at one and the same time' (35).

Turning to the claim that 'myth is already enlightenment' – the other half of *Dialectic of Enlightenment*'s central thesis – this suggests that instrumental rationality, and hence domination, do not begin with modernity, but rather with the beginning of human historical time. To elucidate this claim, Horkheimer and Adorno consider Homer's *Odyssey*, which is not only (in the written form we have access to) the retelling and systematization of ancient myth, but also 'the basic text of European civilization' (46).

Crucially, for Horkheimer and Adorno (1987), the story told in this foundational text is one in which the protagonist survives through self-denial or self-sacrifice in one episode after another. Odysseus' encounter with the Cyclops Polyphemus serves to illustrate how this survival through sacrifice can be understood as the paradigmatic instance of the violence exacted by the ('enlightened') separation of concept and thing. Odysseus survives his encounter with the Cyclops only by cunningly denying his individuality: he tells Polyphemus that his name is '*Udeis*' (Nobody) so that when he blinds the Cyclops and escapes, aid for the Cyclops is not forthcoming because Polyphemus is yelling 'Nobody has blinded me!' Odysseus thus survives this episode by denying his own existence ('I am Nobody'). The downfall of the Cyclops (variously referred to as 'uncivilized,' 'lawless,' 'savage,' and 'stupid' – terms that seem to function practically as synonyms [64–5]) arises from his inability to distinguish between word and thing (60). This episode shares a thematic similarity with the departure from the land of the Lotus-Eaters, during which Odysseus is found to deny bodily pleasures and the possibility of an 'idyll[ic]' relationship with nature 'without work and struggle' (62–4); as well as with the fact that Odysseus can only enjoy sexual relations with Circe by having 'an unassailably firm heart in [his] breast' (quoted in Horkheimer and Adorno 1987, 72) According to the authors, all of these episodes serve to demonstrate the following, more general point: 'Man's domination over himself, which grounds his selfhood, is almost always the destruction of the subject in whose service it is undertaken ... The history of civilization is the history of the introversion of sacrifice' (54–5).

But understanding myth as 'already enlightenment' does not simply consist in reading enlightenment back into the earliest texts of Western civilization. Rather, myth can be viewed in this way because Horkheimer and Adorno understand enlightenment, or demythologization, as a means of controlling nature. For the 'enlightened,' the choice is always between controlling nature and being controlled by it. And to avoid being controlled by nature, one may have to expel nature from oneself. Thus, civilization is not only the progressive domination (or 'rational mastery') of external nature, but also the sacrifice of internal nature.

Myth is 'already enlightenment.' In this regard, Horkheimer and Adorno's statement that 'civilization is ... the introversion of sacrifice' is also a claim that the mythic logic of sacrifice is already an attempt to dominate nature. 'Mythic inevitability,' they write, 'is defined by the equivalence between the curse, the crime which expiates it, and the guilt arising from that, which in its turn reproduces the curse' (58). The emphasis on inevitability and on the cyclical reproduction of the ever same would seem here to distinguish myth from the progressive linearity of enlightenment; however, the notion that myth is defined by *equivalence* warns us against such a neat division. In the book's opening pages, after all, the authors had remarked that '*bourgeois* society is ruled by equivalence' (7; emphasis added). 'Myth is already enlightenment' in the sense that the sacrificial substitution of 'equivalents' already represents an attempt to *control* fate by imposing a matrix of exchange relations: sacrifice is 'a device of men by which the gods may be mastered: the gods are overthrown by the very system by which they are honoured' (49).

Nevertheless, there remains a crucial difference between myth and enlightenment. The shift from myth to enlightenment is marked by a shift from mimesis to conceptual identification. Thus even magic (which predates myth) is 'already enlightenment' in the sense that it is aimed at the control of nature. But the rationality of magic differs from that of enlightenment in the ways this control is to be accomplished: 'Like science, magic pursues aims, but seeks to achieve them by mimesis – not by progressively distancing itself from the object' (Horkheimer and Adorno 1987, 11). This distinction between the proximity of mimesis on the one hand, and the 'distancing' involved in conceptual identification on the other, is noteworthy because it parallels the distinction between art and labour: a few pages later, in a discussion of the decline of the social role of art, the authors note that 'nature must no longer be influenced by approximation [as in art], but mastered by labor' (19).

The fundamental ambivalence that underlies this shift to the mastery of nature by instrumental rationality (represented by science and labour) can be understood by recalling the claim that 'enlightenment reverts to mythology,' and by returning to the authors' reading of the *Odyssey*. The episode with the Cyclops is perhaps the most striking example of the assertion of identity through self-denial; but it is another episode from the *Odyssey* that is privileged in Horkheimer and Adorno's text. In the pages preceding the chapter they dedicate to the *Odyssey* (what we might call their 'prehistory' of the *Odyssey* chapter), Horkheimer and Adorno discuss Odysseus' encounter with the Sirens, which the authors introduce as a crystallization of 'the entanglement of myth, domination, and labor' (32). As with the other adventures of Odysseus, we can see in this episode the psychological repression that is necessary in order to construct the subject's identity: the Sirens' allure lies in their full knowledge of the past, which is heard as 'the irresistible promise of pleasure' (33). The 'price' of this knowledge of the past, however, is 'the future' – the individual cannot survive full knowledge of his own past.[4] 'Men had to do fearful things to themselves before the self, the identical, purposive, and virile nature of man, was formed, and something of that recurs in every childhood. The strain of holding the I together adheres to the I in all stages; and the temptation to lose it has always been there with the blind determination to maintain it' (33).

The Sirens episode is privileged in the text because of the ways it links this allegory of psychological repression with one of class domination. It is especially important because of what it suggests in terms of the social division of labour. Odysseus' men have their ears plugged with wax so that they can row on without being tempted by the Sirens; but Odysseus himself is strapped to the mast, able to hear but unable to act. The authors' recounting and interpretation of the episode is worth quoting at length:

> The laborers must be fresh and concentrate as they look ahead, and must ignore whatever lies to one side. They must doggedly sublimate in additional effort the drive that impels to diversion. And so they become practical ... Odysseus, the seigneur who allows others to labor for themselves ... listens, but while bound impotently to the mast; the greater the temptation the more he has his bonds tightened – just as later the burghers would deny themselves happiness all the more doggedly as it drew closer to them with the growth of their own power. What Odysseus hears is without consequence for him; he is able only to nod his head as a sign to be set free from his bonds; but it is too late; his men, who do not listen, know only the song's danger but nothing of its beauty, and leave him at the mast in order to save him and themselves. They reproduce the oppressor's life together with their own, and the oppressor is no longer able to escape his social role. The bonds with which he has irremediably tied himself to practice, also keep the sirens away from practice: their temptation becomes neutralized and becomes a mere object for contemplation – becomes art. The prisoner is present at a concert, an inactive eavesdropper like later concertgoers, and his spirited call for liberation fades like applause. Thus the enjoyment of art and manual labor break apart as the world of prehistory is left behind. (34)

Numerous points could be made about this very rich passage. The association of repression with deafness was no doubt evocative for Adorno (who was a musicologist, and who once opened an essay on cultural criticism by alluding to the importance of 'thinking with [one's] ears' [Adorno 1967, 19]). In terms of the dialectic of enlightenment, however, and for our purposes here, what seems crucial is the argument that the division of labour, which increases our ability to dominate nature, is no guarantee of greater freedom. In fact, the Sirens episode demonstrates not only how the two can be disconnected, but also how the division of labour perpetuates and even intensifies domination and repression: 'The servant remains enslaved in body and soul; the master regresses ... Mankind, whose versatility and knowledge become differentiated with the division of labor, is at the same time forced back to anthropologically more primitive stages, for with the technical easing of life the persistence of domination brings about a fixation of the instincts by means of heavier repression' (Horkheimer and Adorno 1987, 35).

Like both Rousseau and Marx before them, Horkheimer and Adorno here question the association of increased mastery over nature (an increase in society's productive forces, in Marx's terms) with a betterment of the human condition. For Horkheimer and Adorno, as we have seen, 'enlightenment' has thus far been the hollow triumph of instrumental reason: we are capable of increasingly sophisticated and accurate representations of nature, but these only serve our domination of nature. What is more, Horkheimer and Adorno have access to two important developments that allow them to press these conclusions further than either Rousseau or Marx could. First, advances in evolutionary biology – in particular, the revolutionary claims of Darwinism – have made it more difficult to contain domination by establishing a rigid distinction between the natural and the social.[5] Second – and perhaps even more important – the development of psychoanalysis (in particular by Freud) has blurred the distinction between external and internal nature. In other words, for Horkheimer and Adorno, the control over nature that enlightened rationality affords has thus far been inseparable not only from the domination of external nature, but also from social domination and heavy psychic repression.

The contributions and limitations of the Freudian framework are taken up much more concretely by Marcuse, and will be discussed in chapter 6. But Adorno's discussion of the possibility of a non-instrumental or non-alienated relationship with nature does not end with the critique presented in *Dialectic of Enlightenment*. Although Adorno's treatment of this question is in some ways more oblique than Marcuse's, it raises important questions; it also helps illuminate some important aspects of his philosophical and political project.

Adorno's Conception of Nature: A Sort of Homecoming

> [Proust] lay on his bed racked with homesickness, homesick for the world distorted in the state of resemblance, a world in which the true surrealist face of existence breaks through. To this world belongs what happens in Proust ... it bears a fragile, precious reality: the image.
>
> Benjamin (1968, 205)

It is impossible to 'sketch out,' or represent in any conventional sense, Adorno's conception of nature. This is because, for Adorno, it is impossible to arrive at an accurate positive representation of nature. Any attempt at representation, any attempt to posit a definition of nature, is doomed to be a distortion. The reasons for this can only be made more clear as the discussion proceeds, since a great deal of Adorno's intellectual project hinges on the ways in which ideas can or should be presented. Nevertheless, the possibility of a different relationship with nature demands some sort of understanding of the object that is to be related to. Let us begin by examining an early essay, in which Adorno came as close as he ever would to addressing this problematic head-on.

Adorno begins 'The Idea of Natural History' by recognizing the limitations of the essay form: it can be no more than a development of an already established discussion, meaning 'that it would be wrong always to begin again at the beginning.' Instead of laying out a series of definitions that are foundational for the discussion, Adorno asks his audience only to 'permit me a few words on terminology' (1984, 111). These limitations are a feature of the essay form, which Adorno takes to an especially compelling mode of philosophical investigation and argumentation (Adorno 1991a). Considering that one of these strengths that he identifies is that the essay form allows the author to 'abandon the conventions of discursiveness' (Rose 1978, 15), it is perhaps not too surprising that this essay's thesis is not stated until very nearly its midpoint. At the end of the first of three parts, Adorno declares: 'If the question of the relation of nature and history is to be seriously posed, then it only offers any chance of solution if it is possible *to comprehend historical being in its most extreme historical determinacy, where it is most historical, as natural being, or if it were possible to comprehend nature as an his-*

torical being where it seems to rest most deeply in itself as nature' (Adorno 1984, 117; emphasis in original).

Adorno here is following Georg Lukács in claiming that social relations are experienced as a 'second nature' (118). Much like the postmodernists in chapter 2, Adorno argues that understandings of 'nature' are always rooted in determinate social conditions, and that appeals to 'nature' are always projections of social values. (There are also important differences between Adorno and postmodern theorists such as Baudrillard and Foucault; these will be discussed below.)

Given this, an understanding of Adorno's conception of nature cannot be grasped on the basis of an appeal to 'natural facts.' It is the thesis of this early essay that 'facts' – even the 'facts of nature' – are simply not accessible without the intervening mediation of social relations. So according to Adorno any claim to unmediated access to the natural world (whether in positivism, in Heideggerian 'neo-ontology,' or in deep ecology) can only be described as ideology, or the rationalization of existent social relations that are predicated on domination.

But Adorno's claim goes even further than Lukacs's claim that social relations are experienced as natural. Simon Jarvis notes that for Adorno, just as knowledge of nature cannot be completely voided of any social content, there can also be no such thing as a purely social object (Jarvis 1998, 47). All interactions with the natural world are mediated by social relations, and all social interactions are mediated by our interaction with nature.

But in Adorno's attempt to move beyond Lukács, we notice a certain slippage: while Lukács posits a dialectical opposition between the natural and the *social*, Adorno in this essay is concerned with the relationship between the natural and the *historical*. To understand the significance of this shift, we must turn to the essay's opening propositions. In Adorno's opening 'few words on terminology,' he suggests a preliminary definition of 'nature':

> What has always been, what as fatefully arranged predetermined being underlies history and appears in history; it is substance in history. What is delimited by these expressions is what I mean here by 'nature.' The question that arises is that of the relationship of this nature to what we understand by history, where history means that mode of conduct established by tradition that is characterized primarily by the occurrence of the qualitatively new; it is a movement that does not play itself out in mere identity, mere reproduction of what has always been, but rather one in which

the new occurs; it is a movement that gains its true character through what appears in it as new. (Adorno 1984, 111)

The opposition of nature (the 'mere reproduction of what has always been') to history ('the qualitatively new') is somewhat suggestive of the *Dialectic of Enlightenment*, written a little more than a decade later. This suggestiveness is intensified when we look a couple of sentences earlier, where Adorno notes that this preliminary definition of nature, 'if I translated it into standard philosophical terminology, would come closest to the concept of *myth*' (1984, 111; emphasis added). If 'nature' here comes closest to 'myth,' then surely 'history' (in the longer passage just cited) can be rendered as 'enlightenment.' Jameson, for example, suggests that *Dialectic of Enlightenment* provides precisely a 'representation and ... working out' of the perpetual process of the 'reciprocal defamiliarization of the two incommensurable poles of the dualism of Nature and History' that the early essay advocates (Jameson 1990, 99). However, when we recall *Dialectic of Enlightenment*'s argument that 'myth is already enlightenment; and enlightenment reverts to mythology,' we can also see why Adorno only suggests this preliminary definition of nature (nature as the opposite of history) as one 'that is to be dissolved' (Adorno 1984, 111).

This pairing of myth and enlightenment, or of nature and history, as a unity of apparent opposites, is (not surprisingly) symptomatically visible in the *Odyssey*, in what Horkheimer and Adorno call the 'quintessential paradox of the [Homeric] epic.' Here, the paradox manifests itself in 'the fact that the notion of homeland is opposed to myth – which the fascist would falsely present as homeland' (Horkheimer and Adorno 1987, 78). Earlier in the text, the authors had suggested that it is 'the end of nomadic existence' that fixes a social order and the division of labour (14). If we were to search for an 'origin' for the domination that is 'coeval with sociality,' we might find it here, at the point at which human existence becomes geographically stabilized. The paradox, in other words, is that nature is the eternal recurrence of the same ('the mere reproduction of what has always been' in the citation from the early essay, above) and yet is also to be *contrasted* with the 'fixed' existence of post-nomadic social life. History, in other words, only starts moving when human communities stop moving.

But although in the early essay, Adorno suggests that 'nature' is identified with 'myth,' in *Dialectic of Enlightenment*, he and Horkheimer take pains to *distinguish* nature from myth: 'Novalis' definition, according to which all philosophy is homesickness, holds true only if this longing is not dissolved into the phantasm of a lost remote antiquity, but represents the homeland, *nature itself, as wrested from myth*' (1987, 78; emphasis added). The opposition of nature and history could be used to identify myth with nature, but this opposition is then exploded by *Dialectic of Enlightenment*'s argument that 'myth is already enlightenment,' that mythic sacrifice is a prototype of exchange relations, and that myth is already an attempt to *dominate* nature. Enlightenment narratives might identify myth with nature, but these fail to see that 'aboriginal myth already contains the aspect of deception which triumphs in the fraudulence of Fascism yet imputes the same practice of lies to the Enlightenment' (45). 'Nature' and 'myth' must, in fact, be 'wrested' apart. If nature is to be distinguished from history (in the sense that historical narratives represent the domination of nature), then nature could be identified with 'myth,' or the absence of historicity. But if, on the other hand, 'myth' turns out to be 'already enlightenment,' or another mode of nature domination, then nature must be something else again.

Horkheimer and Adorno assert that 'the homeland' should be identified with 'nature itself'. and not with what is presented as the homeland in fascist propaganda. The fixity of post-nomadic life is in fact the basis of domination and 'grounds the human alienation in which originates all homesickness and all longing for the lost primal state of man' (78). Immediately after this, however, they continue: 'Homeland is the state of having escaped.' If the domination of nature, in either enlightened or mythic form, is predicated on alienation, we might then want to identify nature with the homeland, or a state anterior to alienation. But this turns out to be inadequate as well, since in fact 'all longing and all homesickness are directed' not to nature, but to 'the settled life and the fixed order of property' – a condition that, as noted earlier, is *already* one of alienation from nature. A 'state of having escaped' cannot be a 'state' in the sense of being geographically fixed, nor can it be a temporally originary moment. Nature, then, cannot be accurately presented as a 'state,' or as a foundation on which social life and domination are erected or that could be revealed by stripping away the layers accumulated through successive generations of alienated living. Thus, Adorno suggests that it is impossible to arrive at an accurate positive representation of nature at all, and he does so in the only way that is logically consistent with this position – by discussing the topic in a manner that consistently *resists* positing a definition of it. In its own way, the process of ceaselessly recasting relations of identity and difference provides a better understanding of nature than any static statement or definition could.

Thus the understanding of 'nature itself' as the homeland (indeed, any definition of nature) is best read as a tactical concession rather than an ontological assertion.[6] Such a reading militates against seeing the critique of enlightenment as a reactionary attack on enlightenment, or as a call to return to a pre-lapsarian state. In this sense, *Dialectic of Enlightenment* seems to offer us a more generalized understanding of the apparent paradox with which this chapter began – that the illusion to be demystified is conjured up by the very process that gives rise to demystification. Thus Jameson notes (in a chapter devoted to Adorno's concept of 'natural history'):

> In any case it should be noted that the peculiar originality of Adorno's and Horkheimer's conception of a 'dialectic of enlightenment' is that it excludes any beginning or fixed term, and specifically describes 'enlightenment' as an 'always-already' process whose structure lies very precisely in its generation of the illusion that what preceded it (which was also a form of enlightenment) was that 'original' moment of myth, the archaic union with nature, which it is the vocation of enlightenment 'proper' to annul. If it is a matter of telling a historical story, therefore, we must read Adorno and Horkheimer as positing a narrative without a beginning in which the 'fall,' or dissociation, is always there already; if, however, we decide to reread their book as a diagnosis of the peculiarities and the structural limits and pathologies of historical vision or narrative itself, then we may conclude, in a somewhat different fashion, that the strange after-image of 'primal unity' always seems to be projected after the fact onto whatever present the historical eye fixes, as its 'inevitable' past, which vanishes without a trace when frontal vision is in turn displaced onto it. (Jameson 1990, 100)

Thus, finally, given this well-founded resistance to a hypostasized understanding of 'nature' (and notwithstanding his scathing criticisms of the products of the culture industry), we might see Adorno agreeing with the claim of one of Hollywood's best-known fantasies. Adorno himself described his exile in the United States as being transported to a fantastical yet disturbing and alienating land ('I felt a little as if I were in Kafka's Nature Theater of Oklahoma' [quoted in Jay 1984, 157]), and his experience in America in turn made it impossible for him to experience his return to Germany as any sort of comfortable 'homecoming' (1984, 161–5). Similarly, a character who is mystically whisked away (from a state that borders on Oklahoma) to a strange, fantastical land, and yet who longs to *return* to a place that is only presented as bleak and grey (literally – these sequences, unlike the rest of the film, are shot in black and white), to a 'home' without her real (or 'natural') parents, would surely also be aware of the impossibility of a positive representation of 'nature itself.' A return to the homeland, to 'nature itself,' is a utopian impossibility: for Adorno, too, 'there's no place like home' (Rushdie 1992, 57).[7]

The Fetishism of Concepts

> The concept of sugar does not taste sweet.
>
> Louis Althusser (quoted in Jameson 1990, 20)

For Adorno, however, as was suggested earlier, this problem of representation is not limited to 'nature' but applies to all concepts. Thus the preceding discussion of Adorno's understanding of nature can serve not only to elucidate the reasons behind his suspicions of a romanticized view of nature, but also more generally to illustrate his philosophy's emphasis on non-identity, or on the recognition of that in the object which eludes conceptualization. The thesis that nature cannot be positively represented, but can only be, in a sense, defined negatively, through its relation to a group of other concepts (history, myth, enlightenment, alienation, property), is thus a particular expression of Adorno's materialist dialectic.

As many commentators have noted, this emphasis on negation and on the impossibility of full positive representation is similar to the project of deconstruction. As we have seen, *Dialectic of Enlightenment* emphasizes the violence that is wrought by the separation of concept and thing, as well as the impossibility of covering up that separation. But it is also crucial to point out that Adorno's critical theory allows for the possibility of reconciliation: the notion that a more reflexive reason might be non-instrumental and might allow for a more adequate approach to the object. Hence Adorno's normative claim that 'how one should think instead has its distant and vague archetype in the various languages, in the names which do not categorically cover the thing, albeit at the cost of their cognitive function' (Adorno 1973, 52).

Adorno holds out the possibility for the existence of a non-dominating form of reason. This is why his critical theory remains more concerned than deconstructive approaches with the domination of nature, and thus offers a more fruitful theoretical point of entry for ecological politics. At the most general philosophical level, he makes this point in his essay 'Subject and Object.' Here, he argues that the separation of subject and object, although real enough as an expression of the current human condition, 'must not be hypostasized, not magically transformed into an invariant' (Adorno 1978, 499). Similarly, the domination of nature that is inherent in the 'crude confrontation of subject and object' (502) may yet be replaced by a 'proper' relationship between subject and object, by a reconciliation between human beings and nature that would be 'the realization of peace among men as well as between men and their Other. Peace is the state of distinctness without domination' (500).

The arguments presented in *Dialectic of Enlightenment* suggest that the possibility of such a 'distinctness without domination,' or of a reconciliation with nature, rests on the possibility of our using a non-instrumental form of reason. The treatment of *nature* in strictly instrumental terms is not something we can separate off from instrumental rationality more broadly conceived. And the latter extends for Adorno all the way into thinking as a form of representation. We might say, then, that for Adorno, the domination of nature is rooted in the definition of nature. But it should be emphasized immediately that Adorno's position is more complex than, for example, the claim that conventional modes of accounting for nature fail to account for certain aspects of nature's value (a line of argument that was pursued by ecocentrists in chapter 1). For Adorno, the domination of nature is not simply rooted in *our* definition of nature; rather, it is rooted in *the* definition of nature – in the problem of reification, which necessarily attends representational thinking as such.

Adorno's *Negative Dialectics* thus in a sense generalizes *Dialectic of Enlightenment*'s claim that the domination of nature is predicated on an instrumentalization of nature that ignores its singularity. In *Negative Dialectics*, Adorno argues that conceptual thinking that does not consider itself – regardless of the specific content – renders mute the specificity of those things which are gathered under the concept.

At this point, we may recall Jameson's observation, noted earlier,[8] that Adorno's critique of conceptual thinking 'logically presuppose[s] some prior fantasy about "truth"' and that 'much of the tortuousness of ... Adornian prose results from the need to short-circuit this unwanted implication and to insist over and over again on the 'objectivity' of such errors or illusions.' For Jameson, what is to be preferred is the Marxian notion of 'value,' which 'usefully ceases to imply and entail any of these issues of error or truth' (Jameson 1991, 237). But Adorno's way of thinking about the reification inherent in conceptual thinking is hardly divorced from Marxism. In fact, Adorno conceives his critique of conceptual thinking as an extension of the crucial Marxian category of 'fetishism.'

Marx defines the 'fetishism of commodities' as the treatment of quantitative exchange-value (which is in fact the expression of social relations) as if it were a natural attribute of objects: 'A commodity is therefore a mysterious thing, simply because in it the social character of men's labour appears to them as an objective character stamped upon the product of that labour.' For Marx, commodities have become fetishized when 'the products of men's hands ... appear as independent beings endowed with life, and entering into relation both with one another and the human race' (Marx 1977a, 164–5). But for Adorno, this fetishism can be extended much more broadly, beyond mere economic categories into representational thought itself. Conceptual thinking, as a mode of thought, is not a 'natural' way of thinking, nor is it determined by something that is inherent in the objects themselves. Even though conceptuality is generally understood as a 'natural' (or indeed perhaps the only possible) way of understanding the world, it is in fact historically specific, and both determines and is determined by social relations that are predicated on the domination of nature. What Adorno's *Negative Dialectics* (1973) seeks to expose is that 'all concepts, even the philosophical ones, refer to nonconceptualities, because concepts on their part are moments of the reality that requires their formation, primarily for the control of nature' (11). This can be understood quite properly as homologous to Marx's discussion of the commodity form. So it is hardly a coincidence that Adorno suggests the need 'to get rid of concept *fetishism*' (12; emphasis added). Adorno's indebtedness to the Marxian critique is further evident in his claim that 'the ineffable part of the utopia [which] defies subsumption under identity' is articulated with the opposite of exchange-value, namely, 'use-value' (11).[9]

But this opposition between exchange-value and use-value brings back the spectre of Baudrillard, whose demonstration of the ideological (or perhaps we might now call it 'fetishistic') character of use-value we considered in chapter 2. By this point, however, we can begin to appreciate the strength of Adorno's method and the reasons why his prose is so 'tortuous' – especially relative to Marx's. Marxian terminology locates Adorno's treatment of the problems of conceptuality as historical materialist; in particular, it helps us contrast that treatment with deconstruction (at least the de Manian version).[10] Also deserving emphasis is how Adorno's broader argument works to give Marxian terminology a particular valence – one that effectively short-circuits Baudrillard's critique of Marx: 'use-value' is here set off as merely the 'Marxist terminology' for 'the ineffable' that 'defies subsumption under identity' (1973, 11). Adorno's critique of conceptual thinking, within which the concept of 'use-value' is clearly situated, warns of the problems inherent in too quickly identifying the example with the more general term. As the preceding discussion of the wanderings of the concept of 'nature' has shown, an attentive reading (which is, to a certain extent, demanded by the 'tortuous' prose) should forestall the mistake of conceiving of what the 'Marxist terminology' here stands in for as something that is ontologically given and prior to any social mediation – just as it should alert us to the mistake of equating the concept (or 'Marxist terminology') with the thing itself.

We can now recap some of the problems of conceptual thinking, which Jameson (1991) refers to collectively as 'the mischief of premature clarification' (xxii). Adorno, for whom the problem of conceptual thinking cannot be solved through patient maturation, calls it a problem of 'identitarianism.' A cursory review allows us to see that identitarianism refers to the following specific problems, which we have already discussed: that concepts are never capable of exhaustively describing the singularity of objects, and that therefore the gathering of disparate objects under the same concept necessarily involves a 'representation' (which is always a *mis*representation) of reality; that conceptual thinking posits a model of reality that is static rather than dynamic, in the sense that conceptual categories hypostasize and thereby fix the identity of (or reify) objects over time; and that conceptual categories (including the system of conceptual thinking itself) are wrongly taken to be transcendent categories, not only in the sense of being ahistorical or static, but also in the sense that they are understood to function independently of social mediations. Hence, finally, conceptual thinking is for Adorno a process of identification – 'to think is to identify' (1973, 5) – that is best grasped as a relentless, violent process of assimilation.

At the same time, Adorno's own emphasis on historicity suggests that conceptual thinking cannot simply be dispensed with: it is the product of a particular social form. To paraphrase Marx, we apprehend reality, although not under conditions of our own choosing. The solution posited in *Dialectic of Enlightenment* ('thought must consider itself') reappears in *Negative Dialectics* under the guise of dialectics. Dialectical negation serves as a reminder of the inadequacy, or necessary failure, of identitarian thinking: 'The name of dialectics says no more, to begin with, than that objects do not go into their concepts without leaving a remainder ... Dialectics is the consistent sense of non-identity' (1973, 5). The modifier 'negative' in the book's title emphasizes Adorno's critique of past forms of dialectical reasoning, which posited a false closure on the dialectic; the latter is 'cut short' by its own claims to have reached (or foreseen) an 'end of history' – a point that receives its most extended elaboration in Adorno's (1973) consideration of Hegel (300–60).

But how is it that Adorno preserves the 'utopian' impulse locatable in Marx without instantiating what Derrida calls the 'metaphysics of presence'? Or to put it another way, how does Adorno propose to avoid the problems of conceptual thinking while simultaneously acknowledging that 'necessity compels philosophy to operate with philosophical concepts' (1973, 11). One possibility might be to suggest that Adorno's critique of conceptual thinking provides a critique of philosophy, and that for Adorno, the utopian model of a non-dominating relationship with nature can only be found outside of philosophy, in the realm of art. Albrecht Wellmer, for example, argues that 'because of his understanding of the "repressive" character of "identifying" thought, the aesthetic rationality of the work of art became for [Adorno] the only *possible* model for an alternative form of rationality, in which instrumental rationality would be preserved only as a sublated moment. But then the organization of the work of art *does* become the only possible model for the organization and the rationality of an emancipated society' (Wellmer 1985, 48–9; emphases in original).

Richard Wolin similarly claims that 'art, therefore, may be said to possess a certain epistemological superiority vis-à-vis philosophical truth' (1992, 73). Wolin also suggests, however, that 'the utopian dimension of Adorno's work manifests itself' at the 'intersection' of art and philosophy – that is, in aesthetic theory rather than in art itself (63). Adorno's aesthetic theories (whose importance is emphasized even more strongly by Jarvis [1998, 90–123]) will be considered in more detail below (although even this will be far from a full consideration of the topic). Here we need only briefly consider the claim about the importance of art and aesthetic theory in order to see that it is far from frivolous. That Adorno's thought seeks a sort of non-conceptual truth in art is reflected in his claim that 'autonomous' art, in its mimetic truthfulness to the object (what Terry Eagleton calls 'a memory trace of mimesis' [1990, 51]), presents us with a Kantian 'purposefulness without a purpose' that provides a more radical critique of existing social relations than any art that aims instrumentally to provide such a critique. The treatment of art as a *tool* for social change already capitulates to the instrumental rationality of conceptual thinking, and thus cannot subvert domination. It can only reproduce it: 'The notion of a "message" in art, even when politically radical, already contains an accommodation to the world: the stance of a lecturer conceals a clandestine entente with the listeners, who could only be truly rescued from illusions by refusal of it' (Adorno 1980, 193). Adorno's particular interest in music in part reflects the fact that it is the least representational form of art, and so might most easily and forcefully demonstrate art's proper role, its 'afunctionality' (Rothberg 1997, 69) – or what Jarvis calls a 'fetish against commodity fetishism' – by refusing to present itself as a use-value (1998, 117–8). 'The more socially dissociated art becomes, the more scandalously subversive and utterly pointless it is.' Thus, 'the most profoundly political work is one that is entirely silent about politics' (Eagleton 1990, 50).

Yet Adorno maintains that this critique of conceptual thinking must not 'be turned into a summary verdict against philosophy' (1973, 11). Jarvis is surely correct when he states that aesthetics' 'significance for Adorno's thought ... can hardly be overestimated' (1998, 90); but as we shall see, art cannot provide the only model for a reconciled relationship with nature. Here, we should also heed Susan Buck-Morss's reminder that even if, for Adorno, philosophy and art 'converge in their "truth content," they were nevertheless nonidentical' (Buck-Morss 1977, 133). Philosophy, along the lines outlined in *Negative Dialectics*, is a necessary complement to art, especially in the situation of 'absolute reification' evident in late modernity – a situation which for Adorno is symbolized by Auschwitz (Rothberg 1997, 69).[11] But even if we grant the 'epistemological superiority' of the work of art, it is important for us to remind ourselves of the lesson taught by Freud's analysis of the symptom: that the crucial question is not one of translation from manifest to latent content (by decoding the truth that the work of art presents), but rather the question of *why* the content must be presented in 'disguised' form.[12] Grappling with the question of why truth can be represented more adequately in a work of art than in 'plain language' leads back to the dialectic of enlightenment and the vicissitudes of conceptual thought.

Adorno argues that conceptual thinking contains a mimetic element that gives it a certain affinity with the aesthetic: 'To represent the mimesis it supplanted, the concept has no other way than to adopt something mimetic in its own conduct, without abandoning itself' (Adorno 1973, 14). It then becomes the task of philosophy (driven by dialectics – 'the consistent sense of non-identity') to illuminate the relationship between conceptual thinking and mimesis, the fact that conceptual thinking contains and strives to repress its own mimetic remainder (recalling that the difference between myth and enlightenment was the shift from mimetic to conceptual identification, and also that 'enlightenment reverts to mythology'): 'The esthetic moment is thus not accidental to philosophy ... but it is no less incumbent on philosophy to void its estheticism, to sublimate the esthetic into the real, by means of cogent insights' (Adorno 1973, 15). Properly understood as thought that critically reflects on its mimetic remainder, philosophy can begin to expose and possibly even undo the 'double character' of language, where by 'mimetic' and 'discursive' language, or artistic and scientific representations of the world, are seen as mutually incompatible (Jarvis 1998, 14 and 26; see also Jameson 1990, 215). Following Walter Benjamin, Adorno argues that attention to this mimetic aspect of conceptual thought means that the manner in which philosophical argument is presented is absolutely crucial to its truth-value: 'The presentation [*Darstellung*] of philosophy is not an external matter of indifference to it but immanent to its idea' (1973, 18).

In what Jameson calls 'the most elaborated statement of [Adorno's] conception of heteronomy' (1990, 82), Adorno shows how this 'return of the (conceptually) repressed' unfolds in the Kantian notion of freedom:

> But freedom itself and unfreedom are so entangled that unfreedom is not just an impediment to freedom but a *premise of its concept. This can be no more culled out as an absolute than any other concept.* Without the unity and the compulsion of reason, nothing similar to freedom would ever have come to mind, much less into being; this is documented in philosophy. There is no available model of freedom save one, that consciousness, as it intervenes in the total social constitution, will through that constitution intervene in the complexion of the individual. This notion is not utterly chimerical, because consciousness is a ramification of the energy of drives; it is part impulse itself, and also a moment of that which it intervenes in. If there were not that affinity which Kant so furiously denies, neither would there be the idea of freedom, for whose sake he denies the affinity. (Adorno 1973, 265; emphasis added)

As this passage makes clear, the presence of this antinomical structure is hardly the result of Kant's personal failing; rather, it can be seen as a model applicable to 'any other concept,' and is thus more a result of the way that social relations 'intervene in' the 'constitution' of thought itself. The 'unity and the compulsion of reason,' whose dark genealogy is revealed in Horkheimer and Adorno's reading of the *Odyssey*, is what makes conceptualization and the domination of nature possible. But as we have seen, 'becoming conscious' of this antinomical character of concepts can only occur philosophically. As Adorno notes in a rare discussion of 'method': 'All philosophy, even that which intends freedom, carries in its inalienably general elements the unfreedom in which society prolongs its existence. Coercion is inherent in philosophy, yet coercion alone protects it from regressing into license. The coercive character that is immanent in our thinking can be critically known; the coercion of thought is the medium of its deliverance' (1973, 48)

This brief passage makes frequent reference to the implication of 'coercion' in freedom, yet it would be wrong to suggest that by this insistence – on the necessity of the coercive character of thought to bring about the end of the coercive character of thought – Adorno has in mind something like the Althusserian formulation that 'total alienation is the solution to the problem of total alienation' (see chapter 3). For Adorno, what is crucial is not the totalizing character of coercion – he believes that late capitalist society provides plenty of experiences of total alienation (recall the earlier characterization of late modernity as a situation of 'absolute reification'), most if not all of which seem only to 'hard-wire' us for alienated experience.

Thus, in what may be read as a critique of Donna Haraway *avant la lettre*, Adorno notes in one of the fragments in *Minima Moralia* that 'the organic composition of man is growing.' This metaphor refers to Marx's discussion of the 'organic composition of capital' (the tendency under capitalism for the proportion of machine-power to increase relative to human labour-power, discussed in chapter 4), here transposed to signify late capitalism's colonization and instrumentalization of increasing areas of human life: 'That which determines subjects as means of production and not as living purposes increases with the proportion of machines to variable capital.' Rather than seeing the rise of human/machine 'cyborgs' as a liberatory possibility (Haraway 1991), Adorno insists that colonization of the human by the machinic must be understood *as* the unfolding of the logic of capital itself at the psychological or biological level (a process whose 'consummate organization demands the coordination of people that are dead'), and not as simply the actions of capital on preformed human subjects ('there is no substratum beneath such 'deformations,' no ontic interior on which social mechanisms merely act externally'). The end result is, under late capitalism, the construction of an ego that functions as a schizophrenic and/or psychotic 'business manager,' one that manipulates personality traits (similar in form to 'human' characteristics of an earlier era, but now severed both from the self and from any biological basis) as lifeless, inert tools. 'Accordingly the destructive tendencies of the masses that explode in both varieties of totalitarian state are not so much death-wishes as manifestations of what they have already become. They murder so that whatever to them seems living, shall resemble themselves' (Adorno 1974, 228-31). In a slightly different context, Adorno notes the tremendous psychic energy involved in maintaining a form of subjectivity that is compatible with totally administered life. Commenting on the then-popular 'jitterbug' dance, he observes that 'for people to be transformed into insects they require as much energy as might well suffice to transform them into human beings' (quoted in Jarvis 1998, 76).

Thus, rather than on the totalizing character of coercion (or the absoluteness of reification), Adorno's emphasis falls on the Benjaminian notion of *Darstellung*: the way in which the coercive character of thought is *presented*, or the way in which concepts are deployed. The preceding discussion of how Adorno discusses nature, and of his critique of conceptual thinking more generally, has gone some of the way toward providing us with an understanding of this, in the first instance by providing an illustration or model of this type of thinking, and in the second by a negative elaboration – that is, by pointing out what it seeks to avoid. The closest that Adorno comes to providing a positive and generalizable elaboration, or a methodological statement for this type of thinking (the reasons for his wariness on this score should by now be familiar), comes in his discussion (again, in *Negative Dialectics*) of the Benjaminian notion of the 'constellation.'

Constellations, Models, the Ecology of the Concept

> Some of our long-standing views need to be brought up-to-date for present workableness (16 November 1952, Aries).
>
> Carroll Righter, 'Astrological Forecast' (quoted in Adorno 1994, 93)

In explaining 'constellations,' Adorno approvingly cites Max Weber's dictum 'that sociological concepts be "gradually composed" from "individual parts to be taken from historic reality. The place of definitive conceptual comprehension cannot, therefore, be the beginning of the inquiry, only the end"' (Adorno 1973, 165). As we saw in 'The Idea of Natural History,' for Adorno understanding 'can not be given in preliminary definitions but only in the course of analysis' (Adorno 1984, 111). Definitions are problematic because they fix understanding and foreclose the possibility of a *dialectical* understanding that sees objects as bearers of processes and, because they are the product of historical processes, as subject to historical change. 'Cognition of the object in its constellation is cognition of the process stored in the object' (Adorno 1973, 163). Hence Adorno's notoriously difficult writing 'style': giving definitions in advance, and always using the same word to mean the same thing, is for Adorno a form of reification – a freezing of words and concepts that treats language as simply a tool. To write in this way would be to engage a form of instrumental rationality, and thus to further the domination of nature.

So instead of simply positing or reciting a definition of 'constellations,' this section will engage in the process of working meaning out, by staging an exploration of three metaphors for this sort of gradual composition. Individually, these three metaphors – the Benjaminian notion of the 'constellation,' the musicological notion of the 'model,' and my own suggestion of the 'ecology of the concept' – are inadequate to the process that Adorno is trying to describe. But this, of course, is exactly what Adorno's analysis would lead us to expect. An understanding of a non-instrumental approach to the object, or a way of thinking that avoids the vicissitudes of conceptuality, cannot be achieved by choosing the single right metaphor; instead, we must examine a number of metaphors, each of which may illuminate certain aspects of the process.

The 'gradual composition' of understanding not only aims to develop a sense of the object's *historicity* (the object as a sort of 'storage-box' of processes, but without the box) but also aims to understand the object *relationally*. As we have seen, dialectical thinking focuses on the non-identical – that which is present in the object but not in the concept – but we can grasp this only conceptually. We cannot see the part of the object that eludes conceptualization simply by comparing the concept with the object, because we can only access the object conceptually. The path to a 'proper' (or non-dominating) relationship between subject and object thus lies not through phenomenology (with its motto: 'To the things themselves!' [Heidegger 1962, 50]), but through the development of an understanding of individual concepts in terms of their relationship with other concepts (their conceptual 'environment,' as it were). Coming to terms with a concept's relationality with other concepts – its constellation, or what we might also call the ecology of the concept – thus 'illuminates the specific side of the object, the side to which a classifying procedure [that is, instrumental rationality] is either a matter of indifference or a burden' (Adorno 1973, 162). Indeed, Ariel Salleh notes that the Frankfurt School's 'approach to knowing,' 'reflecting the fluid, dialectical, self-feeding and polyvalent character of things, offers the basis of an epistemology that is peculiarly matched to the study of eco-systems' (Salleh 1988, 135). Thus, understanding constellations as the ecology of the concept highlights the point that this is not simply, as Eagleton (1990) has it, a call for '"All power to the particulars!"' (58). It requires an understanding of mediation, or the general, as much as the particulars. The latter can only be grasped if they are mediated: it is only through the non-particular, the concept, that the particular can attain any power.

We have already seen an example (or 'model') of this in Adorno's development of a concept of 'nature,' which was 'gradually composed' through a series of juxtapositions with other concepts, such as myth, enlightenment, history, and the homeland (all of which are themselves equally to be understood as we proceed, rather than posited at the outset). As in any serious musical composition, the identity of each element is only fully comprehended through the composition as a whole (not to mention other works to which the piece might refer), which can only unfold 'gradually' (that is, diachronically). The comparison with a musical composition is important because, as Jameson points out, although the term 'model' might seem 'inert,' for Adorno it has 'a specifically *musical* provenance.' For Arnold Schoenberg, the term 'designates the raw material of a specific composition or its thematic point of departure: which is to say, for twelve-tone music, the specific row itself ... which ... becomes the composition ... What in classical music was separated – the initial "themes" and their later "development" – is here reunited' (Jameson 1990, 61; emphasis in original). This is concretely demonstrated in a quotation from Adorno's *Philosophy of Modern Music*'s discussion of Beethoven, where in Beethoven's 'model,' 'everything remains 'the same.' But the meaning of this identity reveals itself as non-identity' (quoted in ibid.).

The second half of *Negative Dialectics* also provides three 'models,' which, Jameson points out, are 'full-dress demonstrations of what we have been calling the constellation method' (1990, 60). Here, the identities of Kantian freedom, Hegelian History, and metaphysics are revealed in turn as non-identities. But in contrast to these 'classical' philosophical texts or problematics, Adorno presents us with a Schoenbergian ('modern') philosophy: 'The concept or problem will not be independent of the *Darstellung* but already at one with it, no "arguments" of the traditional kind will lead to truth climaxes; the text will become one infinite variation in which everything is recapitulated at every moment; closure, finally, will be achieved when all the possible variations have been exhausted' (Jameson 1990, 62). It is perhaps for this reason, Jameson concludes, that the final model ('Meditations on Metaphysics') is 'most uncharacteristically for this author' divided into twelve numbered sections, corresponding to the number of steps in the atonal scale.[13]

This discussion of the idea of the 'constellation' has begun with the positing of some alternative metaphors for it, or ways of conceptualizing it, not simply because (as we have just seen) the very content of the concept seems to demand this, but also because the metaphor of the constellation seems, especially for Adorno, to be a singularly inapt one. Buck-Morss notes that Adorno used the term in his inaugural lecture as a member of the Frankfurt philosophy faculty ('The Actuality of Philosophy' in 1931); even then, he 'manifested certain misgivings about the term, suggesting also "a less astrological and scientifically more current expression: ... trial combinations"' (Buck-Morss 1977, 254n84; Buck-Morss's ellipsis). Indeed, that Adorno would continue to use an astrological term seems especially striking in light of the fact that he produced a content analysis of the *Los Angeles Times* astrology column. His first sentence in that analysis describes astrology as a 'social phenomen[on] involving irrational elements ... fused with what may be dubbed pseudo-rationality' (Adorno 1994, 34). In this essay, written in the early 1950s, Adorno notes that a certain social-psychological dysfunctionality, an inability on the part of most members of society to accept responsibility for the social form that they reproduce, accounts for 'why they like so much to project their dependence upon something else, be it a conspiracy of Wall Street bankers or the *constellation* of the stars' (1994, 114; emphasis added). A certain discomfort with the metaphor is also registered in a slip by Jameson (1990), where he refers to constellations as 'astronomical figures' (60) rather than *astrological* ones. Adorno himself, meanwhile, takes pains to remind his readers (in both the introduction *and* the conclusion of the 'Stars' essay) that 'we take up the study of astrology, not because we overrate its importance as a social phenomenon *per se*' (Adorno 1994, 35) and that 'we are not primarily interested in astrology *per se*' (113). It would of course be absurd to suggest that the stars can be brought 'down to earth' in the manner that astrology suggests. Indeed, as Adorno points out, modern astronomy can only be accommodated with astrology through 'an intellectual retrogression ... In a world in which, through popular scientific literature and particularly science fiction, every schoolboy knows of the billions of galaxies, the cosmic insignificance of the earth and the mechanical laws governing the movements of stellar systems, the geocentric and anthropocentric view concomitant with astrology is utterly anachronistic' (1994, 37). Although astrology and astronomy were conflated for thousands of years, the belief that human events can be read off from the movements of celestial bodies now seems nothing more than the mark of a mind that is not fully 'enlightened.'

Yet the bifurcation of human and natural history is perhaps not quite so clear as all that. Why, after all, would Adorno continue to use and valorize a term whose persistence is a painfully obvious symptom of the irrationality of social organization, a term that is 'utterly anachronistic' and associated with 'intellectual retrogression'? Part of the answer surely lies in the fact that no single term can suffice for the mode of thinking that Adorno is trying to develop. 'Trial combinations' certainly has the 'inert' character that Jameson notes might at first thought be attributed to 'models.' That said, this latter term is useful in the way in which (like 'constellations') it emphasizes how 'presentation' can determine 'content.' Indeed, this is even more the case for 'models' (especially, of course, musical models), insofar as Schoenbergian compositions aim at producing 'the realization that the order of presentation is non-binding, that it might have been arranged in an utterly different fashion, so that, as in a divinatory cast, all the elements are present but the form of their juxtapositions, the shape of their falling out, is merely occasional' (Jameson 1990, 50). But the musical associations of 'models' here might serve to distract from the way in which 'the elements' are to be understood as present independently of their presentation. In the case of constellations, there can be no doubt of a certain 'primacy of the object' – that is, no doubt that the elements to be 'arranged' are not in any sense a product of human volition.

And if 'models' risks overemphasizing the idea of subjective choice, then my earlier suggestion of constellations as 'the ecology of the concept' perhaps at first glance takes things too far in the opposite direction. As a branch of the natural sciences, ecology can be understood as simply providing a descriptive analysis of the relationship of an organism to its environment – an analysis in which, as in all 'hard' sciences, the brute objectivity of the facts seems to determine even their 'presentation.' In fact, however, there is a sense in which, in terms of the history of modern science, ecology's role has been to demonstrate the necessary arbitrariness of the choice of object of study in an interconnected system, or the ways in which 'the elements are present but the form of their juxtapositions, the shape of their falling out, is merely occasional.' As we saw in chapter 1, Eckersley's definition and defence of ecocentrism showed how dominant understandings of the natural world are a result of an arbitrary 'presentation' of the world.

As we also saw in chapter 1, what is still missing from this conventional understanding of ecology is a further recasting of this ecological representation of the elements of the natural sciences to focus on the social world. Here, we can return to the thesis of Adorno's 'Natural History' essay, with its injunction *'to comprehend nature as an historical being where it seems to rest most deeply in itself as nature.'* In other words, it is appropriate to understand Adorno's notion of the constellation as the 'ecology of the concept' only if we remind ourselves that 'ecology' has as much to do with history and the social as it does with nature.

This, in a sense, is also part of the aim of the 'Stars' essay, which of course rejects the claim that a natural fact (the arrangement of the stars) can be comprehended as historical in the sense in which astrologists claim, but which nevertheless leaves room for the natural in its 'stud[y] of astrology as a kind of key to more widespread social and psychological potentialities' (Adorno 1994, 113). We can see this if we recall that the thesis of 'The Idea of Natural History,' like the central argument of *Dialectic of Enlightenment*, is formulated as a chiasmus: we must not only *'comprehend nature as an historical being where it seems to rest most deeply in itself as nature,'* but also *'comprehend historical being in its most extreme historical determinacy, where it is most historical, as natural being.'* Here, the crucial point lies in the reason why so many people 'believe' (if only half-heartedly [114; Witkin 2003, 68]) in astrology, especially at a time when such a belief is so patently at odds with other dominant forms of knowledge: 'We thus must assume that only *very strong instinctual demands* make it possible for people still – or anew – to accept astrology' (Adorno 1994, 37; emphasis added). This 'most historical' social phenomenon – that is, a widespread acceptance of astrology at a time when its validity is increasingly untenable – is understood as natural, although not simply in the sense that stars are natural objects (the figures of the constellations themselves, not to mention the interpretation of their relative positionings, are after all social constructions), but rather also in the sense that we can properly understand this social phenomenon only in terms of biological drives.

But then we can reverse the poles again, and understand these 'instinctual demands' as products of human historicity, rather than simply as naturally given. As Robert Witkin points out, astrology as a system of belief depends on a particular personality structure. The program of 'the [astrological] column shifts the concerns of the subject from the questioning of means and irrational conditions to the business of making the best of them from the viewpoint of maximizing the individual's own private interests' (Witkin 2003, 77). But it is only within a particular social system and its analogical configuration of psychological and instinctual drives – monopoly capitalism and the authoritarian personality – a system in which the individual is helpless in the face of apparently arbitrary power, that such a shift makes sense.

The constellation of nature and history in this sense is further spelled out in the final section of *Negative Dialectics*, which, Adorno explains in the preface, aims 'by critical self-reflection to give the Copernican revolution an axial turn' (1973, xx). Copernicus declared, basically, that since the motions of the stars could not be explained by assuming the earth was the immobile centre of the universe, the earth itself must be moving. Kant suggests that such a revolution should also be applied to the field of metaphysics, claiming that an understanding of the object rests not on something inherent in the object, but on the transcendental schemata located in the subject: 'We can know *a priori* of things only what we ourselves put into them' (Kant 1950, 23). As Gilles Deleuze puts it:

> The fundamental idea of what Kant calls his 'Copernican revolution' is the following: substituting the principle of a *necessary* submission of object to subject for the idea of a harmony between subject and object (*final* accord). The essential discovery is that the faculty of knowledge is legislative, or more precisely, that there is something which legislates in the faculty of knowledge ... The rational being thus discovers that he has new powers. The first thing that the Copernican Revolution teaches us is that it is we who are giving the orders ... Kant sets up the critical image in opposition to wisdom: we are the legislators of Nature. (Deleuze 1984, 14; emphases in original)

Reflection on the limits of reason (the 'critical self-reflection' of reason), however, points to the totalitarian potentialities in this 'legislative' power, or the way in which the decline of metaphysics leads from the discovery of this legislative power over nature, to blind submission to the social as a 'second nature.' Adorno aims first to show that modern science has worked to exclude metaphysical problems, but without necessarily solving them. 'All metaphysical speculations' are wrongheaded to the extent that they participate in an 'ideological untruth in the conception of transcendence[:] ... the separation of body and soul, a reflex of the division of labor' (Adorno 1973, 400). At the same time, the decline of metaphysics must be understood as a historical phenomenon: 'Kant's epistemological question, "How is metaphysics possible?" yields to a question from the philosophy of history: "Is it still possible to have a metaphysical experience?"' (372). But of course this philosophy of history is not one of the triumph of the absolute spirit, such that metaphysics, like astrology, can eventually be dismissed simply as superstition. Rather, Adorno's negative dialectics insists on a philosophy of history that represents what Michael Rothberg calls a 'negative teleology of modernity' (Rothberg 1997, 49). The historical context of the decline of metaphysics is 'after Auschwitz,' a time when 'the absolute integration' is 'genocide' (Adorno 1973, 361–2). So-called *human* history leads not 'from savagery to humanitarianism' but 'from the slingshot to the megaton bomb' (320). This development reveals itself to be no escape from blind submission, and works as effectively as a heliocentric cosmology to reveal any hope of transcendence to be a lie: 'The earthquake of Lisbon sufficed to cure Voltaire of the theodicy of Liebniz, and the visible disaster of the first nature was insignificant in comparison with the second, social one, which defies human imagination as it distills a real hell from human evil' (361).

The 'axial turn' that Adorno wishes to bring about here hinges on metaphysics and its concern with the meaning of life in the context of our awareness of human mortality. Metaphysics thus must be understood as the presumed capacity of human beings to 'see beyond themselves' (376) or to transcend that perspective which our consciousness provides – the knowledge that human life is finite. But the current context is one in which metaphysical speculation is dismissed, even though the questions it raises remain unresolved: 'What in an unideological sense ought to be the most urgent concern of men has vanished' (395). The dominant explanation for this, of course, is that this 'most urgent concern' must at some level be repressed for the very sake of itself – for human survival: 'We might be tempted to speculate anthropologically whether the turn in evolutionary history that gave the human species its open consciousness and thus an awareness of death – whether this turn does not contradict a continuing animal constitution which prohibits men to bear that consciousness. The price to be paid for the possibility to go on living would be a restriction of consciousness, then, a means to shield it from what consciousness is, after all: the consciousness of death' (395).

Adorno's characterization of such an argument as 'anthropological,' however, is coloured by his use of the term with respect to Kant, a few pages earlier. Adorno characterizes the Kantian 'block' on knowledge of the objects in themselves in the following terms: 'Human consciousness, says the anthropological argument, is condemned, as it were, to eternal detention in the forms it happens once to have been given' (1973, 386). It is in this context that Adorno argues that 'Kant chimes in with the eminently bourgeois affirmation of one's own confinement' (382) and that Kant's 'critique ... repeats the transformation of the bourgeoisie from a revolutionary class into a conservative one' (383). Thus the Kantian system ('a system of stop signals'), premised as it is on 'the anthropological argument,' must finally be understood as 'the self-maiming of reason, the mutilation inflicted upon itself as a rite of initiation into its own scientific character' – as 'a constant initiation rite' (as Adorno elsewhere describes the culture industry) that is a direct reflection of the social division of labour (388).

The issue of the social division of labour alerts us to the character of '*dialectical* anthropology,'[14] which Adorno might seek to contrast with the anthropological perspective offered earlier. We can now understand this dialectical anthropology by way of the decline of metaphysics: 'Schopenhauer, the pessimist, was struck by the fact how little men *in media vita* are apt to bother with death. Like Heidegger a hundred years later, Schopenhauer read this indifference in human nature rather than in men as products of history' (396). The 'instinctual demands' that lead to the belief that our fates are controlled by astrological constellations must similarly be understood as products of history, rather than as simply embedded in a transhistoric human nature.

Adorno's aim 'to give the Copernican revolution an axial turn,' as well as his 'solidarity [with] metaphysics at the time of its fall' (408), can thus be comprehended as seeing the human 'instinct' for self-preservation as one that is capable of being historically transcended. For Adorno, it is possible for people to genuinely 'see beyond themselves,' but only by breaking through 'the natural-historic cares we share with beetles' (389). But as we have seen (in the earlier quotation about the 'jitterbug' dance), to transform people into genuine human beings rather than insects is not simply a matter of the quantitative expenditure of energy; rather, this requires a qualtative transformation at the levels of the structure of thought and of social relations: 'Socially there is good reason to suspect that [Kantian] block, the bar erected against the absolute, of being one with the necessity to labor, which in reality keeps mankind under the same spell that Kant transfigured into a philosophy. The imprisonment in immanence to which he honestly and brutally condemns the mind is the imprisonment in self-preservation, as it is imposed on men by a society that conserves nothing but the denials that would not be necessary any more' (389).

Before we return to the issue of social relations, there is a final point to make about Adorno's use of the term 'constellation,' since his reasons for deploying this particular word are perhaps still somewhat opaque. Adorno's first use of the term in *Negative Dialectics* is found in his claim that 'the determinable flaw in every concept makes it necessary to cite others; this is the font of the only constellations which inherited some of the hope of the name' (53). But although the singularity of the proper name offers a crucially positive point of reference for Benjamin, Adorno is more sceptical of its use.[15] A couple of sentences earlier, Adorno refers explicitly to Benjamin: 'Benjamin's concepts still tend to an authoritarian concealment of their conceptuality. Concepts alone can achieve what the concept prevents' (53). Although the proper name offers a 'hope,' it conceals an 'authoritarian' tendency insofar as it may seem to promise a fully adequate, positive representation of the object. For Adorno, however, as we have seen, truth cannot be accessed without negation.

Yet Adorno is not willing to give up 'the *hope* of the name.' In the sentence that is inserted in between the discussion of Benjamin's concepts and the first mention of constellations, Adorno says: 'Cognition is a τρωσας ιασεται' (53). A possible translation for the Greek phrase is offered by Rainer Nagele: 'What wounds heals.' Nagele immediately retracts this (or any) translation, however, since 'it would inscribe [the utopia] in the language of our administered world, in which 'healing the wounds' is inseparably linked to the functionalization of body and soul for further exploitation' (Nagele 1983, 75). For Nagele, this suggests why *Negative Dialectics* as a whole is littered with Latin and ancient Greek terms and phrases: 'The strange Greek words are not a demonstration of scholarly erudition, but a gesture of shame to speak the utopian' (ibid.). In his use of 'dead' languages, Nagele suggests, Adorno is telling us that 'only the dead can speak the language of that no-place, utopia, as long as the living do not live yet' (76).

'Constellations,' on the other hand, is not a word from a dead language; rather it refers to a belief that *should* have been rendered 'utterly anachronistic.' The persistence of the word, then, marks the persistence of the instincts that might be transcended if human beings were to escape the prison of natural history. The value of 'constellations' is that it retains 'the hope of the name' and simultaneously demonstrates that this hope has not yet been realized. That the utter anachronism is part of a living language reminds us that the living do not yet live.

Philosophy and Aesthetics: Negation and the Division of Labour

> Culture is the general sphere of knowledge, and of representations of lived experience, within a historical society divided into classes; what this amounts to is that culture is the power to generalize, existing *apart*, as an intellectual division of labour and as the intellectual labour of division.
>
> Debord (1995, 130)

As we suggested earlier, Adorno seems to be offering us two possible modes of knowing that can be construed as alternatives to instrumental rationality. On the one hand, there is the moment of negation that can be found in dialectical thinking ('the consistent sense of non-identity'); on the other, there is the mimetic moment to be found in art (not explicitly presented as such, but rather an 'organizing absent presence' throughout Adorno's work [Jameson 1990, 127]). What the two forms of thinking share is that both are in some sense impossible without a transformation at the level of social relations.

In the case of art, we must be careful not to conflate artistic mimesis with the mimesis that is to be found in magic, as elaborated in *Dialectic of Enlightenment*. Magical mimesis was a sort of proto-(instrumental) reason; it was 'already enlightenment,' in the sense that mimetic approximation was used in an attempt to *control* nature. In contrast, what Adorno calls 'authentic autonomous' artistic mimesis is of the sort that (as in metaphysics) allows for a sense of seeing beyond the immediate. In a telling simile, Adorno remarks: 'Thinking men and artists have not infrequently described a sense of being not quite there, of not playing along, a feeling as if they were not themselves at all, but a kind of *spectator*' (1973, 363; emphasis added). The crucial difference between *artistic* mimesis and the sort to be found in magic is that the latter is felt to be necessary for survival, whereas in the former, mimesis occurs without the impetus of terror in the face of the power of nature. In artistic mimesis, as in metaphysics, there is a suspension of the self-preservation 'instinct' that might allow one to move past the entanglement of thought in domination:[16] '"What does it really matter?" is a line we like to associate with bourgeois callousness, but it is the line most likely to make the individual aware, without dread, of the insignificance of his existence. The inhuman part of it, the ability to keep one's distance as a spectator and to rise above things, is in the final analysis the human part, the very part resisted by its ideologists' (ibid.).

The qualifying clause inserted into the first sentence – 'without dread' – is crucial. In the paragraph that follows the passage just cited, Adorno suggests that it is the only way to forestall the cynical reaction that this stance is simply another form of ideology, that art is simply to record from a distance, like 'Shaw on his way to the theater, showing a beggar his identification with the hurried remark, "Press"' (ibid.). It is a final reminder that the undoing of the social division of labour (on which, as we shall see, this all depends) is not to be taken as a call for a return to simpler times, but rather is premised on a level of development that makes it possible for us to interact with the natural world 'without dread,' or, in the terms of 'Subject and Object,' to be 'fearlessly passive' (Adorno 1978, 506).

It should be clear, though, that overwhelming technological capacity is not what is required for such an experience. The lesson of *Dialectic of Enlightenment* is that if we think of nature as an 'other' to be controlled, the technology we develop will inevitably be turned to control the nature that resides within the self. The natural must be understood as historical, and vice versa. At the end of the previous chapter, we noted Neil Smith's claim that the Frankfurt School misidentifies social relations with nature as natural relations. This is the obverse of Axel Honneth's claim that Adorno and Horkheimer model social domination too closely on the domination of nature. Jarvis's comments on the latter can provide a response to the former, as well: 'For a materialist theory, to dominate other humans – since humans are not pure culture – is *already* domination of nature as well as social domination, not social domination instead of or "modelled upon" domination of nature. Only a theory which itself presupposes mastery of nature can regard intersubjectivity as a separate sphere which has somehow separated itself from the natural' (Jarvis 1998, 35).[17]

Odysseus' psychic repression (his self-denial) does not occur simply because of a weakness in the face of nature that is the result of a lack of technological capacity. What needs explaining is how this experience of weakness is just as true in an era of microprocessors and atomic power as it was at the dawn of Western civilization. For Adorno, it is not that we lack the technological capacity to do away with insecurity, but rather that social relations and our way of thinking remain structured to perpetuate insecurity. Psychic repression is justified by the reification of the social division of labour as an uncontrollable 'second nature.'

The fetishization of technological development as a means to overcome the experience of weakness is ultimately a self-destructive defence mechanism. This much is clear from much of *Dialectic of Enlightenment*. But the text also shows that the 'technology' that is actually required in order to experience nature differently was available to Homer. We noted earlier a passage in *Negative Dialectics* in which Adorno suggests that the capacity to distance oneself from suffering, identified as 'the inhuman part' of metaphysical thinking, is ultimately 'the human part.' This passage has its analogue in *Dialectic of Enlightenment*, in the concluding pages of the chapter on the *Odyssey*. There, Horkheimer and Adorno (1987) identify what might be called a 'metaphysical' impulse in 'eloquent discourse itself, language in contradistinction to mythic song' (78). As with metaphysics, it is 'the inhuman part' of narrative – here its precision, where Homer 'already exhibits the frigidity of anatomy and vivisection' (79) – that can be understood as what is ultimately the human part, that is, the part that would allow us to break through 'the natural-historic cares we share with beetles' and emerge from our prehistory by refusing to naturalize suffering:

> The cold distancing of narration, which still represents horror as if it were a conversational topic, also allows the horror as such to appear for the first time that in song is solemnly represented as fate ... The reticence and composure of the narration [of the execution of prostitutes by Odysseus' son] are the true marks of eloquence. The passage closes with the information that the feet of the row of suspended women 'kicked out for a short while, but not for long' ... As a citizen reflecting momentarily upon the nature of hanging, Homer assures himself and his audience (actually readers) that it did not last for long – a moment and then it was all over. But after the 'not for long' the inner flow of the narrative is arrested. *Not for long?* The device poses the question, and belies the author's composure. By cutting short the account, Homer prevents us from forgetting the

> victims, and reveals the unutterable agony of the few seconds in which the women struggle with death. (78–80; emphasis in original)

The 'device' that prefigures the possibility of a genuinely human existence, an experience of nature 'without dread,' is one that becomes available with the very beginnings of literature. As Horkheimer and Adorno conclude, however, the promise of deterrorized mimesis remains unfulfilled: 'In the narrative account of atrocity, however, hope attaches to the fact that it happened a long time ago. Homer offers consolation for the entanglement of prehistory, savagery, and culture by recourse to the once-upon-a-time device. Yet the epic is *novel* first, and fairy tale after' (80; emphasis added).

Thus, commenting on the 'culture industry,' Horkheimer and Adorno observe that 'despite its size, this bloated pleasure apparatus adds no dignity to man's lives.' The culture industry is understood to be one which 'perpetually cheats its consumers of what it perpetually promises,' one that stages a 'spectacle' that can be seen as an endlessly deferred 'promissory note ... draw[n] on pleasure' (139). The culture industry in this sense compulsively repeats the experience that Odysseus imposes on himself – the perpetual denial of gratification in the present – for the promise of gratification in a future which, however, never arrives.

Nor is this denial limited to the realm of aesthetic pleasure. As Slavoj Žižek (1994) puts it, for the Frankfurt School generally: 'In an alienated society, the domain of "culture" is founded upon the violent exclusion ("repression") of man's libidinal kernel which then assumes the form of a quasi-"nature": "second nature" is the petrified evidence of the price paid for "cultural progress," the barbarity inherent to "culture" itself' (11). In other words, the denial of aesthetic pleasure is intimately linked with the denial of more material or basic needs: 'The idea of "fully exploiting" available technical resources and the facilities for aesthetic mass consumption is part of the economic system which refuses to exploit resources to abolish hunger' (Horkheimer and Adorno 1987, 139). Both the industrialization of culture and the persistence of malnutrition and even famine are indicted as failures to provide an escape from the terror of insecurity, even while the technical capacity for escape exists.

The privileged position accorded to the culture industry in *Dialectic of Enlightenment* can also be understood in the context of Odysseus' encounter with the Sirens, which, we will recall, is seen as the first instantiation of the alienation that makes bourgeois aesthetic experience possible. Thus 'the primal myth of Adorno's aesthetic theory' (Jameson 1990, 129) is the vision of Odysseus, helplessly tied to the mast, as the first 'spectator' – 'an inactive eavesdropper like later concertgoers' (Horkheimer and Adorno 1987, 34).

What deserves to be emphasized, however, is that Odysseus' helplessness, in this instance at least, is not directly a result of a confrontation with the forces of external nature: rather it is self-imposed, and predicated on a particular form of social organization. As was noted earlier, Odysseus can think of two ways to sail past the Sirens: by being tied to the mast, or by relentlessly rowing on, having had one's ears stopped with wax. But the two cannot be experienced simultaneously; Odysseus must enforce a social division of labour in such a way that 'the enjoyment of art and manual labor break apart' (ibid.). The radicalism of the *promise* inherent in the culture industry – although it obviously remains unfulfilled – lies in the possibility of the end of the social division that was, in earlier stages of development, deemed necessary: the possibility of socially universalized aesthetic experience. This promise carries within it the promise of an end to social domination (or the enforcement of a social division of labour), and, analogously, the promise of an end to the psychic repression associated with the hegemony of the survival instinct.

As Jameson (1990) points out, however, at least part of the falseness of the culture industry's promise lies in the fact that its products are not 'art' in Adorno's sense of the term (137–8). Indeed, 'authentic autonomous art' is extended a privileged position in Adorno's theorizing because of the way in which it not only partakes of a 'form' that lends it a universalizing character (mimetic representation seems to offer us the possibility of a more immediate access to the object than that provided by language), and also because it simultaneously necessarily *fails* to provide a totalizing standpoint, one in which all particularity is subsumed into the universal. That a good part of art's 'truth-value' lies in this constitutive failure means that art recapitulates the persistence of the social division of labour (and all the other forms of division and repression entailed by it) – the repressed libidinal kernel that is the price paid for culture itself, as Žižek points out – even while it attempts to represent reconciliation. As Eagleton succinctly puts it: 'Art is an allegory of undeluded happiness – to which it adds the fatal rider that this cannot be had, continually breaking the promise of the well-being it adumbrates' (1990, 54).

The products of the culture industry are not 'genuine' art in this sense. The falseness of the industry's promise lies in this fact and also in the fact that, although it is experienced on a mass scale, it does not aim at a reconciliation of the schism that inaugurated class division. The culture industry's reconciliation is false because it does not try to reunify art and manual labour: the production of art is divorced from its enjoyment. Or as Jameson notes, mass culture is identified as 'popular' only because it is consumed, not produced, by the people (1991, 62–4). In other words, the culture industry's claim to have brought aesthetic enjoyment to the masses is ideological in the sense that it masks the perpetuation of class division as well as the necessity of toil, which remains socially imposed on the masses. For this reason, the 'art' that it presents cannot be genuine art, but only the extension of the rhythms of the work processes, the progressive colonization of the realm of 'free' time:

> Amusement under late capitalism is the prolongation of work. It is sought after as an escape from the mechanized work process, and to recruit strength in order to be able to cope with it again. But at the same time mechanization has such power over a man's leisure and happiness, and so profoundly determines the manufacture of amusement goods, that his experiences are inevitably after-images of the work process itself ... What happens at work, in the factory, or in the office, can only be escaped by approximation to it in one's leisure time ...
>
> Fun is a medicinal bath. The pleasure industry never fails to prescribe it. (Horkheimer and Adorno 1987, 137–40)

But to raise the issue of the identity of the subject that produces cultural objects is to notice that if Marx at least attempted to sketch out (if only roughly) what *labour* might look like from the standpoint of a society that had transcended the current division of labour, Adorno's perspective seems to come from a decided rejection of the idea that the proletariat might constitute a 'universal class.'[18] To be sure, the social division of labour imposes an alienated form of existence on both classes: 'As proprietor, [Odysseus, the master,] finally renounces even participation in labor, and ultimately even its management, whereas his men – despite their *closeness to things* – cannot enjoy their labor because it is performed under pressure, in desperation, with senses stopped by force' (Horkheimer and Adorno 1987, 35; emphasis added). For Adorno, the path to reconciliation requires a *distance* from the immediacy of labour and survival, as much as (if not more than) a 'closeness to things.' We can return to the passage cited earlier: 'The inhuman part of it, the ability to keep one's distance as a *spectator* and to *rise above things*, is in the final analysis the human part' (Adorno 1973, 363; emphases added). If, for Adorno, Odysseus' position (that of the 'spectator') finally represents 'the human part,' then the overcoming of alienation seems only to be possible in the 'cold distancing' from or analysis of the necessity of the labour process and the divisions enforced by it. Marx perhaps held out hope for an immediacy in labour (through its rationalization and universalization). Adorno, in contrast, sees this in terms of the culture industry's colonization of the unconscious, and in its industrialization of leisure. This similarly accounts for the difference – highlighted by Nigel Gibson – between Marx and Adorno on the question of 'utopia' and the human relationship with nature. Gibson contrasts Marx's description of socialism from the *Grundrisse* as 'the full development of human control over the forces of nature' with Adorno's account in *Minima Moralia*: 'Perhaps the true society will grow tired of development and, out of freedom, leave possibilities unused ... lying on the water and looking at the sky, being, nothing else without any further definition and fulfillment ... None of these abstract concepts comes closer to fulfilled utopia than that of perpetual peace' (Gibson 2002, 284–5).

An account of this distancing from the necessity of labour, meanwhile, also appears toward the end of the chapter on the *Odyssey*, in the discussion of the prophecy of Tiresias. Earlier, in the episode with the Sirens (or in the 'prehistory' of the *Odysseus* chapter), we had seen the 'primal myth' of the domination inherent in the social division of labour. In that scene, of course, the labour that is represented is that of the oarsmen, with wax-stopped ears, rowing past the Sirens; Odysseus does not row, but instead is tied to the ship's mast. In contrast, the prophecy of Tiresias tells us of an incident in which Odysseus himself actually does (or rather is supposed to) wield an oar: 'Odysseus is to carry an oar upon his shoulder and continue to wander until he reaches a people "who do not know the sea and never eat food seasoned with salt." When he meets another traveller who mentions the winnowing fan he bears on his shoulder, the right spot will have been reached to make the expiatory sacrifice to Poseidon. The core of the prophecy is the mistaking of the oar for a winnowing fan' (Horkheimer and Adorno 1987, 76–7).

The possibility for expiation – for overcoming the 'mythic curse' of the social division of labour – thus depends not on the fact that Odysseus is eventually made to row like everybody else (or its obverse, that everyone takes his turn being strapped to the mast – an appropriate Adornian metaphor, perhaps, for the Fordist model imposed on art by the culture industry), but on the possibility that the instrument of labour might go unrecognized as such. That such a transcendence of the necessity to labour might be dismissed as impossible under the 'primitive' conditions of Ancient Greece is evident in the sentence that follows the passage just cited: 'The Ionians must have found it comic.' In the laughter lies the possibility of transcendence, as well as the rationalization of the division of labour that perhaps was ideological even for the Ionians. Laughter itself – which, like narration and spectating, relies on a cold distancing – contains both inhumanity and, through a reflexive turn, the possibility of another approach to the world, or the humanity that Adorno terms (as we saw earlier) 'the hope of the name': 'Even though laughter is still the sign of force, of the breaking out of blind and obdurate nature, it also contains the opposite element – the fact that through laughter blind nature becomes aware of itself as it is, and thereby surrenders itself to the power of destruction. This duality of laughter is akin to that of the name, and perhaps names are no more than frozen laughter ... Laughter is marked by the guilt of subjectivity, but in the suspension of law which it indicates it also points beyond thralldom' (Horkheimer and Adorno 1987, 77–8).

Adorno's understanding of labour, and his disagreement with the more orthodox Marxist position taken by Lukács, is conditioned by his historical location, 'after Auschwitz.' Gibson argues that for Adorno, 'the concept of labor always equals "work" and work is always forced labor' (Gibson 2002, 284). Still, Adorno should not be reduced to what Eagleton describes as the 'easily caricatured' view that sees 'Beckett and Schoenberg as the solution to world starvation and threatened nuclear destruction' (Eagleton 1990, 63). That Adorno remains relentlessly critical of any attempt to rationalize the necessity of labour and its divisions simply means that for the category to be maintained as a liberatory one, some crucial 'work' on the concept of labour itself is required. This work is undertaken in the pages of *Negative Dialectics*, especially in the key section titled 'Presentation' (*Darstellung*). Here, in yet another reversal of the normal valences, labour is revealed to be not an act of constructing or positing, but an act of negation. The undoing of the social division of labour then begins with the positing of a fundamental homology between labour and dialectical thinking itself:

> Thought as such, before all particular contents, is an act of negation, of resistance to that which is forced upon it; this is what thought has inherited from its archetype, the relation between labor and material. Today, when ideologues tend more than ever to encourage thought to be positive, they cleverly note that positivity runs precisely counter to thought and that it takes friendly persuasion by social authority to accustom thought to positivity ... The point which thinking aims at its material is not solely a spiritualized control of nature. While doing violence to the object of its syntheses, our thinking heeds a potential that waits in the object, and it unconsciously obeys the idea of making amends to the pieces for what it has done. In philosophy, this unconscious tendency becomes conscious. (Adorno 1973, 19)

That this tendency becomes conscious, however, is not to say that it is realized. As Adorno says in *Negative Dialectics*' opening sentence, philosophy only 'lives on, because the moment to realize it was missed' (1973, 3). Here we must avoid the teleological view that this opportunity or moment cannot recur, but we must do so without succumbing to nostalgia. The sweep of human history can be seen as 'natural,' as the mythic recurrence of the ever-same, and paradoxically, this can provide the most emancipatory of possibilities. The possibility of bursting the fetters of the necessity of labour can be found in the most mundane behaviour, if only the cold distancing of narrative and of laughter were to be turned inward, upon thought itself. In philosophy, which lives on – and even in thought itself, prior to its 'persuasion by social authority' – we are offered a glimpse of the humanity that remains tantalizingly out of reach.

Utopia

What now needs to be finally registered is the familiar compliant or objection regarding Adorno's pessimistic or ultimately apolitical stance. For some, such as Smith, this is located in Adorno's allegedly reading social relations as relations with nature. As we saw earlier, Smith's tendentious misreading rests on a reification of 'the human condition' – a concept that might be understood dialectically in a more sympathetic reading of the Frankfurt School. But even Ben Agger, who is relatively sympathetic to Adorno, contends that 'he paints with too broad a brush in declaring administration total' (Agger 1993, 150). The consequences of this are put most starkly by Gibson: 'Adorno is not simply in the bind between futile activity and passivity, but that even the idea of open thinking is not receptive to new elements outside of thought because the world outside it is totally administered' (Gibson 2002, 284). And although Russell Berman's reminder of the explicitly political content of much of Adorno's work is a laudable attempt to correct this 'posthumous distortion of Adorno as bleakly devoid of political thought' (Berman 2002, 130), it only goes so far in countering the suspicion that Adorno's is a political philosophy of unmitigated despair.

Nobody mistakes Adorno's diagnosis as a celebration (as does sometimes happen with Baudrillard, as we saw in chapter 2). That said, it is often claimed that the 'bad news' of Adorno's message is overstated, and that because he misrecognizes certain aspects of contemporary society (for example, he reads life in late capitalist society as more administered than it actually is), he wrongly rejects certain strategies for political change. Here a certain similarity is suggested between Adorno and Foucault: both are accused of having a 'totalizing' picture of domination in contemporary society, and both reject the possibility of effecting change at a 'macro' level. For Foucault, this means a rejection of a globalizing Marxist praxis, and a reconceptualization of the project of the intellectual as one of being involved in 'specific' struggles (Foucault 1980, 126–8). For Adorno, as Joan Alway points out, there is his comment (in the essay 'Schubert') that 'change succeeds only in the smallest things' (Alway 1995, 67; see also Buck-Morss 1977, 76).

But besides the apparent similarities, there are also crucial differences between the two thinkers. It must be emphasized that for Adorno, 'totality' functions as a critical category. Foucault, in contrast, as we saw in chapter 2, operates with a post-Althusserian conception of subjectivity: the subject, for Foucault, is constructed by nothing but 'ideology.' Foucault of course does not use the latter term, preferring 'discourse' or 'discursive practices,' because the very concept of 'ideology' resists being totalized – if there is 'ideology,' we expect a 'truth' behind or outside of it (Foucault 1980). For Adorno, the persistence of non-identity (what remains 'untrue' about 'the whole') is what gives the category of 'totality' its critical edge, and what allows us always to see Adorno's descriptions of 'totally administered' society as operating at the level of a tendential logic rather than empirical description (which in some sense renders moot the issue of the breadth of Adorno's brushstrokes).

But it must be remembered that if our mode of social organization, which is premised on the domination of nature, produces something like a 'false consciousness,' Adorno also rejects the possibility of a standpoint within our society (such as a Lukácsian Subject-Object of history) that would be capable of identifying a consciousness that is not false. This is the meaning of his dictum in the opening pages of *Negative Dialectics* that dialectics 'does not begin by taking a standpoint' (for further emphasis, the section is titled 'Dialectics not a standpoint') (Adorno 1973, 4–5).

With this in mind, we can now turn to the formulation – perhaps Adorno's best-known on the subject – that was elided in the earlier discussion of Adorno's conception of nature. In *Aesthetic Theory*, Adorno has the following to say about nature: 'Nature, whose imago art aspires to be, *does not yet exist*' (quoted in Jameson 1990, 214; my emphasis). The non- (or not yet) existence of nature is a function of the workings of the dialectic of enlightenment – in other words, of our entrapment in 'the natural-historic cares we share with beetles,' even at the moment we think we have transcended our nature through the construction of civilized society. As Jarvis (1998) puts it: 'Adorno, in effect, is speculatively rewriting the oldest maxim of aesthetics. Art imitates nature: but nothing like "nature" exists as yet: art imitates what does not yet exist. For Adorno it can be said that all authentic art is a mimesis of utopia – yet this mimesis can only be carried out negatively. Art cannot provide an explicit image of utopia. The possible "nature" which does not yet exist can only be imitated by the determinate negation of the falsely naturalized culture which does exist' (100).

Thus, if Adorno, unlike Foucault, offers us the possibility of an outside to the vision of society as constituted ('totally') by domination, it is an outside that can only be indicated through negation. In his suggestion that it might be possible to transcend the 'instinct' for self-preservation, Adorno might be seen as a highly 'utopian' thinker rather than a gloomy pessimist. But as we have seen, this utopian impulse is also properly outside the limits, for Adorno, of what can be conceptualized. The imposition of a *Bilderverbot* (ban on graven images) means that utopia, or even the desire for it, can only be grasped in 'a situation of indirect illumination' (Rothberg 1997, 77). Even utopia's inverse cannot be presented to us directly: in the Sirens episode, we see not the birth of domination, but rather a narrative representation of it, and the name that is offered for the apotheosis of domination, Auschwitz, is both metonymic (a single camp standing in for a continentwide program of genocide) and metaphoric (a place representing an event).

But clearly, even the strongest possible argument that Adorno remains a Marxist must nevertheless concede that he seems more concerned with art and philosophy than with the more explicitly political terrain of class struggle. It might be tempting to suggest that such a move away from class struggle as such also removes from his purview the problematic of non-alienated objectification (which, as we saw in the previous chapter, was a crucial concern of Marx's). As we have seen, however, this concern with art and philosophy is informed and even demanded by Adorno's political commitments. In other words, Adorno's concern with developing a more appropriate or adequate means of encountering the world of objects than that offered by instrumental rationality reveals the problematic of alienation and objectification (albeit expressed in somewhat different terms, as one of a non-dominating relationship with nature) to be one of his central concerns. But since any positive representation of such an 'undamaged' relationship would inevitably participate in precisely the mode of thinking that causes the 'damage' in the first place, the possibilities can only be glimpsed through situations of 'indirect illumination.'

Such indirect illumination, however, is not limited to the representation of the inverse of utopia. Adorno also offers us two 'models' of a more positive kind: the 'deterrorized mimesis' of aesthetic identification, and the self-conscious, persistent negation of philosophical (dialectical) thinking. Both of these can only be revealed negatively, by pointing to the limits of attempts to engage this sort of practice (as in by pointing to the moment where the Hegelian dialectic is untrue to itself and takes an 'affirmative' turn, or by recognizing in Beckett's *Endgame* where 'philosophy, spirit itself, declares itself to be dead inventory, the dreamlike leavings of a world of experience, and the poetic process declares itself to be a process of wastage' [Adorno 1991b, 243]). But in seeing these limits as such, we can glimpse the possibility of a transformed relationship with nature, which would, of course, be a radical transformation of social relations as well.

But it is far from clear how these philosophical and aesthetic models of a non-dominating relationship with nature can be mapped onto other aspects of the transformation of nature. Jameson concludes his discussion of Adorno with the following, somewhat ambivalent, judgment: 'Meanwhile, the vital relationship of Adorno to political thinking lies in the form rather than the content of his thoughts, which, conceptualizing aesthetic form or philosophical content rather than politics as such, is capable of detecting within them – with a starker, more luminous articulation than can normally be achieved within political analysis or social history – the complex mobilities of the historical dialectic' (Jameson 1990, 225).

But we can here again raise the question taught to us by Freud: *Why* does a 'luminous articulation ... of the historical dialectic' manifest itself as an analysis of aesthetics or philosophy, rather than of politics or social history? Adorno's refusal to provide any positive representation of a society that has abolished the division of labour along with the fear of nature that is its cause (or, in Jameson's terms, his seeming inability or unwillingness to mobilize his method to illuminate a truth-content in politics or social history), stems from much more than the ban on graven images imposed by the logic of his arguments. The question of how the relationship with the object that might be found in philosophical negation or genuine aesthetic experience can be mapped onto, say, ensuring that nobody goes hungry, is made more complicated by the fact that the former necessitates precisely a suspension (or at least a relativization) of the 'instinct' for self-preservation, which is taken to be the cause of the latter. That Adorno emphatically rejects any apologias for starvation only indicates, perhaps, the utopic (or at least fleeting) character of Adorno's notion of reconciliation: 'The idea of a fullness of life, including the one held out to mankind by the socialist conceptions, is therefore not the utopianism one mistakes it for. It is not, because that fullness is inseparable from the craving, from what the *fin-de-siecle* called "living life to the full," from a desire in which violence and subjugation are inherent. If there is no hope without quenching the desire, the desire in turn is harnessed to the infamous context of like for like – and that precisely is hopeless. There is no fullness without biceps-flexing' (Adorno 1973, 378).

Adorno thus shows us the depth to which a dominating approach to nature is implicated in our social relations and in the structure of our way of thinking. Although Adorno is not suggesting that there is no possibility of a reconciled relationship with nature, his analysis leaves us with little in the way of an understanding of what such a relationship might look like. Adorno never tells us what social relations might be entailed, or what sorts of lives we might live, or even what sorts of beings might exist, in a genuinely 'human' society that finally breaks from our evolutionary animal past. What Adorno does tell us is that the dilemmas of human ecology are not problems strictly rooted in our relationship with nature, nor strictly in our social relations, but both at once, and that it is only with the elaboration of a genuinely *human* ecology, that the two will in fact become separable. For a more 'positive' elaboration of this problematic, we turn next to the work of Herbert Marcuse.

CHAPTER 6

Herbert Marcuse: Basic and Surplus Alienation

> Indeed, there is a level at which our consciousness must be neither poetry nor science, but a transcendence of both into a new realm of theory and practice ... Poetry and imagination must be integrated with science and technology, for we have evolved beyond an innocence that can be nourished exclusively by myths and dreams.
>
> Bookchin (1991, 20)

> Reason is what engenders egocentrism, and reflection strengthens it.
>
> Rousseau (1987, 54)

The final theorist to be considered in depth here is Herbert Marcuse, who offers the possibility of a more 'positive' elaboration of the dialectic of enlightenment and the vicissitudes of conceptual thinking that were explored in the preceding chapter. More specifically, this chapter will take Marcuse's seminal distinction between 'basic' and 'surplus' repression and show that the basic–surplus trope can be applied to a number of problematics beyond that of psychological repression. Treating the trope in such a modular fashion will allow us, finally, to develop and clarify a distinction between basic and surplus alienation from nature. This approach, whose genealogy can be traced back through Marx's distinction between objectification and alienation, to Rousseau's historicization of alienation, will then provide the starting point for the notion of a genuine human ecology, or a denaturalized ecological politics – something whose possibility Adorno only indicated through 'indirect illumination.'

It is worth emphasizing at the outset, however, that Marcuse's theorizing will not present us with a statement of the problematic of alienation that fully comprehends those laid out in the previous three chapters. Nor will it present us with a fully developed solution to the dilemmas of ecological politics in a post-natural condition that confronted us in the introduction. Marcuse's theorizations *will* provide the final (and perhaps most concretely elaborated) elements that will allow us to develop a political position that avoids the antinomies of ecocentrism and postmodernism that were set out in chapters 1 and 2.

Like Adorno, Marcuse understood the history of modernity as the progressive intensification of domination. Both were critical of what they saw as the increasingly bureaucratic character of life in 'totally administered' societies, and both focused on the similarities at least as much as the differences among liberal capitalist, Soviet, and fascist societies.

Marcuse also pursues Adorno's critique of identitarian thinking, albeit in slightly less abstruse terms, among other ways through the development of the concept of 'one-dimensionality,' which posits that the sources of critical impulses are eliminated in advanced industrial societies. Marx and Engels's *Communist Manifesto* opened with the pronouncement that 'a specter is haunting Europe'; in contrast, Marcuse's *One-Dimensional Man* begins by noting the opposite – that the specter has apparently (but only apparently) been exorcised: 'A comfortable, smooth, reasonable, democratic unfreedom prevails in advanced industrial civilization, a token of technical progress' (Marcuse 1964, 1). With an increasingly rationalized form of social organization, nonconformity and individual liberty (beyond the freedom to choose from pregiven alternatives) are seen as increasingly irrational: 'Thus emerges a pattern of *one-dimensional thought and behavior* in which, ideas, aspirations, and objectives that, by their content, transcend the established universe of discourse and action are either repelled or reduced to the terms of this universe. They are redefined by the rationality of the given system and of its quantitative extension' (13; emphasis in original).

The emphasis here is on the individual (or what is elsewhere called 'bourgeois interiority') as the source of the 'second dimension.' We should note, however, that in this regard, Marcuse elsewhere emphasizes the role of culture. As with Adorno and Horkheimer's understanding of the 'culture industry,' Marcuse problematizes the more orthodox Marxian distinction between an economic base and a cultural superstructure. As Agger notes, for Marcuse and for the Frankfurt School more generally, the logic of advanced capitalism 'involves the penetration of political-economic imperatives into culture and personality' such that 'the superstructural sphere – art, politics, quotidian experience – is increasingly "economized" in the face of the imperatives of social control and profit in late capitalism' (Agger 1992, 132). The decline of the critical potentialities of both the production of culture and the manifestations of individuality are thus aspects of the same phenomenon, in that both involve 'the deep internalization of alienation' (131).

For Adorno, as we saw in the previous chapter, these patterns are visible in the most banal social products, such as those offered by the culture industry; but they are also embossed on the lofty heights of bourgeois philosophy. For Adorno, Kant's ideological block regarding the inability to rid freedom of its grounding in unfreedom, is what leads Kant to 'chime in with the eminently bourgeois affirmation of one's own confinement' (Adorno 1973, 382). For Marcuse, as we shall now see, these patterns are visible in modern science (which, like Kantian philosophy, is not without its truth-value) – in particular, in the concepts and categories of that most bourgeois of the modern sciences: Freudian psychoanalysis.

Beyond Freud: Freedom and Repression

Marcuse's essay 'Freedom and Freud's Theory of Instincts' begins by noting the need to make the case for the political relevance of Freudian theory. This relevance, in the first place, is to be found in what Marcuse (see above) called the 'one-dimensionality' of society: Freudian theory helps explain the tendency toward increasing social rationalization, and away from nonconformity (or what Erich Fromm [1969] famously called the 'escape from freedom'): 'The psyche appears more and more to be a piece of the social totality, so that individuation is almost synonymous with apathy and even with guilt ... Moreover, the totality of which the psyche is a part becomes to an increasing extent less "society" than "politics." That is, society has fallen prey to and become identified with domination' (Marcuse 1970, 1).

This immediately raises the problem of how to define 'domination.' Marcuse offers the following: 'Domination is in effect whenever the individual's goals and purposes and the means of striving for and attaining them are prescribed to him and performed by him as something prescribed. Domination can be exercised by men, by nature, by things – *it can also be internal, exercised by the individual on himself, and appear in the form of autonomy*' (1970, 1–2; emphasis added).

This last point – that domination can take the appearance of autonomy – is crucial. As we saw in the previous chapter with Adorno and Horkheimer's psychoanalytically inflected reading of the *Odyssey* (which focused on Odysseus' survival through self-denial as a prototype of the constitution of subjectivity), Freud's decisive contribution was to show how domination can be internalized and exercised from within by the superego. Marcuse draws the paradoxical, yet obvious, conclusion: 'Under these circumstances, however, freedom becomes an impossible concept, for there is nothing that is not prescribed for the individual in some way or other. And in fact freedom can be defined only within the framework of domination, if previous history is to provide a guide to the definition of freedom. Freedom is *a form of domination*: the one in which the means provided satisfy the needs of the individual with a minimum of displeasure and renunciation' (1970, 2; emphasis in original).

But Marcuse also notes pointedly that bringing psychoanalysis to political science must not only lead to an increasing scientization of the latter discipline (which would only reinforce one-dimensionality) but also politicize – or reveal the power dimensions latent within, and the contested character of – psychoanalysis, political science, and political development. Individuation is thus to be identified 'with the principle of negation, of possible revolution' (1970, 1). Elsewhere, in a statement whose significance will shortly become apparent, he notes that it is the unconscious (more precisely, the pleasure principle) that provides a locus of resistance to one-dimensional society: 'The interpretation of the 'mental apparatus' in terms of these two principles [the pleasure and reality principles] is basic to Freud's theory and remains so in spite of all modifications of the dualistic conception. It corresponds largely (but not entirely) to the distinction between the unconscious and conscious processes. The individual exists, as it were, in *two different dimensions*, characterized by different mental processes and principles' (Marcuse 1987, 12; emphasis added).

Here Marcuse allows us to see both the radical and the conservative elements in Freud's thought. On the one hand, Freudian theory can be construed as progressive insofar as it argues that the development of civilization (the productive forces, in Marx's terms) should lead to the progressive minimization of 'displeasure and renunciation.' Furthermore, the identification of the 'second dimension' with the unconscious suggests a *biological* basis for human freedom – that the revolt against the displeasure and renunciation found in the administered society is 'natural.' On the other hand, Freud in no way suggests that this displeasure and renunciation can ever be entirely eliminated; indeed, he is quite pessimistic about even the extent to which it can be reduced. In the conclusion to *Studies on Hysteria*, for example, Freud and his collaborator, Joseph Breuer, remark rather sanguinely that 'much will be gained if we succeed in transforming your hysterical misery into common unhappiness' (Freud and Breuer 1974, 393). As well, even the freedom and happiness that are available within civilization are only trade-offs: the renunciation of 'momentary pleasure, uncertain in its results,' for the promise of 'an assured pleasure at a later time' (Freud 1984, 41).

As we saw in the previous chapter, however, whether even this promise is actually fulfilled under current social conditions is another question entirely. Thus, for Marcuse – and as we have already seen with Adorno – 'freedom is possible only on the basis of unfreedom, that is, on the basis of instinctual suppression' (Marcuse 1970, 5). This suppression, which Freud identifies as the replacement of the 'pleasure principle' by the 'reality principle' ('transforming [a person] from a subject-object of pleasure into a subject-object of work' [ibid.]), is highly traumatic. The paradoxes of Freudian theory, then, include the simultaneous assertion of the naturality of both instinctual gratification *and* its suppression, and the claim that the securing of happiness can only be achieved through intense suffering:

> Only this transformation [replacing the pleasure principle with the reality principle], which leaves an unhealable wound in men, makes them fit for society and thus for life, for without secure cooperation it is impossible to survive in a hostile and niggardly environment. It is only this traumatic transformation, which is an 'alienation' of man from nature in the authentic sense, an alienation from his own nature, that makes man capable of enjoyment; only the instinct that has been restrained and mastered raises the merely natural satisfaction of need to pleasure that is experienced and comprehended – to happiness. (5–6)

In other words, 'civilization arises from pleasure' (19), but at the same time, 'the more civilization progresses, the more powerful its apparatus for the development and gratification of social needs becomes, the more oppressive are the sacrifices that it has to impose on individuals in order to maintain the necessary instinctual structure' (13).

For Adorno, as we have seen, the emphasis fell decidedly on the latter proposition – that is, on the way the construction of subjectivity is increasingly achieved through the destruction of the subject. In Marcuse's rereading of Freud, however, we can detect a response to Adorno and Horkheimer's *Dialectic of Enlightenment*: the elaboration of a more positive sketch of the possible course of human development, beyond the point at which Adorno's speculations, in particular, break off. Later in this chapter, we will pursue this point at greater length. For the moment (and as a part of the preliminary work necessary in order to compare Marcuse and Adorno), we must examine Marcuse's reading of Freud in a bit more detail.

Eros and Civilization is Marcuse's most systematic attempt to deal with Freudian theory. It might be useful to think of Marcuse's attitude toward Freud as similar to Adorno's attitude toward Kant, mentioned earlier – that the theorist under discussion provides 'the eminently bourgeois affirmation of one's own confinement.' Freud's pessimism regarding the possibilities for circumventing the trauma of alienation, his conclusion that 'freedom' is illusory – that what we call freedom is only possible on the basis of repression – is of a piece with Kant's claim that freedom can only be realized through what Adorno terms a 'system of stop signals.' In *Eros and Civilization*, Marcuse systematically elaborates this point in an effort 'to develop the political and sociological substance of the psychological notions' (1987, xii). He provides, in other words, a Marxian (or Adornian) critique of Freud, arguing that the psychological concepts as Freud deploys them are hypostasized, or stripped of their dynamic, evolutionary, and dialectical character. Or as Slavoj Žižek puts it, rather more pointedly, Marcuse sees Freudian theory as ideological to the extent that biological drives are naturalized: 'The guise in which the unconscious appears as "archaic," quasi-"biological" drives is itself an indication of a "reified" social reality; as such, this appearance is not a simple illusion to be abolished by "historicizing" the unconscious but, rather, *the adequate manifestation of a historical reality which is itself "false"* – that is to say, alienated, inverted' (Žižek 1994, 11).

The opening sentence of *Eros and Civilization* declares that 'Sigmund Freud's proposition that civilization is based on the permanent subjugation of the human instincts has been taken for granted' (Marcuse, 1987, 3). Freud's proposition is not subjected to an overtly Marxian critique (Marx's name does not even appear in the book's index), but rather to an immanent critique: 'Freud's *own theory* provides reasons for rejecting his identification of civilization with repression' (1987, 4; emphasis added). Marcuse's project here is thus to show that Freudian theory itself 'allow[s] the concept of a non-repressive civilization, based on a fundamentally different experience of being, a fundamentally different relation between man and nature, and fundamentally different existential relations'[1] (1987, 5).

Among the most important Freudian categories, for Marcuse, are the 'pleasure principle' and the 'reality principle.' These two principles form the 'governing value system' of the psyche (1987, 12). As we have already seen, this dualistic conception of psychic development – in which the pleasure principle is supplanted by the reality principle as the individual develops from infant to mature adult – is a fundamental supposition of Freudian psychology. Moreover, for both Freud and Marcuse, this development in the individual psyche mirrors the development of the human species: ontogeny recapitulates phylogeny.

Marcuse's intervention, then, is not to deny this supposition about the dualistic conception of human development (both at the individual or psychological and at the social or historical level). Rather, Marcuse suggests that Freud's understanding of the 'reality principle' is reified: 'Nietzsche exposes the gigantic fallacy on which Western philosophy and morality were built – namely, the transformation of facts into essences, of historical into metaphysical conditions ... Nietzsche speaks in the name of a reality principle fundamentally antagonistic to that of Western civilization' (Marcuse 1987, 121). In other words, Freud's pessimism is a result of his misrecognizing the reality principle of his (and our) society as the only possible reality principle, or more precisely, in failing to see the possibility of a non-surplus repressive reality principle: 'The specific reality principle that has governed the origins and the growth of this civilization [a reality principle which Marcuse refers to as the 'performance principle'] is clearly not the only historical reality principle: other modes of societal organization not merely prevailed in primitive cultures but also survived into the modern period' (Marcuse 1987, 44–5).

Marcuse offers two possible responses to Freud's proposed model of human development. The first is the Nietzschean response suggested by the earlier quotation: the 'reality principle' is not unitary, as Freud seems to be suggesting. To describe it as such is to conceal the multiplicity of *possible* reality principles. The second possible response is the Hegelian or Marxian response: that Freud's model is in fact a model of arrested development. Marcuse posits the possibility of a third 'stage,' one that goes beyond the two acknowledged by Freud.[2]

That Marcuse refers to the current reality principle as the 'performance principle' helps us see why his critique of Freud is not so much Nietzschean as Marxian. The 'performance principle' is so called 'in order to emphasize that under its rule society is stratified according to the *competitive economic* performances of its members' (1987, 44; emphasis added). Marcuse in effect is suggesting that the multiplicity of possible reality principles is related to the multiplicity of possible forms of socio-economic organization – in other words, to the multiplicity of *modes of production*.

It is in this context, of allowing for the possibility of different reality principles, that Marcuse makes the crucial distinction between basic and surplus repression.

> The Freudian terms, which do not adequately differentiate between the biological *and* the socio-historical vicissitudes of the instincts, must be paired with corresponding terms denoting the specific socio-historical component. Presently we shall introduce two such terms:
>
> (a) *Surplus-repression*: the restrictions necessitated by social domination. This is distinguished from (basic) *repression*: the 'modifications' of the instincts necessary for the perpetuation of the human race in civilization.
>
> (b) *Performance principle*: the prevailing historical form of the *reality principle*. (Marcuse 1987, 35; emphases in original)

These distinctions then allow Marcuse to argue that advanced civilization does not logically necessitate the sort or extent of represssion and 'traumatic transformation' of alienation from nature that Freud seems to suppose. On this basis, he 'aims at describing the conditions of possibility of a society from which aggression will have been eliminated and in which libidinally satisfying work will be conceivable' (Jameson 1971, 115). Marcuse admits that human life does necessitate some repression ('basic' repression) and thus a certain form of alienation from what might be construed as a 'natural' (that is, animal) mode of being (immediate instinctual gratification). It is only what Marcuse terms 'surplus-repression' that necessitates the sort of alienation that is endemic to modern societies. As Stephen Bronner points out, the very term 'surplus-repression' is an adaptation of Marx's 'surplus-value' (Bronner 1994, 241), and Marcuse's discussion of the former draws quite heavily on Marx's discussion of alienation in the '1844 Manuscripts':

> For the vast majority of the population, the scope and mode of satisfaction are determined by their own labor; but their labor is work for an

> apparatus which they do not control, which operates as an independent power to which individuals must submit if they want to live. And it becomes more alien the more specialized the division of labor becomes. Men do not live their lives but perform pre-established functions. While they work, they do not fulfill their own needs and faculties but work in *alienation*. Work has now become *general*, and so have the restrictions placed on the libido: labor time, which is the largest part of the individual's life time, is painful time, for alienated labor is the absence of gratification, negation of the pleasure principle. (Marcuse 1987, 45; emphases in original)

For Marcuse, the category of 'surplus-repression' offers a way out of the Freudian paradox that the advance of civilization, intended to secure happiness, seems only to lead to an increase in unhappiness. Repression, necessary for civilization, is a denial of pleasure, yet repression should be what makes it possible to experience pleasure (or more precisely, *happiness*, as opposed to the mere gratification of needs). In other words, Marcuse's distinction between repression and surplus-repression is (as the above quotation suggests) homologous to Marx's distinction between labour and alienated labour:[3]

> To be sure, every form of society, every civilization has to exact labor time for the procurement of the necessities and luxuries of life. But not every kind and mode of labor is essentially irreconcilable with the pleasure principle. The human relations connected with work may 'provide for a very considerable discharge of libidinal component impulses, narcissistic, aggressive, and even erotic.' ([Freud,] *Civilization and Its Discontents*, p. 34 note.) The irreconcilable conflict is not between work (reality principle) and Eros (pleasure principle), but between *alienated* labor (performance principle) and Eros. (Marcuse 1987, 47n; emphasis in original)

We can thus extend Marcuse's distinction between basic and surplus repression to include a distinction between alienation from nature that is biologically necessary for human life and alienation from nature that is only made necessary by particular forms of social organization.

At the same time, it should be noted that Marcuse's theorizations provide not only a Marxian critique of Freud, but also a Freudian critique of Marx. Marcuse not only revises Freud's understanding of history by drawing on Marx's distinction between objectification and alienation, but also revises Marx's understanding of history by providing it with a 'biological' (psychoanalytic) grounding. As was noted at the outset of this chapter, Marcuse's particular appropriation of Marx undercuts considerably the adequacy of any sort of base–superstructure distinction. The economic level of the mode of production (capitalism) can be read not only as the 'base' but also as the superstructure, if the psychological level of the reality principle (performance principle) is understood as the base. The 'false needs' generated by advanced capitalism are thus 'real' to the extent that they are biologically grounded, 'introjected into the subjective, psychological "infrastructure" of society's members' (Bronner 1994, 241–2).[4] The point here is not to *reverse* the traditional base–superstructure distinction, nor to suggest that biology determines economy, which then determines ideology or culture. Rather, in recognizing that, for example, personality structure operates at the level of ideology or culture *as well as* at the level of biology, we can see that the levels are interpenetrated, that they reinforce and generate tensions with one another. There is no single level that can be abstracted so that it reveals itself as the one that determines all the others.

Beyond Marx (I): Automated Production and Technological Rationality

From the time of the height of his theoretical currency, Marcuse's relationship with Marxism has been hotly contested. Some, such as Douglas Kellner and Ben Agger, argue that Marcuse remains committed to a reconstruction of Marxism,[5] whereas others, such as Lucio Colletti, claim that Marcuse's 'revisions' are an abandonment or betrayal of Marx's critical project.[6] The question of whether Marcuse ultimately is or is not a Marxist is of little concern for our purposes here; even so, the claims that he has abandoned Marxism are worth exploring critically and in some detail for the light they can shed on Marcuse's own project and on its relevance for contemporary ecological politics.

Colletti provides two main objections to seeing Marcuse as a Marxist theorist. The first is that Marcuse's critique of science and of technology abstracts these from the social relations within which they are produced. Marcuse thus provides 'not an indictment of capital but of technology' (Colletti 1972, 138). In other words, Marcuse is seen as providing an argument about technology that is precisely the mirror image of the one provided by bourgeois economists. Bourgeois economists equate machinery and capital so that 'whoever wants modern productive forces, i.e. machinery and modern industry, must also want capitalist *relations of production*' (139; emphasis in original). Similarly, according to Colletti, Marcuse's putatively romantic critique equates machinery with capital so that 'whoever does not want exploitation, or rather ... 'integration,' must return to patriarchal conditions of life, or even perhaps to feudalism' (139).

This view of Marcuse's position might seem to be supported by his claim (at the conclusion of *One-Dimensional Man*'s chapter on technology) that 'technology has become the great vehicle of *reification* – reification in its most mature and effective form' (Marcuse 1964, 168–9; emphasis in original). But a closer examination of how Marcuse reaches this conclusion (along with a recollection of some of the points raised in the previous chapter) can show that Marcuse – like Adorno and Rousseau – is not calling for anything like a return to feudalism. Colletti's argument rests on the fact that although Marcuse claims to be in agreement with Marx's assertion that 'the social mode of production, not technics is the basic historical factor,' he goes on to add this important caveat: 'However, when technics becomes the universal form of material production, it circumscribes an entire culture; it projects a historical totality – a "world."' (154). If we live in a society in which technics or scientific rationality is the universal form of material production, then it should not be surprising that our way of viewing the world, our senses (as Marx himself had argued in the '1844 Manuscripts'), and indeed our very subjectivity are determined by the demands of technics. We saw in the previous chapter the various ways that Adorno argued that social domination and the domination of nature are closely linked. Timothy Luke (1994) makes the same point in a discussion of Marcuse: 'The rationalizing technical hierarchy based on humans dominating nature merges with the disciplinary social hierarchy of humans dominating other humans' (197).

For Colletti, Marxism remains a scientific enterprise – one that precisely because it is scientific, is capable of developing an understanding of the true nature of social forms. Although the emergence of Marxism as a scientific discourse can be understood as the result of certain particular historical developments, it is nevertheless necessarily capable, like any science, of providing an understanding of the world that is not historically circumscribed. In this sense, 'science' is transhistorical.

For Marcuse, however, Colletti's claim that science or scientific rationality, as a mode of apprehending the world, can be divorced from a mode of production, is ill-considered. Colletti rejects Marcuse's claim that a genuinely liberatory mode of production must be founded on a different mode of apprehending the world. But for Marcuse (following Adorno and Horkheimer), modern science in itself, whatever its claims to neutrality, is tied to specific social practices and relations, and thus indissolubly linked to domination:

> Scientific rationality makes for a specific societal organization precisely because it projects mere form (or mere matter – here, the otherwise opposite terms converge) which can be bent to practically all ends. Formalization and functionalization are, *prior* to all application, the 'pure form' of a concrete societal practice. While science freed nature from inherent ends and stripped matter of all but quantifiable properties, society freed men from the 'natural' hierarchy of personal dependence and related them to each other in accordance with quantifiable qualities – namely, as units of abstract labor power, calculable in units of time. (Marcuse 1964, 156–7; emphasis in original)

It follows that the establishment of 'qualitatively new relations between men and between man and nature' – a form of social organization or a *mode of production* that is not based on exchange-value – would be possible only on the basis of a post-Galilean science that allows for the transcendence of the present '*Lebenswelt* [world of practice]' and the establishment of 'a qualitatively new mode of "seeing."' (165).

For Colletti, all this suggests that Marcuse provides little more than a revamped Bergsonianism, whose idealism ultimately betrays its progressive intentions:

> The 'fetish' is the natural object investigated by science. 'Reification' or, as Bergson said, *le chosisme*, is the product of the scientific intellect that breaks up (the famous *morcelage*) the fluid and 'living' unity of the real into the 'fictitious' outlines of the objects that have to be used for practical-technical action. Alienation, in short, is science, technology ...
>
> The kernal [sic] of Marcuse's philosophy is precisely here. Oppression is science. 'Reification' is to recognize that things exist outside ourselves. (Colletti 1972, 134)

This critique of science that Colletti imputes to Marcuse is not unlike the ecocentric critique of modern science discussed in chapter 1. And indeed, both Marcuse and certain strands of deep ecology share a commitment to certain Heideggerian themes (Marcuse was a student of Heidegger's).[7] Both see modern science's positivist and quantifying approach to the world (what Heidegger calls an experience of things as 'present-at-hand') as impoverished or even 'inauthentic.' But their divergent attitudes toward the experience of things as 'ready-to-hand' (immanence in the artisanal labour process, for example) reveal certain important differences. At the risk of oversimplification, we can say that Heidegger – at least at certain important moments – rather uncritically valorizes artisanal production, in particular as this mode of 'being-in-the-world' was structured in pre-Socratic Greece.[8] For Heidegger (1977), this requires us to see the history of the West (and in particular the rise of modern science and technology) as one of decline. Marcuse, in contrast, retains a materialist view of history that sees it as (dialectically and at least potentially) progressive. For Marcuse (here siding with Marx and against Heidegger), technological advances, although they *have been* used to rationalize domination, are nevertheless a fundamental precondition of human liberation. Hence Marcuse's very un-Heideggerian claim in *An Essay on Liberation*: 'Utopian possibilities are inherent in the technical and technological forces of advanced capitalism and socialism: the rational utilization of these forces on a global scale would terminate poverty and scarcity within a very foreseeable future' (1972a, 13).

Nor should the fact that this quotation is extracted from Marcuse's later work be taken to suggest that he only eventually reversed the critique of science developed in *One-Dimensional Man*. Marcuse notes in the concluding pages of the latter book: 'If the completion of the technological project involves a break with the prevailing technological rationality, the break in turn depends on the continued existence of the technical base itself.' (1964, 231). Marcuse's argument hinges on a distinction here between 'technological rationality' and the 'technical base' – a distinction that seems to elude Colletti.

This distinction between 'technological rationality' and the 'technical base' does not quite parallel the distinction between surplus and basic repression (not least because, for Marcuse, it is equally plausible to see the form of rationality as the [biological] base, with the productive forces thereby relegated to the 'superstructural' level). Rather, the relevant distinction must be seen as one between 'basic' technological rationality and the 'surplus' technological rationality that is characteristic of advanced industrial societies. The latter has a totalizing character, similar to Adorno and Horkheimer's notion of 'instrumental rationality.' Basic technological rationality, on the other hand, is circumscribed by some other form of rationality – human, ecological, self-reflexive; its precise character is not specified, but it does provide an exterior standard against which the demands of technological (or instrumental) rationality can be judged: 'The reification of human labor power, driven to perfection, would shatter the reified form by cutting the chain that ties the individual to the machinery – the mechanism through which his own labor enslaves him. Complete automation in the realm of necessity would open the dimension of free time as the one in which man's private *and* societal existence would constitute itself. This would be the historical transcendence toward a new civilization' (Marcuse 1964, 36–7; emphases in original). As we shall see below, this form of rationality, without which instrumental and technological rationality would be unchecked, is closely connected to the aesthetic faculty of judgment.

So if Colletti sees Marcuse's critique of the scientific mindset as a call to return to feudalism, we can see how a Marcusean response to this criticism might take the same form as Marcuse's critique of Freud. Just as Freud seemed to be suggesting that the 'performance principle' was the only possible 'reality principle,' Colletti similarly seems to be incapable of imagining a 'scientific' understanding of the world that is not predicated on the domination of nature. And just as Freud transformed the 'fact' of the 'performance principle' into an 'essence' (*the* reality principle), Colletti similarly essentializes the fact of Galilean science (a science predicated on the domination of nature).

To be sure, this problem of reification is not simply a failure of individual imagination on the part either of Freud or Colletti. We have already seen how important Marcuse considers it 'to develop the political and sociological substance of the [individualizing] psychological notions' (Marcuse 1987, xii). In other words, Freud's inability to conceptualize any reality principle other than the one in force in his society – the ultimately ideological character of his work, noted earlier – should be understood as a condition that was not strictly an individual pathology, but rather one that was determined by the particular social conditions in which he lived – the final stages of European imperial expansion and the rigorous strictures of Victorian morality.[9]

This view of the historicity of psychic development allows us to see that Marcuse is not in fact arguing against technology or science 'as such'; that said, its emphasis on the malleability of subjectivity makes its Marxian commitments more problematic in another sense: the experience of contradiction as a source of suffering is one that must be seen, like all experience, as conditioned by social relations. A more economistic version of Marxism might see socialist revolution arising more or less ineluctably out of the laws of motion of the capitalist economy, as factory production is increasingly concentrated and the working class is increasingly immiserated; or at the very least it would see Marxism as a science capable of revealing the truth about capitalism (specifically, its irrationality). But the Frankfurt School's analysis of advanced capitalism notes the ways in which domination is increasingly rationalized. The very historicity of 'human nature' allows for the development of a working class that can experience alienation and domination as not only untroublesome, but indeed as a source of libidinal pleasure.

This is of course not to suggest that the contradictions of capitalism are made to *disappear* through the adaptive strategies of the subject. Contradictions continue to be generated, but this psychological adaptation makes it that much more difficult to identify the experience of contradiction as such. For Marcuse, therefore, the struggle against capitalism – which remains a 'biological' as well as a socio-economic imperative – takes place not only in the ambit of the state and the workplace, but also (and perhaps even more importantly) on the psychic terrain of the construction of subjectivity itself. The construction of a working-class subject who actually *wants* to lose her or his chains – something that Marx scarcely even imagined to be a problem – is for Marcuse a vexingly necessary precondition for a viable socialist revolution (in advanced capitalist countries, at least). As we shall now see, the necessity of a biological or psychological grounding for radical political theory leads Marcuse to the realm of aesthetics.

Beyond Marx (II): Beauty and Sublimation/Necessity

Colletti's second point of criticism of Marcuse is that the latter's prescriptions for overcoming alienation amount to an endorsement of interiority (or a 'flight into inwardness') complicit with the bourgeois defence of the private sphere. Colletti objects that Marcuse's focus on the overcoming of one-dimensionality through the cultivation of individuality and aesthetic sensibilities is ultimately protective of, rather than threatening to, bourgeois society. This objection is, of course, similar to the accusations of paralysing 'gloomy pessimism' that we saw levelled against Adorno in the previous chapter, and is a familiar charge against Frankfurt School theorists in general (even if Marcuse's more 'political' works, such his *Essay on Liberation*, are sometimes excepted). The charge that the retreat into the private sphere is strategically misguided is made by Colletti in an almost offhanded fashion. It receives a more sustained treatment by Timothy Lukes, who unlike Colletti is sympathetic to Marcuse and takes issue only with this '"last step" in Marcuse's philosophical syllogism ... his reliance on "the aesthetic dimension" – the flight into inwardness – as a means to relieve the more negative aspects of modern technological society' (Lukes 1985, 15). As we shall see, however, Lukes's claim that we can follow Marcuse for a certain distance but then shift directions at the moment of his 'last step' is one that cannot be sustained. Marcuse's 'flight into inwardness' is not a strategically guided choice of one possible option among many; still less is it a 'strategic retreat' dictated by an assessment of the current balance of forces; rather it is dictated by the logic of Marcuse's arguments themselves. In particular, as we shall see, it is dictated by the way that the aesthetic and the political cannot be neatly separated out, but can only be posited as separable at some future hypothetical moment. In this sense, the entanglement of aesthetic and strategic or political concerns (of the demands of beauty and the demands of necessity), can be seen as homologous to the complex intertwining of basic and surplus repression.

Although some have seen Marcuse's valorization of the 'aesthetic dimension' in his later work as a more or less abrupt turn away from more explicitly political concerns – a turn perhaps caused by Marcuse's disillusionment with the failure of the countercultural and student movements of the late 1960s and early 1970s[10] – Lukes compellingly argues that the aesthetic functions as a crucial political category even in Marcuse's earlier works. The aesthetic and the imagination ground his critiques of advanced capitalism (in *One-Dimensional Man*) and of state socialist societies (in *Soviet Marxism*); furthermore, they are crucial to Marcuse's rereading of Freud in *Eros and Civilization*. Lukes sees aesthetics as crucial to Marcuse's project of overcoming the Freudian opposition between civilization and primal desire: 'It is the aesthetic imagination which can maintain complex reorganizations of reality within the universe of sensual satisfaction. The aesthetic imagination, capable of translating immediacy into the highly complex images conforming to aesthetic form, can accommodate the complexity of technology, and integrate technology into the realm of sensual fulfillment' (Lukes 1985, 49). In other words, certain kinds of aesthetic practice can be understood as a way of achieving 'nonrepressive sublimation' (81). Aesthetic practice is thus for Marcuse a crucial political category, insofar as, through its expression of a non-surplus repressive form of subjectivity, it points to the possibility of a 'pacified' existence, or a form of social organization that is not predicated on the domination of nature.

This is not, of course, to suggest that any and all forms of artistic expression are inherently liberatory or even politically progressive. Liberatory artistic practice, for Marcuse, is that which does not shrink from the demands of the aesthetic form, or in which the autonomy of the work itself is not circumscribed, but in which the work of art also leads beyond itself. In other words, the demands of the aesthetic form can be seen in the commitment to Kantian formal purposiveness ('purposiveness without purpose') of 'genuine' works of art, in their expression of the ontological propensity to universalize. To attempt to discover or express universally valid harmonies is – or (taking Adorno's cautions about our current level of humanity into account) should be – no less than an essential aspect of the human condition. This link between 'genuine' art and 'genuine' humanity is also found in Joel Whitebook's observation that 'insofar as the ego possesses a synthetic function, and insofar as *Eros* is defined as the drive to establish and preserve "ever greater unities," we can locate something like *Eros* in the ego itself' (Whitebook 1985, 145–6). Or as Marcuse himself puts it, emphasizing the socio-political imperative that should go along with the demands of aesthetic form: 'In the aesthetic imagination, sensuousness generates universally valid principles for an objective order' (Marcuse 1987, 177).

Genuine art's commitment to autonomy and universalization thus suggests that what Lukes terms 'scientific art' (examples of this include socialist realism and 'art of the technologically rational society,' such as art commissioned by NASA) is not genuine art because it 'attempt[s] to render art an auxiliary to scientific "progress"' (Lukes 1985, 88). Marcuse argues that these forms of art, in celebrating the triumph of science, wrongly imply that the scientific domination of nature is a situation of harmony. In Adornian terms, they posit a false universality that ignores the moment of non-identity.

In contrast, in 'affirmative art,' such as bourgeois high art, this moment of non-identity is acknowledged, although what might be otherwise recognized as a *political* issue of domination and the denial of sensual gratification, is deflected (sublimated) into the realm of the spiritual. In 'The Affirmative Character of Culture,' Marcuse notes that

> only in art has bourgeois society tolerated its own ideals and taken them seriously as a general demand ... When this beautiful world is not completely represented as something long past ... it is deprived of concrete relevance by the magic of beauty ...

> [Beauty] displays what may not be promised openly and what is denied the majority. In the region of mere sensuality, separated from its connection with the ideal, beauty falls prey to the general devaluation of this sphere. Loosed from all spiritual and mental demands, beauty may be enjoyed in good conscience only in well delimited areas, with the awareness that it is only for a short period of relaxation or dissipation. (1968, 114–15)

Marcuse's understanding of aesthetics obviously shares a great deal with that of Adorno; even so, their views are not identical. Lukes summarizes the distinction by noting that 'for Marcuse, the truth of art is more the transcendence of reality; for Adorno, it is more the dissection of reality' (Lukes 1985, 111). This distinction will be taken up later in greater detail; for the moment, let us simply note that Marcuse's emphasis on the possibility of transcendence makes him more committed to what Lukes terms 'liberative' art, and less content than Adorno to rest with the admitted political impotence of 'anti-art' or 'critical art' (which includes surrealism and atonal music). For Marcuse, even the most critical forms of art, by remaining within the 'aesthetic form,' betray what he calls 'the internal ambivalence of art' (1972a, 49): 'The aesthetic necessity of art supersedes the terrible necessity of reality, sublimates its pain and pleasure; the blind suffering and cruelty of nature (and the "nature" of man) assume meaning and end – "poetic justice" ... The indictment is cancelled, and even defiance, insult, and derision – the extreme artistic negation of art – succumb to this order' (50).

A final point Lukes makes is that for Marcuse, the distinction between 'liberative' and 'affirmative' art – whether the work's glimpse of the possibility of reconciliation fosters political action or confines those universalizing impulses to the spiritual realm – is not one that rests in the work of art itself, but rather in the context in which it is deployed. Following Kant, Marcuse suggests that it is no more than art's *sensitization* of the 'aesthetic insight' (the ontological propensity to universalize that is contradicted by lived experience in contemporary society) that makes genuine art potentially revolutionary. A work of art is accorded 'revolutionary' status to the extent that 'it represents, in the exemplary fate of individuals, the prevailing unfreedom and the rebelling forces, thus breaking through the mystified (and petrified) social reality.' But although this makes 'every authentic work of art ... revolutionary,' some remain more subversive than others: 'The obvious difference in the representation of the subversive potential is due to the difference in social structure with which these works are confronted'

(Marcuse 1978, xi). It is thus 'affirmative culture' (that is, the cultural context within which the work is embedded) that, through sublimation, cancels the revolutionary potential of 'affirmative art.' The performance principle represses the aesthetic insight in order to uphold civilization against what are seen as the destructive forces of human nature. 'Liberative' art in this sense is identical to bourgeois 'affirmative' art, but with the former occurring in the context of an increasing recognition that the technological 'base' has rendered superfluous such repression (or the opposition of human 'nature' and beauty) (Lukes 1985, 120–1).

This apparent detour into the different forms of art has been necessary in order to put us in a position to fully appreciate the reasoning behind Lukes's dissatisfaction with Marcuse's aestheticism. According to Lukes, Marcuse wants to have it both ways: on the one hand, in order to be politically effective, art must be completely autonomous. For it to express its truth, it must not be subordinated to political concerns. On the other hand, this very autonomy means that an aesthetic sensibility can be disconnected from a drive for political action. The question of whether genuine art's sensitization of the aesthetic insight will lead to revolutionary action is, after all, a question about the political context in which art is produced and received, rather than about the content of the work itself.

In an extended consideration of William Shakespeare's *King Lear*, Lukes notes that it is the character of the Fool, with his disregard for conventional morality, 'who is best able, through play and autonomy, to counterpose a vision of a wholly new reality to the accepted, "prescribed" one' (1985, 136). As the play progresses, the king's descent into madness can be seen as his acceptance of the fool's vision – a rejection of the prescribed reality principle: 'Lear's imagination allows him to die joyfully, for his imagination maintains his daughter's animation. Lear's imagination, apparently substantiating Marcuse's hypothesis, seems to overcome deficient reality' (138). But for Lukes, it is crucial to bear in mind that this is only an *imaginary* overcoming of reality, and that it simultaneously leads to impotence in reality: 'The great irony of the fool, then, is that the qualities of detachment and playfulness that make possible the fool's superior insights, are the same qualities that make the fool's existence such a precarious one' (139). Lukes agrees with Marcuse's quest for a society in which a 'complex imagination' can successfully harmonize internal drives with the external environment, thereby pacifying what are often taken to be 'natural impulses' to violence; nevertheless he argues that 'the promotion of the feeling of a natural receptiveness to sensibility will erode the political drive prematurely, and will not assist in the material construction of a "pacified" environment' (126). For Lukes, in other words, although the development of a society that fosters a 'complex imagination' is a worthy *end*, the *means* to that end are the creation of the appropriate political context – a task that requires, for Lukes, not an aesthetic sensibility, but hard-headed political sense.

Stated in terms of means and ends, the Machiavellian overtones of Lukes's argument become more clear. And in this sense, the strategic considerations that motivate the choice of *King Lear* also become more obvious. Against Marcuse's prescription of a generalized cultivation of aesthetic sensibility, Lukes recommends that we 'encourage and foster "politicians" like Lear as king, who while treating aesthetics as a diversion (affirmative art), would still be dissatisfied with existence without such a diversion' (163). Lukes thus concludes: 'If the integration of politics and aesthetics, humanity and nature, sensibility and reason, is ever to take place, it will owe its chance to "politicians" – those who resisted the premature 'flight into inwardness,' and retained an obligation to instrumental interests' (165).

However, as we saw especially in the previous chapter's discussion of the dialectic of enlightenment, whether such a hard and fast distinction between means and ends can be maintained is precisely what is thrown into question by the Frankfurt School. One can imagine that Lukes might have been less sanguine in his conclusions on this score had he chosen to analyse a different Shakespeare text: *Macbeth*, for example, seems to offer an object lesson in the impossibility of achieving a pacified existence through an economy of violence. Macbeth asserts early on the Machiavellian sentiment that 'if it were done when 'tis done, then 'twere well / It were done quickly,' yet his attempts to economize the violence necessary for him to assert the throne spiral out of control and lead to an uncontainable orgy of bloodshed, foreshadowed by his acknowledgment that 'we but teach / Bloody instructions which, being taught, return / To plague th'inventor' (I, vii, 1–2 and 8–10).

Indeed, even a different reading of *King Lear* might also lead us to reject Lukes's view. Jonathan Dollimore, for example, argues that the play is notable for its insistence on the ways in which identity is socially and ideologically constructed rather than essential. Instead of seeing Lear as someone who wholly accepts the liberative views of the Fool, Dollimore insists that the play's characters, – including the king himself – 'cling even more tenaciously to the only values they know, which are precisely the values which precipitated the disintegration' (1989, 200). What *King Lear* in fact shows us, according to Dollimore, is precisely that ideological structures can be perpetuated and strengthened even as social conflict is generated out of them. The character of Edmund, for example, achieves a 'liberation' from the 'myth of innate inferiority' without a liberation from the ideology of property. And in fact, the liberation from the myth of innate inferiority, and the strengthening of the ideology of property, go hand in hand: 'Edmund embodies the process whereby, because of the contradictory conditions of its inception, a revolutionary (emergent) insight is folded back into a dominant ideology. Witnessing his fate we are reminded of how, historically, the misuse of revolutionary insight has tended to be in proportion to its truthfulness, and of how, as this very fact is obscured, the insight becomes entirely identified with (or as) its misappropriation. Machiavellianism, Gramsci has reminded us, is just one case in point' (201–2).

In his call for a division of labour – his exhortation for 'politicians' to liberate us from the barbarians so that the aesthetic sensibility might be cultivated – Lukes arguably ends up reproducing just those problems of affirmative culture that he recognizes Marcuse being at pains to point out. In his discussion of affirmative culture, Lukes notes that for Marcuse, it is in classical philosophy 'that one can discover the idea, crucial to affirmative culture, that existential satisfaction can never be achieved in the "factual world."' (Lukes 1985, 100). In the works of Plato and Aristotle, the happiness of philosophical contemplation is made possible only by the subjugation of the masses (and, at least in Aristotle's case, the naturalization of slavery). This division of labour is reproduced in Lukes's demand that some (the 'politicians') remain subject to the concrete and ruthless pragmatism of the performance principle.

In seeking to avoid the problems of the premature integration of aesthetics and politics, Lukes, like the Greeks, suggests that the disentanglement of basic and surplus repression can (at least for now) only happen at the level of individuals fulfilling particular social roles. But if the development of the aesthetic sensibility (or in Plato or Aristotle's terms, philosophical contemplation) really does lead to greater happiness – a point that Lukes does not dispute – this division of labour would require precisely the sort of social domination it is supposed to overcome. For Marcuse, following Adorno and Horkheimer (and also

Plato, whose reflection of the social division of labour in the individual psyche was in this sense honest), the retention of politicians with 'an obligation to instrumental interests' cannot help but reproduce domination rather than overcome it. A politically free society is one in which aesthetic needs are satisfied precisely *without* being confined to the 'artistic' sphere. It is 'the "end" of art through its realization' (Marcuse 1972a, 51). Even though Lukes's argument would seem to have some prima facie merit on strategic grounds, the logic of Marcuse's theorizations seems to suggest instead that what is to be distinguished is not political insights from aesthetic ones, but rather those political or strategic considerations which are necessary for human social life, and those which function to perpetuate domination.

Marcuse's only concession to 'strategic' considerations, in this sense, is his unwillingness to categorically embrace non-violence. Rather, he insists on a rather vague distinction in *Counterrevolution and Revolt* between 'violence' and 'revolutionary force.' In a 'counterrevolutionary situation,' Marcuse writes, 'violence is the weapon of the Establishment.' What Marcuse terms, 'revolutionary force,' on the other hand, is a 'coordinated action by masses or classes capable of subverting the established system in order to build a socialist society.' Marcuse bluntly admits that at the time of his writing (the early 1970s), 'in the United States, the conditions for such action do not prevail' (1972b, 53). In this sense, Marcuse's prescription for the cultivation of an aesthetic sensibility is (paradoxically) a strategically considered retreat from strategic considerations. It is a laying of the groundwork (at the most basic level of the biological constitution) for what Marcuse, like Adorno and Marx, would identify as a 'genuinely human' society.

As with the first point of criticism raised by Colletti, Lukes's criticism illuminates the ways in which Marcuse's project can be understood as a reconstruction of Marxism through its articulation with a Freudian account of the construction of subjectivity. The encounter of Marx and Freud in Marcuse's work allows for a historicization of the 'bourgeois science' of Freudian psychoanalysis, one that allows not only for the reversal of some of Freud's more pessimistic views on the possibilities for historical progress, but also for an understanding of certain psychological pathologies as being rooted in determinate social conditions, rather than being simply a result of individual weakness or misfortune. At the same time, the encounter provides a more thorough 'biological' grounding to Marxian social science, undercutting both a strict economism and its attendant claims to the 'historical inevitability' of socialist revolution. The twentieth century has shown that both the expansion of capitalism to the global level and its increasing penetration into the interstices of everyday life can proceed along with an apparent decline of working class–based politics. Marcuse's marriage of Freudianism and Marxism allows him to point to the moments of truth in both the appearance and the underlying reality: the ways in which subjectivity is constructed under advanced capitalism, such that libidinal pleasure can be derived from situations of domination, and the ways in which a basis for liberation can be found in the id or the unconscious. To understand this fully requires an examination of Marcuse's treatment of the category of labour – the transformation of nature – itself.

Beyond Adorno: Play and Labour

Among other things, the preceding sections of this chapter have sought to point to the ways in which the linchpin of Marcuse's political project is the possibility of, as Jameson puts it 'libidinally satisfying work,' or what Luke calls 'the fusion of Eros with *techne*' (1994, 201). This section and the following one pursue this concept in a bit more detail. It is on this point that the differences between Marcuse and Adorno can be registered most clearly. It should first be noted that both are (like Marx and Rousseau) interested in overcoming the established division of labour. As we saw in the previous chapter, however, Adorno's understanding of liberation involved interrogating Marx's claim that the proletariat constituted a 'universal class.' For Adorno, liberation equally required universalization of the (bourgeois) position of the 'spectator,' able to experience the world 'without dread.' It is in Odysseus' escape from the Sirens that 'the enjoyment of art and manual labor *break apart*' (Horkheimer and Adorno 1987, 34; emphasis added).

For Marcuse, Adorno's metaphor is telling: the claim that these two things 'broke apart,' and thus were once fused, is one that deserves to be explored. This goal of a '*recherche de la temps perdu*' fuels Marcuse's insistence on the importance of a Freudian framework for understanding human society. Following Freud, Marcuse claims that 'the "struggle for existence" is originally a struggle for pleasure: culture begins with the collective implementation of this aim. *Later*, however, the struggle for existence is organized in the interests of domination: the *erotic basis of culture is transformed*' (Marcuse 1987, 125; emphases added). Moreover, for both Marcuse and Freud, what occurs at the level of the history of the social – the establishment of domination and the necessity to labour – is homologous to the establishment of a repressive 'reality principle' in the formation of the human individual. In this sense, Marcuse asserts, Freud is wrong in his 'basic assumption that the "struggle for existence" (that is, for the "satisfaction of the great vital needs") is *per se* anti-libidinous in so far as it necessitates the regimentation of the instinct by a constraining reality principle' (213).[11] At both the level of the social and the level of the individual, in the mists of prehistorical time, there is a model of gratification that is not based on the repression that Freud thought necessary for civilized life.

For Marcuse, this model of gratification can now finally be recuperated, given that advanced technology has the potential to abolish scarcity. But it should be emphasized that both the prehistory of the individual subject and the prehistory of society provide only a *model* of non-surplus repressive gratification. Marcuse's call for a rejection of the established reality principle is not to be taken as a call for a return to either an infantile personality structure or a paleolithic mode of social organization.

Such a goal would in any event be impossible, given the irreversible historicity of human development. We may recall that for Adorno, the dialectic of enlightenment suggests that the goal of abolishing scarcity and recuperating the rule of the pleasure principle is an impossible one, if the means employed are the ones traditionally associated with establishing of security in the face of nature's hostility. The totalizing logic of instrumental rationality is such that domination is only intensified as technological progress makes these goals 'objectively' realizable. The addition of a psychological dimension to the Marxian dialectic, for Adorno, only serves to show how the working class has internalized repression, in that it too often struggles not for socialism, but for barbarism. Marcuse, in contrast, emphasizes that the rule of the reality principle never completely eclipses what preceded it. The 'logic of gratification' lives on in the 'unreal' dimension of phantasy and in cultural archetypes such as Orpheus and Narcissus. Moreover, for Marcuse, a recuperation of the rule of the pleasure principle is more than just possible; contrary to what is asserted by Adorno and Horkheimer, the intensification of domination may in fact *increase* the likelihood of liberation.

Marcuse notes some striking similarities between Freud's understanding of the development of civilization and Adorno and Horkheimer's notion of the dialectic of enlightenment:

> Recurrently Freud emphasizes that, as civilization progresses, guilt feeling is 'further reinforced,' 'intensified,' is 'ever-increasing.' The evidence adduced by Freud is twofold: first, he derives it analytically from the theory of the instincts, and, second, he finds the theoretical analysis corroborated by the great diseases and discontents of contemporary civilization: an enlarged cycle of wars, ubiquitous persecution, anti-Semitism, genocide, bigotry, and the enforcement of 'illusions,' toil, sickness, and misery in the midst of growing wealth and knowledge. (78)

That Freud found psychoanalysis to be of use primarily to the afflicted bourgeoisie further suggests that his theory was confirmed by the practice. Thus, as with the dialectic of enlightenment, Freudian theory implies that this growth of enforced illusions and mental illness alongside the progress of science and enlightenment humanism is a thoroughly *logical* prediction for the development of civilization:

> Since culture obeys an inner erotic impulse which bids it bind mankind into a closely knit mass, it can achieve this aim only by means of its vigilance in fomenting an ever-increasing sense of guilt ... If civilization is an inevitable course of development from the group of the family to the group of humanity as a whole, then an intensification of the sense of guilt ... will be inextricably bound up with it, until perhaps the sense of guilt may swell to a magnitude that individuals can hardly support. (Freud, quoted in Marcuse 1987, 80)

The conclusion, which Marcuse applies perhaps as much to Adorno as to Freud: 'Originating in renunciation and developing under progressive renunciation, civilization tends toward self-destruction' (1987, 83). The progress of civilization, or enlightenment, itself points to the 'inner limits' of the reality principle (77).

Up to this point, Marcuse seems to differ from Adorno only in temperament. As Steven Vogel quips: 'Marcuse is sometimes just Adorno in a good mood' (Vogel 1996, 137). For Vogel, a crucial feature of both Adorno and Marcuse is that both are 'deeply suspicious of activity *as such*: it is too closely bound up for [Marcuse] with "productivity," "the performance principle," and hence domination' (138). Vogel's reading of Marcuse thus emphsizes the importance of the prehistorical (or 'subhistorical') sources of latter's utopianism: 'The deep "subhistorical" past [Marcuse] yearns for is one that precedes human action. His dream is of a world without difference or change ... *This* is why real human practice always appears in Marcuse's work as "toil" and why he repeatedly returns to the daydream of a totally automated world where labor would be unnecessary' (139; emphasis in original).

But such a tendentious judgment ignores the fact that Marcuse's political theory focuses centrally on the category of labour and on the possibilities for deriving libidinal satisfaction therefrom. Rehearsing the central hypothesis of *Eros and Civilization*, Marcuse notes: 'The elimination of surplus-repression would *per se* tend to eliminate, not labor, but the organization of the human existence into an instrument of labor. If this is true, the emergence of a non-[surplus] repressive reality principle would alter rather than destroy the social organization of labor: the liberation of Eros could create new and durable work relations' (1987, 155). In an endnote, Vogel does qualify the above judgment; nevertheless he insists that the eroticization of work, as described by Marcuse, 'doesn't really sound like work at all.' It 'doesn't sound like work,' for Vogel, because it is explicitly 'purposeless': 'The fundamental ontological characteristic of labor as conscious world changing is something [Marcuse] never emphasizes' (Vogel 1996, 203n140).

Again, Marcuse's challenge to Freud's essentialization of the 'reality principle' can serve as a model for his response to the division that structures this 'fundamental ontological characteristic of labor.' For Vogel, something that is 'purposeless' self-evidently cannot be 'work.' 'Work' is the project of consciously changing the world, and thus is purposive by definition. Activity that is 'purposeless,' since it is not work, but that even so is activity, is defined as 'play.' 'Play' is activity that is undertaken with *itself* as its purpose: 'Play is entirely subject to the pleasure principle: pleasure is in the movement itself in so far as it activates erotogenic zones ... Work, on the other hand, serves ends outside itself – namely, the ends of self-preservation' (Marcuse, 1987, 214). But the idea that activity *either* serves the end of self-preservation *or* is governed by the pleasure principle is precisely the one that Marcuse is attempting to counter. 'Eroticized labour' is not purposeless labour, but rather an activity that is both purposive (in Vogel's sense) and simultaneously in accordance with the demands of the pleasure principle. The dissolution of the performance principle becomes possible if a form of social organization is possible such that 'work pleasure [i.e. sublimated pleasure] and libidinal pleasure usually coincide' (219). Marcuse thus is not suggesting that the conscious transformation of the external environment can be dispensed with (even under conditions of a 'pacified' nature), but rather that such activity need not be divorced from desublimated pleasure. From a Marcusean perspective, 'work per se is a biological/ontological necessity; work as toil is an historical phenomenon, the consequence of domination, a specific "organization of scarcity"' (G. Horowitz 1977, 187).

It was at this point that Adorno's analysis was seen to break off. As we saw at the conclusion of the previous chapter, for Adorno, pleasure – an experience of the 'fullness of life' – seemed inextricably tied to violence and subjugation. The transformation of nature (both external and internal) that is necessary to sustain a recognizably human existence has thus far been made possible only through an instrumental rationality – one which is capable of a violence that both demands repression and that inexorably returns. For Adorno, this perpetual scarring has been the unshakable foundation of human subjectivity. The possibility of its removal, for Adorno, lies at the very limits of the imaginable and is not susceptible to positive representation. Marcuse, in contrast – especially in his *Essay on Liberation*, with its discussion of the 'new sensibility,' provides a theorization of 'a concrete acting out of the Utopian impulse' (Jameson 1971, 111): the possibility of work without this (surplus) repression. Marcuse's discussions of the possibility of a 'new sensibility' can be understood as a response to Adorno as well as to the 'dark philosophers of Enlightenment,' whose 'honesty' Adorno admired: Nietzsche, Sade, Freud, Weber. These thinkers all point to the limitations of the form of subjectivity characteristic of 'Enlightenment,' and to the implication of domination in instrumental reason, but they do not acknowledge the possibility that such forms of subjectivity and rationality are historical rather than transcendental categories.

It is important to emphasize from the start, however, the critical distance that is to be inserted between Marcuse's discussion of the 'new sensibility' and the particular form taken in its 'concrete acting out' – that is, between the theorization and the practice of the 'Utopian impulse.' The 'psychedelic search,' for example, contains a 'kernel of truth' in its search for 'a revolution in perception, for a new sensorium,' but this truth content is 'vitiated [by] its narcotic character' (Marcuse 1972a, 44). As with art, the new sensibility is only liberative if the issues it raises are confronted at the level of social organization. If this distinction between the theory and the practice of the new sensibility were to be collapsed, then works such as *The Aesthetic Dimension* could indeed be understood as a retreat from politics, and Marcuse's relevance as a *political* thinker, in the wake of the failure of the countercultural movements of the 1960s and early 1970s, could be dismissed. Instead, however, following Jameson

(1971), we might read Marcuse's understanding of the new sensibility 'as a dress rehearsal of Utopia, as a foreshadowing of ultimate concrete social liberation. The immediate contingent freedom of the new life-style must therefore function as *figures* of Freedom in general; and without this characteristic movement in them from the particular to the general ... from individual experience to that universal liberation for which the experience stands, they remain a matter of individual narcosis, of individual salvation in the midst of the collective shipwreck' (111–12; emphasis in original).

With this in mind, we can return to note some of the new sensibility's specific characteristics. The new sensibility is, first and foremost, characterized by a need to liberate the erotic drives by abolishing the surplus-repression that characterizes life under the 'performance principle.' New 'vital needs' are stimulated by advanced technology, which has rendered certain forms of repression superfluous to social life, although they have remained because they are necessary in order to perpetuate domination. 'Utopian possibilities are inherent in the technical and technological forces of advanced capitalism and socialism' (Marcuse 1972a, 13). Thus while keeping the fruits of technological progress, Marcuse advocates an abandonment of science and technology's current orientation for one that is 'in accord with a new sensibility – the demands of the life instincts,' a sensibility that is itself 'expressive of the needs of a new type of man' (28). We could than satisfy the demands of the life instincts through a form of activity that entails 'the development of needs *beyond* the realm of necessity and of necessary waste' (Marcuse 1987, 93; emphasis in original). Such activity would combine the features of work and play: the transformation of nature that is necessary for human survival could be accomplished in a manner that is in itself instinctually gratifying. Purposive activity would meld with 'purposive purposelessness.' In other words, finally, human beings would be able to produce 'according to the laws of beauty.'

The argument for the possibility of 'libidinally satisfying work,' by drawing a careful distinction between basic and surplus repression – between the technical base and a technological mindset requiring ever-increasing specialization in the division of labour, and between alienated toil and unalienated praxis, aims to undermine the dichotomies between labour and leisure, between sublimated artistic freedom and desublimated political freedom, and between freedom and necessity. In so doing, it also begins to undermine the distinction between action and fantasy. In its relative autonomy from the reality principle, fantasy remains closely connected with the pleasure principle. If the 'truth-value' of fantasy 'corresponds to an experience of its own – namely, the surmounting of the antagonistic human reality' (Marcuse 1987, 143), the erotic drive to 'establish ever-higher unities' can be seen as a 'vital need' to bring 'human reality' into line with fantasy and the pleasure principle.

But Vogel (1996) reminds us that 'practice already contains within itself the moment of what Adorno calls nonidentity. Indeed, it is just this that distinguishes it from "theory": unlike thinking about the world, changing the world is difficult, is fallible, encounters resistance, requires planning, and so on' (96). This idea is what grounds Vogel's critique of Marcuse: 'Real practice ... in fact crucially involves the moment of resistance and otherness in the world; that is what separates it not just from theory but from "phantasy"' (139). For Vogel, Marcuse's claim that action and fantasy can be reconciled in a 'new science' is grounded in an unsustainable teleological view of nature, one that is rendered especially visible in certain passages of *Eros and Civilization*. At one point, Marcuse writes that natural objects, 'to be what they are they *depend* on the erotic attitude: they receive their *telos* only in it.' Even more strongly, he claims: 'The world of nature [at present] is a world of oppression, cruelty, and pain, as is the human world; like the latter, it awaits its liberation.' Marcuse's Hegelianism or romanticism here seems to shine through, in that he sees all forms of contradiction and conflict as moving toward an ultimate beneficent resolution: 'The song of Orpheus pacifies the natural world, reconciles the lion with the lamb and the lion with man' (Marcuse 1987, 166; emphasis in original). In *One-Dimensional Man* Marcuse argues that scientific understanding is historical and that scientific rationality 'projects a world' as much as it describes one. Does he mean that if human beings adopt the right frame of mind ('erotic attitude'), all forms of oppression and pain – in the non-human world as well as the social realm – will disappear? Is it really sufficient to 'project' a liberated or pacified world?

Before declaring Marcuse guilty of this sort of idealist relativism, we might recall the distinction that was asserted earlier in the context of the 'new sensibility,' between its theorization and its existence in practice. Marcuse is indeed sensitive to the difference between, on the one hand, the way the 'new sensibility' might be unfolded theoretically through a historicization of Freudian psychological topography and Kantian aesthetics, and on the other hand the practice of the new sensibility among the members of the Woodstock generation (the latter, as we noted at the very outset, also taking place during an era of dramatic expansion and intensification of capitalist relations). This sensitivity, along with the very *excess* of the rhetorical formulations cited earlier (the reconciliation of lion and lamb, for example), should perhaps caution us against taking fantasy too literally. The 'reconciliation' of lion and lamb is perhaps best understood – as Jameson notes of the relationship between the new sensibility and freedom – as a *figure* of a pacified nature. To suggest that Marcuse's understanding of a pacified nature would be one in which lion and lamb were actually reconciled would be akin to suggesting that, according to Marcuse, under socialism everybody would be required to ingest LSD on a regular basis.

This is not to suggest that Marcuse's speculations are to be dismissed as mere flights of fancy. As we saw in de Man's reading of Rousseau in chapter 3, the literal is not easily distinguished from the metaphorical; and Marcuse does, after all, in some sense want us to take fantasy literally – or more precisely, to recognize its truth content. That truth content, as we have seen, lies in fantasy's connection to the pleasure principle and the 'logic of gratification.' Moreover, technological development, and even more importantly the erotic drive that manifests itself as a cultural force, emphasize the tendential movement toward fantasy's realization:

> In light of the idea of non-repressive sublimation, Freud's definition of Eros as striving to 'form living substance into ever greater unities, so that life may be prolonged and brought to higher development' takes on added significance. The biological drive becomes a cultural drive. The pleasure principle reveals its own dialectic. The erotic aim of sustaining the entire body as subject–object of pleasure calls for the continual refinement of the organism, the intensification of its receptivity, the growth of its sensuousness. The aim generates its own projects of realization: the abolition of toil, the amelioration of the environment, the conquest of disease and decay, the creation of luxury. All these activities flow directly from the pleasure principle, and, at the same time, they constitute *work* which associates individuals to 'greater unities'; no longer confined within the mutilating dominion of the performance principle, they modify the impulse without deflecting it from its aim. There is sublimation and, consequently, culture; but this sublimation proceeds in a system of expanding and enduring libidinal relations, which are in themselves work relations. (Marcuse 1987, 211–12; emphasis in original)

Vogel (1996) notes that Marcuse's understanding of the possibility of a 'new science' is correct in the sense that it recognizes the extent to which our environment is a social construction: 'If a new social order would produce for itself a new worldview, this also means that it would inhabit a new world' (135). 'Science,' be it old or new, is in this sense always ideological, and neither sort can claim to be a value-free projection of the world. Thus Vogel asserts that Marcuse's view is also wrong, to the extent that it anthropomorphizes nature; he contends that nature itself 'awaits liberation' and thus might prefer one ideology over another. A new understanding of nature, embedded in a new form of society, will not prevent hungry lions from devouring available lambs.

But to suggest that all projections of the world are 'ideological' is not to reduce the choice to mere subjective preference. Marcuse's claim is that a 'new' science would be *objectively* preferable. This objective preference is, first of all, aesthetic: 'The Orphic Eros transforms being: he masters cruelty and death through liberation. His language is *song*, and his work is *play*. Narcissus' life is that of *beauty*, and his existence is *contemplation*. These images refer to the *aesthetic dimension* as the one in which their reality principle must be sought and validated' (Marcuse 1987, 171; emphases in original). Following Kant, Marcuse reminds us that the realm of the aesthetic – the faculty of judgment – is itself governed by objective laws: 'In the aesthetic imagination, sensuousness generates *universally* valid principles for an *objective* order' (177; emphases added). These universal principles, in turn, are 'hard-wired' into our very biological constitution – in the erotic drive and the need to establish greater and greater unities.

The Ego and Alienation

Marcuse's argument is thus that the biological constitution of the human being predisposes us to thrive under conditions in which our interactions with the external world are governed by something resembling the 'new sensibility,' rather than the 'domination of nature' approach afforded by instrumental or 'one-dimensional' rationality. But his claim to having discovered a 'biological foundation for socialism' here refers not so much to the drives of the id as to the synthesizing function of the ego. This is a crucial distinction, the ignorance of which can lead commentators on Marcuse to either confusion or easy caricature. Although the continued repression of desire testifies to the persistence of unfreedom in contemporary society, Marcuse's program does not simply call for the anarchic liberation of the drives. As Gad

Horowitz (1977) puts it: 'It is perhaps too easy not to notice that what Marcuse is describing is not a simple regression but a dialectical one, a regression under the control of and in the service of the ego (civilization)' (202).

Here we can see the significance of Horowitz's insistence (see note 11) that the development of the ego and the processes of (basic) repression and sublimation be seen as precisely *natural* aspects of human development, and that sublimation be understood 'as a "condominium" of the ego and the id.' (191, citing Robert Waelder). On this account, it is not the development of the ego per se, but rather the radical separation of the ego from the id, that is the mark of human alienation.

Horowitz's claim is both confirmed and complicated by Marcuse's insistence that 'repression is a historical phenomenon. The effective subjugation of the instincts to repressive controls is imposed not by nature but by man' (Marcuse 1987, 16). In part, the complication stems – as Horowitz notes elsewhere – from Marcuse's apparent carelessness in distinguishing 'repression' from 'surplus-repression' within the text. Horowitz's reading makes sense as long as the 'repressive controls' are understood as referring to *surplus*-repression. But if this passage refers to surplus-repression (that is, repression imposed 'by man') as the 'effective subjugation of the instincts,' then we would have to insist on seeing the ego – or more precisely the 'condominium' of ego and id, with the drives already under some control or direction – as itself 'instinctual.'

A similar argument is implied in John Bokina's claim that 'Marcuse's central point [is] his concept of an erotically instinctual individual' (Bokina 1994, 14). Here again, we should be wary of oversimplification. It would be easy to suggest that this concept points to an essentialist humanism at the heart of the Marcusean project – to the notion that all human beings are endowed with an instinctual erotic drive that both renders 'aesthetic' judgments objective and provides the 'biological foundation for socialism.' Marcuse's postmodern critics, for example, suggest that this essentialist universalization of aesthetic experience – the insistence, noted earlier, and crucial to his theorizations, that there is a vital human need to establish greater and greater unities, rooted in the erotic drive – raises troublesome questions. According to these critics, the claim that the 'vital need' for this type of experience transcends a variety of subject positions seems to trap Marcuse's putatively radical politics within an ultimately conservative, colonizing discursive framework, one that again reveals Marcuse's ideological biases. Carol Becker provides a typical example of this line of argument: 'But Marcuse's concept assumes a unified subject and a coherent self that can escape alienation ... In the same vein, Marcuse implies that art can transcend racial, gender, and cultural differences through certain aesthetic forms. These forms are undoubtedly Eurocentric, grounded exclusively within the Western tradition' (1994, 179–80).

But it is possible to read the notion of an 'erotically instinctual individual' in a different way. Instead of reading it as an expression of an ahistorical 'human nature,' we might read it as (to return once again to Jameson's formulation) a 'figure for Freedom.' On this reading, the 'erotic instinct' is one whose ontological status is less certain. True, Marcuse asserts that 'morality is a "disposition" of the organism, perhaps rooted in the erotic drive to counter aggressiveness' (Marcuse 1972a, 19). However, the next sentence adds: 'We *would then have*, this side of all "values," an instinctual foundation for solidarity among human beings – a solidarity which *has been* effectively repressed in line with the requirements of class society' (19–20; emphasis added). The future conditional tense at the sentence's beginning is at odds with the sentence's conclusion, which looks backwards, suggesting that this 'human nature' is perhaps no more than a possibility. The next paragraph goes on to note that 'this foundation is itself historical' and that 'changes in morality may 'sink down' into the 'biological' dimension and modify organic behaviour.' (20). Marcuse's 'central point' may thus be the (objective) desirability of getting to the point where Eros may at last sink down to the instinctual level.

A similar reading strategy can be deployed with the second part of the term: the 'instinctual individual.' The oxymoronic character of the phrase can be highlighted by noting that 'individuality' (personality, character) is generally understood to be a reflection of the *transcendence* of instinct, which is common to all members of the species. Vogel notes that at the conclusion of Marcuse's *Essay on Liberation*, this contradiction is especially clear: 'The last paragraph of *An Essay on Liberation* begins by calling once again for new and noncompetitive "incentives" to be "built into the instinctual structure" of humans as the basis for a free society, but ends by quoting "a young black girl" who speaks of such a society as one where "for the first time in our life, we shall be free to think about what we are going to do." There is no recognition shown that acting from instinct and "thinking what we are going to do" are *mutually exclusive*' (Vogel 1996, 204n 152; emphasis in original).

But if, as Gad Horowitz suggests, the basic repression necessary for the development of the ego is itself necessitated by human biology, rather than by a particular form of social organization, then it becomes possible to see 'thinking what we are going to do' precisely as an expression of 'instinct.' The two are in conflict under the rule of the current reality principle. With the absence of surplus-repression, it could become possible to express individuality through obedience to instinct: through the discharge of erotic energy in the form of desublimated or unalienated labour. Also in that final paragraph, Marcuse speaks of 'the social expression of the liberated work instinct.' This 'instinct' can be 'socially expressed' in the form of cooperative labour – that is, through engagement in the project of (re)building society (right down to the level of the rebuilding of human instincts) in accordance with the laws of beauty.

One final elaboration of what Bokina identifies as Marcuse's 'central point' remains to be explored, through the pairing of 'erotic' and 'individual.' With this pairing, we raise the issue of whether Marcuse's particular psychoanalytic framework remains valid in the face of the rise of object relations theory. According to C. Fred Alford, more recent developments in psychoanalytic research suggest that Marcuse's 'key failure ... is his insensitivity to human relatedness, to the way in which not eros but relationships fulfill the self – or rather, the way in which eros is always already part of a relationship with another subject' (Alford 1994, 131). This criticism is especially important for our purposes, since such a *relational* view of the self and of Eros seems to mirror the ecological critique of atomistic science and liberal individualism.

Marcuse's optimism regarding the alleviation of surplus-repression hinges on his seeing repression as a consequence of the confrontation with the father (that is, the reality principle), whereas Freud's pessimism stems from his understanding of repression as primarily a consequence of the prohibition on incest (the need to separate from the mother). In this sense, Alford is suggesting that Marcuse fails to distinguish adequately between necessary and unnecessary forms of repression: 'Marcuse seeks not merely freedom from labor so that the entire body might remain libidinally cathected – that is, what he calls polymorphous perversity. Rather, Marcuse seeks an erotic relationship to the self so complete that others are unnecessary and become a burden, their presence reminding us of the pain of separation, incompleteness, loss, and death that accompany us throughout life' (1994, 136). Nowhere is this more clear, for Alford, than in Marcuse's 'selective' readings of the myths of Orpheus and Narcissus. Marcuse suggests that these two figures represent 'the image of joy and fulfillment,' but he neglects to highlight the fact that each was 'fixated on himself unto death' (137). Alford, for his part, does concede that for Marcuse, orphic and narcissistic impulses, just like art and the new sensibility, are in themselves insufficient and must have a social component to be fully realized. The deaths of the mythic individuals in the face of a hostile reality principle do not necessarily entail their inability to function as the governing drives of a new reality principle under a changed social order: 'Only when the protest against the reality principle is *shared* may eros become a social force, the builder of culture and communities and a medium of human relationships' (ibid. emphasis added).

We might recall then, in this context, that in the realm of social labour, Marcuse's vision remains one of a *social order*, rather than one of individualistic, anarchic abandonment. Erotic individuality remains embedded in social relationships. As Agger explains, 'the erotization of labor ... does not mean that human beings would act with total abandon, heedless of each other and of the collective imperatives of survival. Rather, a new division of labor and organizational rationality can emerge that fosters erotized nonalienated work' (Agger, 1992, 175). Marcusean freedom is thus not a total absence of authority so much as 'nonauthoritarian authority' (176–8). Even in the absence of surplus repression, there is an undeniably social (or relational) character to the mode of 'instinctual' gratification. For Agger, Marcuse's vision of free and non-alienated labour (or 'libidinally satisfying work') relies on 'two integral components' that operate at the level of the social organization of production: 'workers control of decision making regarding investment strategies and day-to-day operations of the plant or office; and workers control of the technological apparatus such that workers do not become estranged from the productive means and dominated by those who have mastered them' (189).

But Agger's response remains at the level of the social, and whether it can function adequately as a figure for psychic freedom remains an open question. Whether the 'erotic' (the drive to establish unity) and 'individual[ization]' can be reconciled at the psychic level seems to rest finally on the question of the status of the ego – its 'instinctuality' (the central term of Marcuse's 'central claim') or in other words finally its 'naturality.' As we have seen, the distinction between basic and surplus repression requires us to see the ego as in some sense instinctual. The ego is natural, and only *surplus* repression is historical. But toward the end of *Eros and Civilization*, Marcuse seems to be suggesting something rather different. Quoting Horkheimer and Adorno, he asserts: 'All pleasure is societal – in the unsublimated no less than in the sublimated impulses. Pleasure originates in alienation.' Marcuse then provides his own elaboration of Horkheimer and Adorno's claim: 'What distinguishes pleasure from the blind satisfaction of want is *the instinct's refusal* to exhaust itself in immediate satisfaction, its ability to build up and use barriers for intensifying fulfillment. This *instinctual refusal* has done the work of domination, it can also serve the opposite function: eroticize non-libidinal relations, transform biological tension and relief into free happiness' (Marcuse 1987, 227; emphases added). The 'refusal,' capable of 'eroticizing' relations and transforming brute satisfaction into pleasure, is the work of the ego. But this work is a refusal to gratify the instincts immediately, *and* at the same time is itself 'instinctual.'

It is perhaps for this reason rather than from simple carelessness that Marcuse in fact says only that 'repression is historical' and nor that surplus-repression is historical (1987, 16). The moment of instinctual refusal of the instincts – the moment of basic repression – is the moment at which the historical begins. The ego, the *'temps perdu'* of non-surplus repression, is historical – and even if it is not ascertainable as historical fact, we can at least have recourse to it as a historical 'figure.'

Thus, for Marcuse, alienation – or what we should term, to avoid confusion, 'basic alienation' – is necessary: a 'vital human need.' 'No longer employed as instruments for retaining men in alienated performances, the barriers against absolute gratification would become elements of human freedom; they would protect that other alienation in which pleasure originates – man's alienation not from himself but from mere nature: his free self-realization' (1987, 227).

Yet the distinction between 'man's alienation from himself' and alienation from 'mere nature' is a troubling one. First of all, this 'mere nature' is what Marcuse elsewhere seeks to 'liberate' or to be 'reconciled' with. This difficulty can be dispensed with if we suggest that Marcuse here is using the term 'mere nature' interchangeably with 'blind necessity' (ibid.). More difficult to deal with is that the foregoing discussion of the ego and the instincts has suggested that 'free self-realization' does require a certain amount of 'man's alienation from himself.' This is necessary both at the individual psychic level (the ego's refusal and direction of the drives) and at the social level (the establishment of a social order). That it is to be non-surplus repressive is not to say that it is not alienation.

The same distinction also raises a problem that is not unrelated to the question of the status of the ego. Marcuse suggests that the freedom that originates in 'that other alienation' would take the following form: 'Beyond want and anxiety, human activity becomes *display* – the free manifestation of potentialities' (1987, 190; emphasis added). Furthermore, 'in a genuinely humane civilization, the human existence will be play rather than toil, and man will live in *display*, rather than need' (188; emphasis added). For Marcuse, in other words, 'that other alienation' – the alienation from 'mere nature' necessary for the development of an ego – is what allows for freedom. Distinct from the alienation of human beings from themselves that manifests itself in surplus repression and social relations of domination, this alienation makes possible the activity of 'display.' However, this activity of display must lie in constant tension with the desire for 'public esteem,' which Rousseau saw as 'the first step toward inequality' (Rousseau 1987, 64). Marcuse does not offer us a utopia that can be achieved once and for all, but rather the vision of a humane society, which would require constant vigilance and work to be sustained.

Although the approach that I have been arguing is central to Marcuse's work – the distinction between 'basic' and 'surplus' – is without question of crucial importance to discussions of alienation from nature, the identification of 'basic' alienation with alienation from 'mere nature' and of 'surplus' alienation with 'man's alienation from himself,' is too simple. As we saw in this chapter and the previous one, when it comes to the transformations undertaken for the purposes of survival and securing gratification, at least under current conditions there can be no reliable distinction between 'mere nature' and the social. 'Alienation' is an overdetermined phenomenon, always caused both by alienation from 'mere nature' (itself always socially conditioned, in any event) and by human beings' alienation from themselves. The project of an ecological politics should be to distinguish between those forms of interaction with the natural world which are *necessary* to the flourishing of human and other forms of life, and those forms of interaction which are *surplus* to it. Human existence necessarily involves 'alienation from nature' in some form. And an adequate understanding of this category is necessary to an ecological politics that can no longer rely on the category of 'nature.'

CHAPTER 7

Denaturalizing Ecological Politics

The previous four chapters have sought to open the terrain of alienation from nature, seeing this as a useful location from which to think about the problems of ecological politics in a postmodern (or postnatural) age. In an era in which a widely professed commitment to 'sustainable development' sits rather comfortably beside the voracious consumption of non-renewable resources and a related intensification of stark social inequalities, what seems to be needed is an ecological politics that is 'denaturalized,' or that does not rely on an abstract, reified, 'anti-social' conception of nature. Before any concluding reflections, however, and before a return to the problems posed in the first two chapters, a clarification about the character of this project, by way of a highly abbrieviated summary of the previous four chapters, is in order.

The particular readings of Rousseau, Marx, Adorno, and Marcuse I have presented go at least some of the way toward developing the foundations for such an ecological politics that is appropriately denaturalized. All four theorists suggested that ecological problems, or problems in the human relationship with nature, are intimately connected with social problems, and therefore that meaningfully addressing the issue of environmental sustainability will require a fundamental reordering of social relations. At the same time, each of the four previous chapters concluded by noting an ambiguity or difficulty in how the theorist at hand dealt with the problematic of alienation. In each case, an examination of divergent readings or interpretations allowed these ambiguities to be highlighted.

For Rousseau, the troubled human relationship with nature is inseparable from social inequality. He recognizes that an unmediated return to nature is impossible, and he attempts to work out a solution to these problems at a number of levels. That none of his posited 'solutions' is workable serves to highlight the complex relations among the various levels at which the problematic of 'alienation from nature' can be seen to operate: alienation from nature is indispensable for human social life, and at the same time it is the cause of social domination. Rousseau's insistence on seeking a solution to the problem of alienation suggests that he felt that the latter characteristic of alienation – that it is the cause of social domination – need not be seen as a necessary feature. Colletti's reading of Rousseau highlights for us that Rousseau's apparent self-contradictions are the result of an inability to distinguish between the social division of labour and commodity exchange (an inability that plays out only slightly differently in de Man and Asher Horowitz).

Colletti then notes that this distinction is made by Marx, for whom the distinction between alienation and objectification increases the sense that not all alienation need have pernicious consequences. For Marx, the 'humanization of nature and the naturalization of man' – that is the overcoming of the alienation (properly so-called) that leads to domination – could be realized by achieving a certain transparency in social organization, or a rationalization of heretofore mystified social relations. For Marx, socialist production relations would allow for an 'incorporation' of nature into the social; this would turn the transformation of nature into a social project whose goal would be beauty rather than domination.

In Marx's later works, however, there is a shift in the focus of his discussion of labour. In his 'exuberant' early works, he suggested that production might be organized entirely 'in accordance with the laws of beauty'; now he suggests that a distinction be made between the 'realm of freedom' and the 'realm of necessity.' The persistence of the latter, wherein some of the alienating characteristics of objectification that obtained under capitalism might continue to exist under socialism, prevents us from too hastly identifying either objectification with alienation from (non-human) nature, or alienation properly so-called with alienation from social processes. Without a doubt, Marx does seek to distinguish between alienation from nature and alienation from social processes; but that distinction is not easily drawn. The absence of a clear dividing line asserts itself in the shift away from the 'exuberance' and 'utopianism' of the '1844 Manuscripts,' as well as within the later works themselves – in particular, in the insistence that precapitalist social relations are 'quasi-natural,' such that domination in premodern societies is understood as inevitable. This is the outcome of necessarily mystified relations with external nature. This last claim, with its corollary that socialism can only be erected on the basis of the realization of the 'alienation from nature' (and denaturalization of the social) that occurs under capitalism, highlights for us the limits of Marx's theorizations. Marx's analysis breaks off prior to the point at which 'the rational mastery of nature' might be revealed to be yet another ideological cover for social domination, rather than the necessary precondition for its abolition.

The complex relations between alienation from 'mere nature' and alienation from social processes receive extended consideration in the work of Theodor Adorno. For Adorno, the two have historically been fused, with the result that all previous attempts to liberate human beings from the vicissitudes of nature have resulted only in the displacement and intensification of domination rather than its elimination. Adorno's analysis emphasizes the continuity between modern and premodern social forms, but does so without lapsing into a conservatism that would naturalize domination. In this account, the instrumentalization of nature, which also entails both the domination of other humans and psychological repression – is rooted in the identitarian impulses of conceptual thinking and in the separation of 'the enjoyment of art and manual labor.' A non-dominating approach to the object would thus require a reflexive turn in thought itself, whereby the violence of conceptuality would be brought to light. It is only through a 'suspension' of the survival instinct that it would be possible to genuinely separate nature from the social, instead of reproducing the blind domination of nature through a socialized second nature.

The weight of Adorno's own arguments, however – in particular, his insistence that unreflexive conceptual thinking is part of what prevents the emergence of a real distinction between humanity and nature – means that Adorno is unable or unwilling to offer any but the most elliptical positive representations of what a non-dominating approach to nature might look like. Thus Adorno leaves us with what is often read as an overwhelming pessimism, or what might more usefully be characterized as an insufficiently elaborated sense of how a non-dominating relationship with nature might be possible.

For a somewhat clearer picture of this, we turned to the work of Herbert Marcuse – in particular to his psychoanalytic rearticulation of the problematic laid out in *Dialectic of Enlightenment*. Marcuse's distinction between (basic) repression and 'surplus-repression' was seen to be mobilizable across a variety of categories. In the case of alienation from nature, we sought to develop out of Marcuse's arguments a distinction between alienation that is necessary for human social existence and alienation that reproduces social relations of domination. The distinction is one that must get beyond the antinomy with which this book began: we require this distinction if we are to steer clear of both the reifications of nature found in ecocentric deep ecology and the paralysing pessimism that seems inevitable when postmodern critiques of 'nature' are deployed in environmental politics. Marcuse's analysis shows us that the distinction is not an easy one to make. 'Basic' and 'surplus' forms of alienation are constantly evolving; furthermore, they are equiprimordial, in the sense that there can be no retreat to a point where one existed without the other. As well, the fact that social relations remain a 'second nature' (in Adorno's words, that nature 'does not yet exist') means that the distinction between basic and surplus alienation cannot be identified with a distinction between alienation from 'mere nature' and alienation from social processes, at least as these are presently figured. For Marcuse as for Adorno, social relations remain a 'second nature.' The materialist commitments of both thinkers prevent them from allowing for the possibility of purely 'cultural' objects.

The distinction between 'basic' and 'surplus' alienation from nature is not made explicitly by Marcuse; rather, it has been teased out of the logic of his other arguments, which were grounded in the more traditional concerns of political theory and which dealt less explicitly with those of human ecology. But Marcuse's theorizations, and his more 'positive' articulation of the dialectic of enlightenment, remain troubled by the persistence of the human–nature distinction that the Frankfurt School sought to undermine. This points out the more general theoretical problem when it comes to developing a Marcusean ecological politics (for all of its promising possibilities). This problem reflects the fact that Marcuse himself barely sketched the ecological implications of his theories.

Thus, although Marcuse is the final theorist whose work is considered here in depth, he is not to be exempted from the dialectical structure of the project. As was the case with the other thinkers discussed in this study, the divergent interpretations of Marcuse are symptomatic of a need for further development. Marcuse's theorizations – in particular, the basic–surplus trope – do not provide a solution or a 'last word' on the subject; they only open up the terrain on which such a development can take place. Althusser (1971) once noted that Marx's contribution was that he opened up a 'continent' for scientific exploration. (71–2). Marcuse's contribution in this sense may not be on the same scale, but it is of the same kind. At the same time, it should also be emphasized that if Marcuse does not provide us with the last word on the subject, he also did not provide the first. Post-colonial criticism teaches us that those who 'discover' new continents are rarely (if ever) the first to arrive. As I have tried to show, there is a sense in which the terrain that was 'discovered' by Marcuse was also discovered by Adorno, Marx, and Rousseau. Moreover, although Marcuse's perspective does not fully comprehend the insights of the three thinkers discussed before him, it does perhaps provide the most fully developed account of the point at which discussions of a denaturalized ecological politics can begin.

At this point, we can turn finally to consider some more recent work that has brought together the concerns of ecology with those of political theory, and that in at least some cases has developed in promising directions the sort of distinction whose importance I have been trying to assert here. The following is not intended as any sort of comprehensive overview of the current literature on ecological politics; rather, I intend it to be highly selective – to point in what has been argued is the most promising direction, that of a denaturalized ecological politics.

Let us begin these concluding reflections by turning to Andrew Dobson's *Justice and the Environment,* which is conceived explicitly as an attempt to engage with environmental issues on the terrain of political theory (and vice versa): 'This book ... is written as a conscious attempt to – at least in part – interest political theorists in environmental questions, and encourage those writing from within the environmental matrix to engage more systematically with political theory' (1998, 11).

This manifest lack of engagement between environmentalists and political theorists[1] is one that Dobson seeks quite rightly to correct. But at the end of his carefully reasoned study, he concedes. 'The suspicion that has ghosted the whole of this book is that the justice and sustainability agendas are different, and it may also be that the agenda for the defence of non-human nature is different from both of these' (262). In other words, perhaps these discourses have so little to say to each other because the concerns of many environmentalists (the defence of non-human nature), while often framed in the language of 'justice' (the just treatment of other species, or intergenerational justice in the case of sustainability), are ultimately irreconcilable with the social or political aspects of justice that are the central concern of political theory.

Dobson is surely correct to conclude that 'it would be a mistake to take common interest for granted' (ibid.). Where my approach has differed from Dobson's (which is more firmly grounded in the analytical tradition) is that I have been trying to sketch in very broad strokes the particular social circumstances in which these common interests might emerge. In his introduction, Dobson suggests two possible objections to the thesis that environmental and social justice agendas inevitably conflict. The first is that the testing of that assumption can only occur 'empirically,' and that this empirical testing has not yet been done: 'Before we can draw any firm conclusions, we need a raft of different studies designed to explore this relationship under a number of different conditions, ranging from pastoral farmers in Sudan, through the urban poor in Brasilia and New York, to stockbrokers in south-east England – and all points in between and beyond' (4). The second possible objection to the thesis that 'political' and 'environmental' justices are incompatible is that 'both environmental sustainability and social justice are contested concepts.' (5). It is to this latter objection that Dobson devotes the bulk of his book. But his careful analysis of the compatibility (or lack thereof) of various prevailing definitions of 'environmental sustainability' and 'social justice' betrays the promise announced in the first potential objection. There, what was seen to be necessary was to survey the spectrum of present conditions of existence (Sudan to Brasilia to New York to southeast England), and also to look *'beyond'* those present conditions. Dobson's logical rigour makes it clear how important it is not to *assume* that the environmental and social justice agendas are compatible. But, as all four thinkers discussed in the previous chapters argued, any emphasis on the empirical risks hypostatizing the world as it is. That is why this book has focused on thinkers who demand that we look beyond the empirically given facts of social life.

At the same time, an insistence on the importance of 'utopian' thinking should not be allowed to overwhelm real physical or biological limits. The thinkers discussed in this book have been chosen because they provide 'utopian' speculations that are nevertheless carefully circumscribed, or grounded in the real but contradictory truths of lived experience. Just as Dobson reminds us that we cannot assume that environmental and social justice agendas are compatible in the present, we equally cannot assume that they will be harmonized in the future, simply on the basis of wishful thinking. The thinkers discussed in the previous four chapters show (perhaps most forcefully in the case of Adorno) that the fact of human frailty, the fact that we depend on particular conditions in our environment for our existence, and that this necessitates a transformation of our environment, means that a thoroughly non-disruptive relationship with the natural environment is impossibile.

A more promising approach than Dobson's is taken in the recent work of Michael Zimmerman. Zimmerman's impressively catholic *Contesting Earth's Future* moves away from the more explicit Heideggerianism of his earlier work (see note 7, chapter 6), and seeks to press against the connections between reactionary politics and the defence of nature: 'Hence, one aim of this book is to encourage radical ecologists to take into account not only the political dangers facing every revolutionary movement, but also the specific dangers posed by movements seeking to improve humanity's relation to "nature." A related aim is to examine the extent to which the views of radical ecologists are consistent with emancipatory political orientations' (1994, 7). Zimmerman's suggestion that the connection between reactionary politics and much of radical ecology is rooted in 'death denial' or 'death anxiety' (181–3 and passim) highlights a certain affinity between Zimmerman and Adorno.

But there are important differences between the two, as well. For Zimmerman, who ultimately defends a heterodox deep ecology that entails 'adhering to a progressive view of human history, one that emphasizes compassion and development of nondual awareness' (232), overcoming death anxiety requires the development of something akin to a 'transpersonal' psychology. For Adorno, as we saw, the 'suspension of the law' of self-preservation occurs through the reflexive critique of conceptual thinking, but this is rooted in a historical materialist understanding of the nature of thought (the 'dialectic of enlightenment'). In Zimmerman, in contrast, there is a greater emphasis on the 'insight into an eternal domain that transcends, yet includes the phenomenal realm' (107), and less attention to the social structures and social relations that form the conditions of possibility of 'insights' of whatever sort. Thus Zimmerman assures us that 'those who have attained such identification [with 'Atman,' the eternal level of consciousness], however, spontaneously care for and seek to alleviate the suffering of all finite phenomena' (135). But he also acknowledges that this provides little in terms of 'concrete guidance for adjudicating complex ecological disputes' (ibid., 135) for those who have not attained the requisite level of enlightenment to solve these ecological problems 'spontaneously' – a particular weakness, given his admission that 'progress would be understood as a *very* long-term affair, not something that can be completed in a few centuries' (107; emphasis in original).

If even Zimmerman's reconstructed deep ecology is susceptible to the depoliticizing tendencies that, as we saw in chapter 1, are associated with more orthodox versions of deep ecology, we can briefly consider the other major forms of ecological thought that are more explicitly attuned to issues of social relations. Let us now consider in turn social ecology and ecofeminism.

The single person with whom the term 'social ecology' is most commonly associated is, of course, Murray Bookchin. On the first page of what is widely regarded as his most important book, *The Ecology of Freedom*, Bookchin provides the following 'fairly crisp formulation' of his central thesis: 'The very notion of the domination of nature by man stems from the very real domination of human by human' (1991, 1). Unlike deep ecologists, Bookchin sees the problem of the 'domination of nature' as one that is rooted in determinate social relations.

Perhaps even more importantly for our purposes, however, Bookchin's focus on the problem of 'hierarchy' provides a key to distinguishing – at least at a fairly high level of generality – those social relations which lead to the domination of nature. Bookchin defines hierarchy as 'the cultural, traditional and psychological systems of obedience and command, [including but not limited to] the economic and political systems to which the terms class and State most appropriately refer.' (4). Opposed to a 'hierarchical' understanding of phenomena for Bookchin is a properly 'ecological' understanding, one that emphasizes 'unity in diversity' and 'symbiotic mutualism.' As we saw was the case for ecocentrists in chapter 1, for Bookchin, ecology as a scientific discipline tends to subvert dominant understandings of the world insofar as these reify the assumptions of possessive individualism. Bookchin, however, examines hierarchy (a 'macrosociological' category) with a view to seeing whether it is necessary for social existence.

Bookchin first insists that hierarchical relations are unique to human communities and are not found in non-human nature. The categories of 'hierarchy' and 'dominance' or 'submission' are found exclusively at the level of the "social" (that is, in institutionalized human communities), and the projection of these categories onto other animals is, for Bookchin, a gross anthropomorphism. Human behaviour is more flexible than the instinctual, drive-based behaviour of 'social insects' like bees; but at the same time, human relations are institutionalized, unlike the 'specific acts of coercion by individual animals' of the sort that can be observed in non-human primates (29). 'Hierarchy,' in other words, is for Bookchin a uniquely human form of social stratification, one in which the social strata 'have a life of their own apart from the personalities who give them substance' (30).

But what makes Bookchin's analysis especially compelling for our purposes is that hierarchy is not criticized because it is simply 'unnatural' in the sense of only being found among human communities. Instead, it is subjected to a more dialectical critique, one which suggests that hierarchy can be construed as what we might term a form of 'surplus alienation from nature.' The critique of hierarchy rests on its destructiveness, both in terms of society and nature: 'But the case against hierarchy is not contingent on its uniqueness as a social phenomenon. Because hierarchy threatens the existence of social life today, it *cannot* remain a social fact. Because it threatens the integrity of organic nature, it will not continue to do so, given the harsh verdict of 'mute' and "blind" nature' (37; emphasis in original).

So it is worth underlining that Bookchin, notwithstanding all the talk of 'dialectical *regression*' (the category applies to him as well as to Marcuse), emphasizes that the elimination of 'surplus' alienation would render human life more complex rather than les: 'Society, in turn, attains its "truth," its self-actualization, in the form of richly articulated, mutualistic networks of people based on community, roundedness of personality, diversity of stimuli and activities, an increasing wealth of experience, and a variety of tasks' (Bookchin 1987, 59) Such increasing complexity and diversity through social evolution is not a mark of society's distance from nature, but a reflection of what occurs in nature. According to Bookchin's view of 'dialectical naturalism,' 'biological nature is above all the cumulative evolution of ever-differentiating and increasingly complex life-forms and a highly vibrant and interactive inorganic world' (Bookchin 1990, 41).

Bookchin's views thus flirt with teleology, whatever his insistence that the potentiality for, and desirability of, ever-increasing complexity and diversity should not be taken to imply either the existence of a finalized, totalizing end point to evolution (either natural or social), or a narrowly determinist view of the process. In the first instance, the dialectical notion of 'unity in diversity' is to be taken as always referring to 'varying degrees of the actualization of potentialities' (Bookchin 1987, 60). As for the charge of determinism, Bookchin insists that the claim that subjectivity and freedom constitute an *outcome* of evolution means that the directionality imputed to evolution remains something objectively desirable, but not necessarily realized in every instance at the empirical level:

> That the *potentiality* for freedom and consciousness exists in nature and society; that nature and society are not merely 'passive' in a development toward freedom and consciousness, a passivity that would make the very notion of potentiality mystical just as the notion of 'necessity' would make it meaningless by definition; that natural and social history bear existential witness to the potentiality and processes that form subjectivity and bring consciousness more visibly on the horizon of the very natural history of mind – all constitute no guarantee that these latent desiderata are certainties or lend themselves to systematic elucidation and teleological explanations in any traditional philosophical sense. (63–4; emphasis in original)

This tension, which asserts a directionality to natural and social evolution while at the same time resisting 'teleological explanations in any traditional sense,' is a result of the antinomy that structures the relationship between 'nature' and 'freedom' in Bookchin's work. Bookchin sees freedom (the development of conscious subjectivity) as the apotheosis of natural evolution. Freedom, in the sense of self-conscious evolution, is the highest potentiality to be found in nature. Note well, however, that this development does not occur through fitful, random change, since there is a clear directionality to natural evolution. Nor does it occur through the labour of a preordained, totalizing motor of history that churns through everything in its wake, since the directionality must be toward freedom, not toward whatever sort of resigned passivity such a totalizing logic might imply.

In terms of social evolution, according to Bookchin the development of this potentiality for freedom is *arrested* by hierarchical social institutions. Because of its surplus-alienating character, hierarchy ultimately impinges on the 'natural' development of human freedom. This notion that the natural course of social evolution is arrested by the imposition of hierarchy is what gives Bookchin's work its *political* thrust – what and allows him to criticize contemporary social arrangements. His work receives its *ecological* inflection in its insistence that human society is a function of natural evolution. The two come together in his overarching claim that certain patterns of social evolution (such as the development of non-hierarchical relations) are more in line with natural evolutionary flows.

On the one hand, therefore, is an insistence that human behaviour is natural, the implication being that social evolution, were it not arrested by hierarchy, would tend in the same direction as natural evolution (that is, toward increasing complexity and diversity). On the other hand, the claim that 'freedom' – more precisely, the development of free, self-conscious subjects – is the apotheosis of natural evolution, suggests that beyond a certain point, the work of natural evolution (the development of increasing complexity and diversity) is in some sense taken over by human subjects (although these are, of course, still a part of nature). That "free" interactions with nature would tend in the direction of *natural* evolution must be accepted unquestioningly, since this assumption is what holds Bookchin's notion of human 'freedom' in delicate balance between passive resignation to blind natural (and social) evolution on one hand and an anti-ecological detachment from nature on the other. Without minimizing the tremendous importance of the ecological critique of hierarchy that Bookchin develops, his theorizations remain troubled by this antinomy, which is a function of the fact that his 'social ecology' rests on a positive vision of 'nature.'

This issue of ascribing essential characteristics to 'nature' is one that has received particular attention in ecofeminist theory as well. The basic structure of ecofeminist argument is quite similar to Bookchin's social ecology. The main difference is that instead of arguing that the domination of nature is rooted in simply 'the domination of human by human,' ecofeminists contend that the domination of nature is intimately connected with patriarchy, or the domination of women by men.[2] But the complex development of ecofeminist thought – which has recently been characterized as 'the predominant position within ecological thought' (Hay 2002, 72) – has generally tended to move away from essentializing associations of 'women' with 'nature,' especially insofar as these were grounded in an assertion that women's *biological* differences made them 'closer' to nature.

Partly in response to this essentialist or biological ecofeminism, a cultural or historical strand of ecofeminism has developed, which sees patriarchy and the domination of nature as intertwined owing to the historical development of particular and historically contingent associations between 'women' and 'nature.' As Michael Zimmerman (1994) explains this 'cultural ecofeminism,' 'ecological issues are often related to women's issues *not* because women are "essentially" closer to nature or superior to men, but because women's social roles are often made more demanding by short-sighted, destructive practices masquerading as economic development' (281). Thus ecofeminism provides a 'contextualist, structurally pluralistic' ethic (Warren 1993, 332–4).

Among those who argue that the identification of women with nature is historically and socially rather than naturally constructed, there are important differences. At one extreme, for example, is Janet Biehl, whom Zimmerman (1994, 259) characterizes as a 'left-Green' ecofeminist, but who has rejected the label of 'ecofeminism' entirely because it 'has by now become so tainted by its various irrationalisms that I no longer consider this a promising project' (Biehl 1991, 5). The tendentiousness of Biehl's critique of ecofeminism aside, the major difference between a more 'mainstream' cultural or historicized ecofeminism and Biehl's social ecology with feminist sympathies, seems to rest on the question of whether it is patriarchy or hierarchy that lies at the heart of social domination. This difference is not entirely unrelated to what Zimmerman identifies as the key difference between 'cultural' and 'left-Green' ecofeminisms – namely, the question of whether 'cultural changes – such as changes in mythic attitudes or religious beliefs – can effect basic alterations in economic and social structures' (1994, 260).

A quite different approach is taken by postmodern ecofeminism, which is exemplified by Catriona Sandilands. For her, 'the fact that "nature" is not a singular, coherent entity to be spoken' stands as an especially vivid confirmation of the Lacanian critique of the fully identical subject: 'The subject, then, is opposed to identity; it is, instead, the point of failure of identification' (Sandilands 1995, 82). Giving Laclau and Mouffe's 'post-Marxist' project (Laclau and Mouffe 1985, 4) an ecological spin, she thus argues that the 'radical contingency' of political identity (including the identity of 'nature') means that 'the subject of environmentalism is always contingent on its articulation with other subject positions in some chain of equivalences,' and that 'the radical potential of environmentalism can be achieved *only* through its articulation with other democratic struggles' (Sandilands, 1995, 84–6; emphasis in original). Elsewhere, Sandilands has argued for a 'queer' ecofeminism, one that involves an even more radical destabilization of 'woman,' 'nature,' and the ecofeminist connection between the two, on the grounds that even 'strategic essentialism is never simply "strategic."' (1997, 28).

Although it is not clear to what extent Sandilands succeeds in avoiding the pitfalls of anti-essentialism that were outlined in chapter 2, her emphasis on a postmodern critique of the subject serves well to refocus our attention on the impossibility of representing (in the terms set out in chapters 1 and 2) nature rather than 'nature': 'Any language of nature is destined to fail, and this failure requires recognition of a moment of nature that overflows any attempt to capture its positivity. It is this process of questioning the positivity of nature that underscores the radical potential of ecology. If nature is impossible, then, as [William Irvin] Thompson has noted, ecology is the study of what lies *within* our horizons, the study of the construction of nature as a social process' (Sandilands 1995, 88; emphasis in original). The consequence for environmentalism, she argues, should be a downplaying of the importance of science in favour of more explicitly political elements, most notably the formation of 'something like a green public culture – meaning here a cultivated practice of reflection and imagination by which individuals' opinions about nature might be debated and refined in public' (Sandilands 2002, 123).

The intersection between ecology on the one hand, and deconstructive or post-structuralist feminism on the other, is also crucial for Val Plumwood.[3] Like many ecofeminists, Plumwood focuses on the conceptual dualisms (human/natural, rational/emotional, universal/particular, and so on) that structure the oppression of both women and nature. The persistence of these dualisms tends to reinforce an understanding of the self 'that stresses sharply defined boundaries, distinctness, autonomy, and separation from others – that is defined *against* others, and lacks essential connections to them' (Plumwood 1993, 300; emphasis in original). From both feminist and ecological perspectives,

> it has been objected that this [dualist] account does not give an accurate picture of the human self – that humans are social and connected in such a way that such an account does not recognize. People do have interests that make *essential* and not merely accidental or contingent reference to those of others. [This account further] gives a misleading picture of the world, one that omits or impoverishes a whole significant dimension of human experience, a dimension which provides important insights into gender difference, without which we cannot give an adequate account of what it is to be human. Instead we must see human beings and their interests as *essentially* related and interdependent. (301; emphases in original)

For Plumwood, ecofeminism provides an alternative conception of the self – the 'self-in-relationship.' Like object relations theory (mentioned in the previous chapter), this view emphasizes mutualistic relationality rather than antagonistic dualisms. Plumwood's concept of the self is both ecological in the sense that it is defined by relationality, and specifically feminist in the sense that the self is defined by relations with concrete others rather than by abstract categories (Benhabib 1987).

For Sandilands, in contrast, even such a relational view of the self might be overly essentialist. For her, the critique of the self-identical subject leads to the sort of coalitional politics advocated by Laclau and Mouffe, where feminism and ecology can be contingently articulated within what Laclau and Mouffe term the 'democratic matrdix.' Sandilands's anti-essentialism thus leads her to note that Bookchinian 'libertarian municipalism' is to be admired, except, crucially, for its 'reification of democracy as tied solely to a sense of *place*, not to mention a rather *static* notion of the 'public sphere."' (Sandilands 1995, 90n; emphases added).

This provides an important point of contrast with Plumwood, for whom the 'self-in-relationship' view is useful precisely for how it undermines the dominant view that instrumentalizes nature and that sees one's relationship to place as accidental or contingent to one's identity. For Plumwood, place-based attachments are a crucial part of identity. But a peculiar slippage makes Plumwood's account of this worth citing at length:

> The relational account of self can usefully be applied to the case of human relations with nature and to place. The standard Western view of the relation of the self to the nonhuman is that it is always *accidentally* related, and hence the nonhuman can be used as a means to the self-contained ends of human beings. Pieces of land are real estate, readily interchangeable as equivalent means to the end of human satisfaction ... But of course, we do not all think that way, and instances of contrary behavior would no doubt be more common if their possibility were not denied and distorted by theoretical and social construction. But other cultures have recognized such essential connection of self to country clearly enough ... If instrumentalism is impoverishing and distorting as an account of our relations to other human beings, it is equally so as a guiding principle in our relations to nature and to place. (302; underlining indicates emphasis added)

The shift from 'place' to 'country' seems to highlight precisely Sandilands's point – that attachments to place are all too often reifications, which (especially in the case of an intense affective relationship to one's country that is seen as essential to one's identity) can have disastrous political consequences.

This negotiation through ecofeminist debates over questions of 'nature' and essentialism thus echoes debates between deconstructive (de Man) and Marxian or Frankfurtian (Colletti, Asher Horowitz) readings of Rousseau, and indeed a whole series of other debates that have been restaged throughout the pages of this book. The point, throughout, has been to chart the development of a denaturalized ecological politics, or a politics that retains a sense of the essentiality of one's connection to place but does not rely on reified naturalizations of these places. Such a politics requires a sense of the importance of attachment to place that – to borrow Adorno's phrase – sees the natural as historical. Drawing on postmodern feminism, Jim Cheney argues that bioregionalism can provide the basis for an environmental ethic that is appropriate for the postmodern moment. Cheney has been criticized for his implicit claim that postmodernity, with its skepticism toward totalizing narratives, has important similarities with premodern ('mythic') societies. Mick Smith argues that Cheney 'presents a myth of a past Golden Age and in terms of it describes a prehistorical tribal humanity at one with itself and nature, a modern alienated society uprooted from the natural world, and a future postmodern millennium' (1995, 262). Although Smith's charge has some merit, what might deserve to be retained is Cheney's insistence in the article's conclusion that 'authentic existence is not a matter of discovering a "real" self (it is still a social self, a construct); there is just the project of bringing into being healthy communities, healthy selves – an *achievement*, not a discovery of something that is hidden, covered over' (Cheney 1995, 38). It is not only the naturalization of place that risks being reified, but also the ongoing construction of human communities, as well as the connections of particular individuals to those communities. Attachment to place, even if an essential part of identity, is constructed – or to use Cheney's term, 'an achievement.' And this remains true whether 'place' is figured as a bioregional space or, as we shall see momentarily, as an urban one.

Along with ecofeminism, one of the more fruitful possibilities for the development of such a politics is through a linkage of ecological politics with the politics of 'race.' Non-white peoples have long been associated with 'nature' – in fact, intensely so; yet a racialized 'version' of ecofeminism has barely been developed. It does exist, however, and to some extent its later start has allowed it to avoid some of the pitfalls of essentialism that proved troubling for earlier ecofeminists. In the First World, the articulation of ecological and progressive 'race'-based politics began with the 'environmental justice' movement, rooted in Robert Bullard and others' pioneering studies of the ways in which non-white communities in the United States were bearing a disproportionate amount of environmental risks (Bullard 1990, 1993). Meyer (2001) notes that this movement did not begin from an essentialist connection between 'race' and nature; rather, 'the basis for the concerns of this movement's members can be found in the places where they live and work.' (146).

With this, we can turn, finally, to the claim that urban space constitutes a 'local environment' suitable for ecological study. Andrew Ross claims as much in the opening sentences of his book, *The Chicago Gangster Theory of Life*: 'Why not begin, as ecology has ordained, with a local environment? As a city-dweller who does not regard himself as much of a nature-lover, it is important to start with the stores in my neighborhood. Living in Manhattan's SoHo ...' (1994, 1). As we saw with the discussion of Goodin's 'green theory of value' in chapter 1, we cannot logically accept the dualism that underpins the claim that Manhattan is 'unnatural.' As Harvey succinctly puts it, 'the distinction between environment as commonly understood [i.e., the natural environment] and the built, social, and political-economic environment is artificial' (1996, 435). The treatment of urban space in an ecological context – the ecology of what is commonly understood to be unnatural spaces – provides perhaps one of the best opportunities for elaborating a denaturalized ecological politics. Ross goes on to argue later in the same book:

> Many components of urban life are not yet configured to the public mind as 'green' issues: adequate housing and health care, access to basic services and inexpensive education, the right to a healthy workplace, freedom from police surveillance and harassment, participation in neighborhood self-management, the right to the city both inside and outside racially segregated enclaves, and so on. And yet surely these are all aspects of how people relate to each other within their social and physical environments – a minimal definition of human ecology. (1994, 103)

Eric Klinenberg, for example, shows compellingly how 'new and dangerous forms of marginality and neglect endemic to contemporary American big cities' – in other words, *social* factors – are playing a crucial role in the morbidity associated with natural disasters (specifically, he discusses the 1995 Chicago heat wave) (Klinenberg 1999, 240). According to him, what is 'disastrous' about extreme weather events is the constant incipient *social* breakdown characteristic of many urban environments, through which meteorological events are mediated. 'When government fails to secure the basic welfare of its citizens, external forces beyond its control (such as the weather) can be uncontrollably dangerous' (275). Far from asserting that disaster lies in the inability to control nature, Klinenberg shows that failure at the level of the social is what causes human disaster. In the case of Chicago in 1995, the 'the heat fail[ed] even to explain deaths officially attributed to the weather.' (243).

Davis (1998) makes a similar point about the various sorts of 'natural disasters' in the Los Angeles region, the effects of which are often intensified by misguided attempts to achieve total control over nature, such as the strategy of 'total fire suppression' in natural wildfire corridors (1998, 101). For Davis, the case of fire patterns in the Los Angeles region is an especially compelling one, insofar as it offers the possibility of seeing the pernicious consequences of both the socialization of nature (the attempts to make areas such as Malibu impervious to fire) and the naturalization of the social (resignation in the face of frequent tenement fires in Westlake):

> Stand at the mouth of the Malibu canyon or sleep in the Hotel St. George for any length of time and you eventually will face the flames. It is a statistical certainty. Ironically, the richest and poorest landscapes in Southern California are comparable in the frequency with which they experience incendiary disaster ...
>
> But the two species of conflagration are inverse images of each other. Defended in 1993 by the largest army of firefighters in American history, wealthy Malibu homeowners benefited as well from an extraordinary range of insurance, landuse, and disaster relief subsidies. Yet, as most experts will readily concede, periodic firestorms of this magnitude are inevitable as long as residential development is tolerated in the fire ecology of the Santa Monicas.
>
> On the other hand, most of the 119 fatalities from tenement fires in the Westlake and Downtown areas might have been prevented had slumlords been held even to minimal standards of building safety. (Davis 1998, 98–9)

William Cronon makes a similar point about Southern California wildfires (1995, 31–2), and also the effects of earthquakes:

> Neither the underlying geology nor anything else in nature explains why some of the most severely damaged buildings were apartment complexes with unreinforced garages on their first floors ... Likewise no feature of the natural environment can explain why some neighborhoods ... were

> able to rebuild so quickly following the quake, while others ... became virtual ghost towns. (30)

A similar understanding of the contemporary urban environment as a reified 'second nature' (although he does not use this term) is found in Matthew Ruben's reading of the film *Twelve Monkeys*. Taking seriously director Terry Gilliam's claim that 'it's a documentary I'm making!' Ruben notes how the film's delinearization of time mirrors the lived experience of urban uneven development under postmodern capitalism. In Philadelphia (where the film is set and was shot), the number of abandoned buildings in poor sections of the city remains roughly constant at just over twenty thousand, as the rate of abandonment almost precisely matches the rate of demolition:

> Within the landscape of Philadelphia's poor neighborhoods, time seems simultaneously to stand still and move in a circular fashion. Abandoned buildings disappear from some locales and newly abandoned structures 'pop up' out of nowhere to replace them, month after month and year after year. Linear temporal logic is subordinated to a seemingly random series of events in a seemingly endless time loop of abandonment and stagnation. (Ruben 1998, 112)

In Ross's treatment of SoHo as an appropriate object of ecological study, we seem to encounter the obverse of these 'social autopsies' (the term is Klinenberg's) of natural disasters. But although urban centres certainly constitute a stark contrast to the 'pristine wilderness' so highly valued by Goodin and other deep ecologists, Ross provides at least one other example of an 'unnatural' space, which is, unlike the city, not even a source of ambivalent praise.

To set the stage, we should note that Ross is among the figures who might be considered most distant from the blind praise of 'nature' associated with deep ecology. He not only introduces himself as 'a city dweller who does not regard himself as much of a nature lover' (1994, 1), but also argues against discourses of 'scarcity' as primarily products of social rather than ecological conditions – a thesis most overtly formulated as follows:

> Scarcity is a political tool, skillfully manipulated by the powerful whenever it suits their purpose. It is not a natural condition ... Contrary to popular belief, capitalism's primary effect is not to create wealth; it creates

> scarcity, first and foremost. The period, far from over, in which the West pillaged the world's resources, was not a temporary respite from some natural condition of scarcity; it was a period that established and defined scarcity as a condition and effect of unequal social organization, maldistribution, and political injustice. (16)

What is more, Ross works to deconstruct the 'straight choice between the natural world and the manmade world' posited by deep ecologists like Bill McKibben (1994, 179), arguing that McKibben's call for people to 'leave their TVs and invade what's left of the Adirondacks' (ibid.) is ultimately not nearly as 'subversive' as McKibben seems to think. In fact, Ross says, it 'is exactly what the well heeled urban or suburban readers of his books are likely to do anyway' (ibid.). McKibben's argument is ultimately complicit with the hegemonic system of (post)industrial capitalism, Ross argues; furthermore, there is something about McKibben's attitude that is, perhaps, *unnatural*: 'Yikes! For a 32-year-old, McKibben often sounds like Gramps on lithium. This is a man who prefers the mating dance of cranes to seminaked club kids shaking their Lycra-clad booties on MTV' (1994, 179).

The naturalism that Ross seems to imply here (isn't it natural for a thirty-two-year-old to prefer MTV to cranes?) is surprising for someone who elsewhere rejects so adamantly the thesis that 'biology is destiny' (1994, 237–73). In the context of his critique of McKibben, it is perhaps attributable to rhetorical excess, and an attempt to highlight the arbitrariness of the values, that McKibben selects to indict 'the couch potato, tawdry symptom of the recline of Western Civ.' (178). Yet later in the same chapter, Ross resorts to a similar sort of naturalism when describing a bombing range in the Nevada desert. Ross also seems to approve of the non-anthropocentric perspective afforded by Richard Misrach's photographs of this site in *Bravo 20: The Bombing of the American West*:

> There is no ostensible human activity on the ground, and the photographer's point of view is that of an isolated visitor to an isolated spot where, in the absence of humans, some kind of war is being waged against the environment. The war victim is quite literally the desert ... All we need to recognize (and question) is the impunity with which these and other areas of desert land are chosen to be systematically pounded, despoiled, and contaminated, simply because desert lands (and their low-density populations) are considered 'expendable.' Who gives permission for this?

... The source of cultural authority lies ... deeply inscribed in a long history of social values that can sanction such aggression towards the natural environment. (Ross 1994, 196)

Ross' impulse to identify this 'aggression towards the natural environment' is surely laudable, but he does not go beyond locating it 'in a long history of social values.' (Davis goes some of the way in his account of the same area and of 'the most extraordinary social movement to emerge in the postwar West,' a consequence of the extraordinary militarization of 'national sacrifice zones' [Davis 2002, 46 and 33].) Without a more specific accounting of these 'social values,' however, we are unable to distinguish adequately between the 'systematically pounded, despoiled, and contaminated' Nevada desert and the 'fancy amalgam of art, commerce and fashion' (Ross 1994, 1) that is SoHo. Or at least we are unable to do so without slipping into the sort of deep ecological mode that we should not expect from someone who by his own confession is 'not ... much of a nature lover.' But this is the only way to account for Ross's apparent blurring of the human-nonhuman divide, and for his insistence that the desert is ('literally'!) the 'victim' of human aggression.

It might be tempting to read this shortcoming in Ross's work as a failure to complete the inversion of the natural and the social (Ross, in spite of himself, experiences some sort of loss of nerve in his attempt to thoroughly rid his argument of any 'nature-loving' impulses). But the same problem arises – albeit in different form – in the analyses of Klinenberg and Davis. Here, it is a question of the nature of the project itself. This shortcoming in Ross's project involves a return of the repressed love of nature; the shortcomings in Klinenberg and Davis's projects can be seen only negatively, in terms of their resolute focus on the local. A similar point might be made about the otherwise highly promising 'environmentalism of the poor,' which rightly challenges the notion that environmentalism is a 'postmaterialist' concern that only highly developed economies can afford (Guha 2000, 98–124). Although it articulates ecological concerns about the maldistribution of wealth between the First and Third worlds, and the global politics of 'race,' it generally does so through the analysis of geographically circumscribed case studies (Guha and Martinez-Alier 1997).

If we can characterize the foregoing ecologies of urban environments as Adornian, in the sense that they attempt to naturalize the historical and to historicize the natural, then they are also Adornian in the sense that the study of individual local cases suggests the difficulty, if not near impossibility, of undertaking this sort of ecological analysis at the global level.[4] At the most extreme, these denaturalized urban ecologies might be taken to suggest the sort of resignation that seems to be found in Adorno's claim that 'change succeeds only in the smallest of things.'

As we saw in chapter 6, however, the ecological implications of Adorno's project are extended considerably by the work of Herbert Marcuse. Indeed, it would be fair to conclude by saying that a denaturalized ecological politics can be seen as a two-pronged approach, one that is most fully developed through the particular readings of Adorno and Marcuse offered here. The Adornian aspect – the negative or critical moment – emphasizes seeing the natural as social (as in denaturalized urban ecologies) and the social as natural. Its focus is on a persistent 'reciprocal defamiliarization' (Jameson 1990, 99) of the natural and the social – a process that receives perhaps its fullest expression in the working out of the *Dialectic of Enlightenment*'s claim that 'myth is already enlightenment; and enlightenment reverts to mythology' (Horkheimer and Adorno 1987, xvi).

In contrast, the Marcusean aspect, although negative or critical in its own way, offers the possibility of elaborating a more positive or constructive moment to a denaturalized ecological politics. Marcuse's distinction between basic and surplus repression provides a basis for developing a distinction between basic and surplus forms of alienation from nature. The distinction, in other words, is between the distance from nature that is necessary for human life as such on the one hand, and attempts to dominate 'nature' that end up naturalizing social domination on the other. This Marcusean aspect is positive in the sense that such a distinction lays the foundation for constituting beneficent (non-dominating) social relations and institutions, as well as human–nonhuman relations – in other words, it offers a yardstick for articulating insightful local analyses with analyses of the global logics of natural and social processes. But it is also negative in the sense that the maintenance of such a distinction between basic and surplus alteration requires the constant operation of critical reason – a persistent 'scouring' of our relations with nature (including, to be sure, our constructions of 'nature').

So while in some ways a denaturalized ecological politics involves a juxtaposition of Adornian and Marcusean theories, in other ways it is considerably more complex than that. This book has sought to bring out both positive and negative aspects in the context of the writings of and interpretive debates surrounding all four of the theorists discussed, as well as, more recently, in the context of the debate over ecofeminism staged between Sandilands and Plumwood. I have sought out these complexities in order to refute the objection that these moments are to be understood as a temporally two-staged process. Basic and surplus forms of alienation co-evolve, so that the removal of the latter cannot be achieved simply by stripping back the historical layers until only basic alienation remains. Alienation from nature is an ongoing process, so the basic–surplus distinction is not a quantitative but a qualitative one. So, similarly, the project of reconstituting social relations in line with such a distinction cannot wait until the project of critique is thought to be complete. The critical moment can never be completed, so it is crucial to avoid falling into the trap of believing that a distinction between basic and surplus forms of alienation from nature can be found once and for all. To make this mistake would be to reify alienation from nature, making it, in a sense, just another word for 'nature.' Maintaining a certain dialectical volatility in our understanding of alienation from nature – a project to which the bulk of this book has been devoted, in excavating it from the works of Rousseau, Marx, Adorno, and Marcuse – is a requirement for the denaturalization of ecological politics, and for the development of a genuinely human ecology.

Notes

1. Ecocentrism and the Defence of Nature

1 The term is from Verena Andermatt Conley, who uses it to characterize Derrida's critique of Levi-Strauss (Conley 1997, 43–4; cf. Derrida 1974, 101–40).

2 Devall and Sessions cite the example of native Alaskans who were hunting endangered bowhead whales. A complete ban on the hunting practice would have been impossible, both because it would have rendered the people 'more dependent on canned meat from the "lower forty-eight" given them by welfare departments' and because, for native Alaskans, 'it was part of their tradition to kill whales, their myths and lifestyles were dependent on it.' The solution that Devall and Sessions approved of was the one advanced by the environmentalist group Friends of the Earth: the number of whales killed was to be regulated, and the killing could only be done 'using their traditional methods (no advanced technology for killing them was allowed),' (1985, 148–9).

3 Devall and Sessions employ a slightly different tactic, arguing that 'humans have a vital need for wilderness, wild places, to help us become more mature' (1985, 111). The constellation of issues raised by this claim (vital needs, wilderness, maturity) will be considered at various points throughout the remainder of the book, and especially in the discussion of Herbert Marcuse (chapter 6).

4 Goodin admits that English village life is not 'more natural' than life in Los Angeles; rather, villagers 'are living more in a context that is outside of themselves, individually or even collectively' (1992, 51–2). As we shall see, however, this presumes precisely the point contested here – that the appropriate external context is natural rather than social.

5 Hence Edward Soja's claim that postmodern geography 'all comes together in Los Angeles' (1989).

6 Nor is the case that English village life 'requires less ... human intervention into various natural processes in order to sustain it' as obvious as Goodin seems to think (1992, 51) Certainly, Los Angeles requires more intervention in natural processes than St Mary Mead, but Los Angeles supports a vastly greater human population. In order to make the comparison meaningful, we would have to compare the impact of a single urban centre with hundreds or even thousands of villages. In this case, it is by no means obvious that cities, with their high population densities, are less efficient in terms of their impact on nature. Indeed, even McKibben suggests that 'perhaps it would be best for the planet if we all ... crammed into a few huge cities like so many ants' (1989, 191).

2. Postmodernism: The Critique of 'Nature'

1 Similarly, many environmentalists view social constructivism with suspicion, if not outright hostility. For a critical summary of environmentalist responses to Cronon's *Uncommon Ground*, see Chaloupka (2000).

2 Baudrillard's use of 'symbolic exchange' and 'symbolic economy' is derived from the work of Georges Bataille (1988; see also Gane 1991, 37–41). Baudrillard takes 'symbolic exchange' to be most closely approximated in our society by 'the gift' (1981, 64–5; 1996, 31). It is also, he claims, the form of 'economy' prevalent in 'primitive' societies, and as such can be used as a critical lever against both modernity and postmodernity (Gane 1991, 102–3), insofar as both modernity and postmodernity aspire to an economy based on 'real time' (instantaneous) exchanges (Baudrillard 1995, 31).

3 In Baudrillard's famous formulation of the homology between commodities and signs, Ev/Uv = Sr/Sd. The relationship between the top and bottom terms in each case is arbitrary; furthermore, in both cases the bottom term is only an *effect* of the top term, providing the latter with a 'guarantee of the real,' it being understood that 'the real' is itself in fact only an effect, rather than an ontological foundation on which the system of exchange value or signifiers is constructed: 'Use value and the signified do not constitute an *elsewhere* with respect to the systems of the other two; they are only their alibis' (1981, 137).

4 The expressions in quotation marks in this sentence are all titles of sections of Part III of *Discipline and Punish*.

5 Baudrillard, perhaps not surprisingly, draws a similar conclusion, stating

that 'prisons are there to conceal the fact that it is the social in its entirety, in its banal omnipresence, which is carceral' (1983b, 25).

6 In the introduction to his *Archaeology of Knowledge*, Foucault famously declared: 'Do not ask who I am, and do not ask me to remain the same: leave it to our bureaucrats and our police to see that our papers are in order. At least spare us their morality when we write' (1972, 17).

7 Theoretical imprisonment in a 'total system' is a recurrent motif in Jameson's analysis of postmodernism. In one of the book's first mentions of it, he notes that 'the Foucault of the prisons book is the obvious example' (1991, 5).

3. Jean-Jacques Rousseau: Modernity and the Historicization of Alienation

1 The use of the same word – 'depraved' – is not limited to the English translation; the original French has the quotation from Aristotle in Latin (*'depravatis'*), and Rousseau's phrase is *'L'homme qui médite est un animal dépravé'* (1964, 109 and 138).

2 Rousseau notes that 'there are a thousand kinds of ideas that are impossible to translate in the language of the populace ... Since, therefore, the legislator is incapable of using either force or reasoning, he must of necessity have recourse to an authority of a different order, which can compel without violence and *persuade without convincing*' (1987, 164; emphasis added).

3 'The dogmas of the civil religion ought to be simple, few in number, precisely worded, without explanations or commentaries' (Rousseau 1987, 226).

4 Rousseau claims that 'men cannot engender new forces, but merely unite and direct existing ones' 147; cited in Althusser 1982, 123.

5 Brewster notes that the translation is necessarily imperfect: in other works of Althusser (also translated by Brewster), *'décalage'* is rendered as 'dislocation' (Althusser 1982, 113n2).

6 Jameson also provides an interesting discussion of the historical specificity of systems of 'exchange' (1991, 231–7) Of particular interest for my purposes are his claims – which arise from a comparison of Marx and the reading of Rousseau provided by de Man in *Allegories of Reading* (see below) – that 'philosophical and linguistic abstraction is itself an effect and a by-product of exchange' (233) and that it might be possible 'to transcode "commodity fetishism" into a vast process of abstraction that seethes through the social order' (1992, 235). For Jameson, ultimately, 'the advantage of the Marxian code of "value" – as opposed to DeManian "rhetoric" or Adorno's notion of "identity" or the "concept" – is that it displaces or

transforms the philosophical problem of "error" ... It is too facile, but not wrong, to suggest that conceptions of error, as they inform the positions of both DeMan and Adorno, logically presuppose some prior fantasy about "truth" – the adequation of language or of the concept to their respective objects – which as in unrequited love, is perpetuated in its henceforth disabused and skeptical conclusions.... The terminology of error always suggests, in spite of itself, that we could somehow get rid of it by one last effort of the mind ... The notion of value, however, usefully ceases to imply or entail any of these issues of error or truth' (1991, 237).

We will have occasion in later chapters to consider to what extent Adorno's framework is compromised by a 'prior fantasy about truth,' or – to transcode it into more immediately relevant terms – by a fantasy of unalienated human existence; as well as to what extent Marx's framework is constructed to avoid this problematic.

7 For Starobinski (1988), this interpretation is epitomized by Frederick Engels. We might recall as well Colletti's comment (cited earlier) that for Rousseau, 'the problem of the elimination of evil from the world comes to coincide with the problem of revolution' (1972, 145).

8 This point is similarly made by Cassirer (1954), who asserts that Rousseau 'made it unmistakably clear right at the beginning of [the *Second Discourse*] that he neither could nor wanted to describe a historically demonstrable original state of mankind' (50) For Cassirer, too, the two texts, 'in spite of all apparent contradictions interlock and complement each other. They contradict each other so little that each can rather be explained only through and with the other' (65).

9 The sentence in parentheses was added by Rousseau for the 1782 edition.

10 De Man notes that the term is misleading 'since "perfectibility" is just as regressive as it is progressive' (1979, 140n10). Such a reading of '*perfectibilité*' is supported by, for example, Rousseau's 'Letter to Voltaire': 'I do not see that one can seek the source of moral evil anywhere but in man, free, perfected, hence corrupted' (1997a, 234).

4. Karl Marx: Objectification and Alienation under Capitalism

1 Unpublished in Marx's lifetime, these are also known as the 'Economic and Philosophical Manuscripts' and the 'Paris Manuscripts.'

2 A rather different reading of the arguments of *Capital* on this score, presented by Moishe Postone, will be considered in the final section of this chapter.

3 On the other hand, both James O'Connor's well-developed notion of capi-

talism's 'second contradiction' (1998), and Joel Kovel's more recent analyses (2002), provide two examples of such an ecological Marxism, which diagnoses ecological crises as emergent from the dynamic of the capitalist system as such, and thus sees environmental issues as eminently susceptible to Marxian analysis.

4 The argument that Marx was not a teleological thinker is further bolstered by his comments on Darwin. Although Marx was eventually critical of Darwin's work to the extent that he found in it a projection of capitalist society and values onto nature ('Darwin recognizes among beasts and plants his English society with its division of labour, competition, opening up of new markets, "inventions" and the Malthusian "struggle for existence"'), he nevertheless initially praised it for providing a decisive refutation of teleological conceptions of natural history (Marx 1977b, 525–6).

5 On the other hand, Leninist and post-Leninist *policies* with respect to the 'peasant question' in Russia were quite consistently (which is not to say inevitably) in line with Warren's reading of Marx. And Russian policies of course set the standard adopted by the many other countries that adopted the 'Soviet model' of central economic planning. In light of this, David Mitrany has gone so far as to claim that 'Marxist theory ... has been invariably and dogmatically opposed to' the interests of peasants, including those whom he claims were the actual revolutionary subjects of the 1917 revolution (1961, 19).

6 Edward Soja takes some of the sting out of this phrase by suggesting that 'the population beyond the reach of the urban is comprised of *idiotes*, from the Greek root *idios*, "meaning 'one's own, a private person," unlearned in the ways of the *polis* ... Thus to speak of the "idiocy" of rural life or the urbanity of its opposition is primarily a statement of relative political socialization' (1989, 235).

7 Althusser, on the other hand, does extract from Marx a defence of the Leninist thesis (that a socialist revolution must begin in the most backwards of the capitalist countries, because such a point is capitalism's 'weakest link' [1977, 94–8]). Althusser's thesis is complex, and its details bear only a tangential relevance to our discussion here. It will suffice to note that although Althusser does resort extensively to Lenin's arguments regarding the situation in Russia in the early twentieth century ('the political requirements of the Russian revolution,' as Warren puts it), his defence is in fact grounded in Marx's own writings. Althusser asserts that, viewed from the perspective of the basic contradiction between the forces and relations of production, the revolutionary situation in Russia indeed seems to have been an 'exceptional' one. But Althusser goes on to ask: 'exceptional ...

but *with respect to what*? To nothing but the *abstract*, but comfortable and reassuring idea of a pure, simple "dialectical" schema, which in its very simplicity seems to have retained a memory (or rediscovered the style) of the Hegelian model and its faith in the resolving "power" of the abstract contradiction as such: in particular, the "beautiful" contradiction between Capital and Labour' (104; emphases in original). Thus Althusser might claim that Warren's schema ignores Marx's *transformation* of Hegelian dialectics, and in particular, that for Marx, unlike for Hegel, contradictions must be understood as 'overdetermined.'

8 'Exchange-value appears first of all as the quantitative relation, the proportion, in which use-values of one kind exchange for use-values of another kind' (Marx 1977a, 126). On the other hand, use-values 'constitute the material content of wealth, whatever its social form may be. In the form of society to be considered here [i.e., capitalist society] they are also the material bearers of ... exchange-value' (ibid.,; ellipsis in original).

9 But as with Rousseau, the status of this implicit distinction between the social division of labour and commodity exchange is not entirely clear in Marx's theory. In the '1844 Manuscripts,' Marx faults liberal political economists for assuming a necessary connection between the division of labour and exchange (private property): 'In political economy *labour* appears only in the form of *wage-earning activity*' (1977a, 289; emphases in original). But in volume 3 of *Capital*, Marx notes that 'even after the capitalist mode of production is abolished, though social production remains, the determination of value still prevails in the sense that the regulation of labour-time and the distribution of social labour among various production groups becomes more essential than ever, as well as the keeping of accounts on this.' (1981, 991).

10 Nearly every study of Marx considers this question in one form or another. Two classic book-length studies of Marx's understanding of alienation are Ollman (1971) and Meszaros (1970). An excellent treatment of the character of Marx's understanding of unalienated existence, discussed briefly earlier, is Booth (1989).

11 Alienation from species-being (which also includes alienation from nature) is an aspect of alienation that is 'derive[d] ... from the two we have already looked at [alienation from the object and the act of production]' (Marx 1975, 327). Alienation from other human beings is 'an immediate *consequence* of man's estrangement from the product of his labour, his life activity, his species-being' (329–30; emphasis added).

12 Marx says in 'On the Jewish Question' that 'an organization of society which would abolish the preconditions and thus the very possibility of

huckstering, would make the Jew impossible' (1978, 48), and in the *Communist Manifesto* that 'no other person than the bourgeois, than the middle-class owner of property ... must be swept out of the way, and made impossible' (486).

13 According to Neil Smith, this is precisely the point that Schmidt overlooks (as does the Frankfurt School more generally). For Smith: 'The Frankfurt School thesis treats certain social relations with nature as natural relations, in the sense that they are deemed eternal and inevitable.' This 'rather subtle fetishism' results in the Frankfurt School's 'politics of despair,' where 'the "human condition" not capitalism, becomes the historic villain and political target' (1990, 28–9). Smith's claim that recognizing a propensity to domination in 'the human condition' rules out effective political action, however, participates in precisely the sort of universalizing anthropology that, he argues, a dialectical analysis should discount. As we shall see in more detail in the next two chapters, the Frankfurt School does, to a certain extent, recognize nature domination as rooted in 'the human condition' (or to put it more explicitly, 'human nature'), but understands this 'human nature' as historically conditioned by determinate social relations rather than universally given.

5. Theodor W. Adorno: From *Udeis* to Utopia

1 This is, of course, not an uncontroversial claim. A thorough argument tying Adorno to Marxism can be found in Jameson (1990). This represents a revision of Jameson's own earlier claim that despite its 'theoretical merits,' Adorno's understanding of contemporary society, 'where it does not lead out of politics altogether ... encourages the revival of an anarchist opposition to Marxism itself' (1980, 208). A comprehensive and balanced overview of the numerous 'approaches to Adorno' can be found in Hohendahl (1995, 3–20).

2 This term occurs frequently, in the English translation of *Negative Dialectics* in particular. Jameson suggests, however, that this rendering of '*Tauschverhaltnis*' is among the translator's 'most urgent howlers' and that a better translation would be '"exchange system" (very much as in "exchange value")' (1990, x).

3 Freud's discovery of the dynamics and internal conflicts motivating individual behaviour thus seems to belong (to some extent) singularly to the bourgeois era, and is thus an instance of Minerva's owl flying at dusk: the moment that Freud elaborates a theory of bourgeois psychology is also the moment that bourgeois subjectivity is eclipsed. 'The individual,' Horkhe-

imer and Adorno write – metaphorically connecting the economic and the psychological realms in mass society – is 'the psychological corner shop.' The bourgeois ego is correlatively 'the internal "small business"' that negotiates the atomistic drives and desires of the 'instinctive economy': 'But in the era of great business enterprises and world wars the mediation of the social process through innumerable monads proves retrograde. The subjects of the economy are psychologically expropriated, and the economy is more rationally operated by society itself. The individual no longer has to decide what he himself is to do in a painful inner dialectic of conscience, self-preservation and drives ... The committees and stars serve as the ego and super-ego, and the masses, who have lost the last semblance of personality, shape themselves more easily according to the models presented to them than the instincts ever could' (1987, 203). As Jameson puts it, the 'economic homology' here provides 'a full-dress theory of the psyche under monopoly capitalism' (1990, 70).

4 The use of the gendered pronoun here is deliberate. Although there can be little doubt that Horkheimer and Adorno did not intend to exempt women from the dialectic of enlightenment, they also seem to be suggesting (in particular by the use of the term 'virile' in the quotation that follows) that it is more strongly associated with the formation of masculine identity.

5 Darwin's writings were, of course, available to Marx, as the *Origin of Species* was published in 1859. (For Marx's assessment of Darwin, see note 4 in chapter 4, above.)

6 This distinction, too, is necessarily imprecise, not only because Adorno's project does not especially lend itself to martial metaphors such as those of 'tactics,' but also because Adorno asserts in 'The Idea of Natural History' (1984) that 'the question of ontology, as it is formulated at present, is none other than what I mean by "nature"' (112).

7 I would like to thank Jonathan Warren for drawing my attention to this remarkable text. Rushdie also suggestively notes that in *The Wizard of Oz* Kansas is represented through simple geometric figures, that 'home and safety are represented by such geometrical simplicity, whereas danger and evil are invariably twisty, irregular, and misshapen' (1992, 21). One might thus also argue that through this representation of Kansas as both a place where nature is controlled through the imposition of geometric regularity, and a place that is colourless and alienating (Dorothy is swept away by the tornado because she is trying to run away), the film restages the dialectic of enlightenment itself.

8 See note 6 in chapter 3, above.

9 Jameson takes this 'crucial phrase' to be 'the decisive clue ... to the ultimate

identity of "identity" itself.' For Jameson, the 'uniformity' enforced by philosophical abstraction is in the last instance determined by (or at the very least homologous to) the uniformity demanded by the exchange processes of capitalist society (1990, 23).

10 Jameson (1991) notes that for Adorno (but also for Derrida), 'hints abound that some radical transformation of the social system and of history itself may open the possibility of thinking new kinds of thoughts and concepts: [this is] something quite inconceivable in De Man's view of language' (237). These 'hints' (insofar as they appear in Adorno's work, at least) were alluded to in the discussion of 'Subject and Object' (above) and will be dealt with at a bit more length presently.

11 Adorno concludes his essay on cultural criticism with the oft-cited claim that 'to write poetry after Auschwitz is barbaric' (1967, 34). The claim seems to be rescinded in *Negative Dialectics*: 'It may have been wrong to say that after Auschwitz you could no longer write poems.' On the other hand, Adorno there continues: 'But it is not wrong to raise the less cultural question whether after Auschwitz you can go on living' (1973, 362–3). Rather than one version contradicting or correcting the other, both may aim to highlight the dilemmas of living with 'the drastic guilt of him who was spared' (363), and who continues to live, moreover, in a culture that has not renounced or even fully recognized the extent of its implication in the horrors of totalitarianism. 'Whoever pleads for the maintenance of this radically culpable and shabby culture becomes its accomplice, while the man who says no to culture is directly furthering the barbarism which our culture showed itself to be. Not even silence gets us out of the circle. In silence we simply use the state of objective truth to rationalize our subjective incapacity, once more degrading truth into a lie' (367).

12 'What is the origin of the remarkable and puzzling form [the dream] in which the wish fulfilment is expressed?' (Freud 1976, 200–1). 'Why is it that dreams with an indifferent content, which turn out to be wish fulfilments, do not express their meaning undisguised? ... Why did it not say what it meant straight out?' (216). Slavoj Žižek (1989) provides a good account of this – in particular, of its articulation (through Lacan) with Marx's analysis of the commodity form.

13 Jameson's observation comes at precisely the mid-point of his own discussion of *Negative Dialectics*: the end of chapter 6 of twelve chapters. Although Adorno was a musicologist, Jameson is a literary theorist, so it is perhaps not too surprising that while the section on *Negative Dialectics* in Jameson's *Late Marxism* is divided into twelve chapters, the book as a whole is divided into twenty-six.

14 The term is used to describe the concern of the 'Notes and Drafts' section of the *Dialectic of Enlightenment* (Horkheimer and Adorno 1987, xvii). For more on Adorno's use of this term, see Jarvis (1998, 70).

15 'In general, the name – to which magic most easily attaches – is undergoing a chemical change: a metamorphosis into capricious, manipulable designations, whose effect is admittedly now calculable, but which for that very reason is just as despotic as that of the archaic name' (Horkheimer and Adorno 1987, 164–5). For a more detailed treatment of the differences between Adorno's treatment of 'the name' and that of Benjamin, see Buck-Morss (1977, 88–90).

16 My understanding of artistic mimesis has been very helpfully clarified through discussions with Shane Gunster and Steven Hayward. In particular, Shane Gunster deserves credit for the understanding of artistic mimesis in Adorno as 'deterrorized.'

17 For a fuller discussion of the relationship between social domination and the domination of nature, see Leiss (1974). The arguments are more concisely (albeit less accurately) rehearsed by Eckersley (1992, 97–106).

18 Adorno's main point of reference here is not so much Marx himself as Lukács (Buck-Morss 1977, 24–42).

6. Herbert Marcuse: Basic and Surplus Alienation

1 As we shall see below, in part because Marcuse is dealing with a future-hypothetical distinction, his formulation is not as precise as it should be: Freudian theory in fact allows for the possibility of a non-*surplus* repressive civilization (cf. G. Horowitz 1977).

2 The adequacy of a temporal model should not be overstated, however. The claim that the rule of the pleasure principle and of the reality principle represent discrete 'stages' of development should not be taken to suggest that there is a point where the rule of either principle is uncontested. Freud admits that 'an organization which was a slave to the pleasure principle and neglected the reality of the external world could not maintain itself alive for the shortest time' and is 'a fiction' (1984, 37n), but also that the rule of the reality principle 'implies no deposing of the pleasure principle' (41).

3 Just as, for Marcuse, Freud failed to distinguish between 'repression' and 'surplus-repression,' for Marx, Hegel failed to distinguish between 'objectification' and 'alienation' (see the section titled 'The "Early Marx" and the Transformation of Labour,' in chapter 4, above).

4 Williams notes that Marx's use of the terms *Basis* and *Grundlage*, rendered

in English as the (economic) 'base,' are translated in French as *'infrastructure'* (1977, 77).

5 Kellner suggests that 'even in works where Marx is never mentioned, such as *Eros and Civilization*, or in those where traditional Marxism is radically questioned, such as *One-Dimensional Man*, Marcuse is using Marxian concepts and methods to expand the Marxian theory' (1984, 5). Agger admits only that Marcuse 'is hazy enough about Marx' to allow for anti-Marxist interpretations of his work to emerge, but that Marcuse does not abandon such crucial Marxian notions as class struggle and alienation of labour (1992, 89). Both argue that Marcuse's 'deviations' from more orthodox Marxist positions are necessitated by the development of advanced capitalism, and are thus necessary to ensure Marxism's continued relevance.

6 Colletti asserts that Marcuse is 'a fierce critic of Marx and of socialism' who at best provides only 'the old liberal rhetoric.' (1972, 140).

7 For sympathetic accounts of the resonances between Heideggerian philosophy and deep ecology, see, for example, Zimmerman (1979) and Foltz (1995). Revelations in the late 1980s of the depth of Heidegger's involvement with the Nazis complicated this connection considerably, causing some Heideggerian deep ecologists, such as Michael Zimmerman, to rethink their position and ask 'to what extent is deep ecology (perhaps unwittingly) compatible with ecofascism?' (2003, 150; see also Zimmerman 1994, 104–33).

8 There are many sources that offer considerably more detailed treatment of Heidegger's views on this score. Among the best are Dreyfus (1991) and Caputo (1993).

9 Historicizing Colletti's inability to see this is more difficult, since he is a contemporary of Marcuse's. But if, as was suggested earlier, Colletti's misreading rests on a failure to distinguish between the ('superstructural') technological rationality and the technical 'base,' we might then see this misreading as one that is 'determined' at a certain level by the nature of advanced capitalism, and that is a function, moreover, of precisely the problematic of advanced capitalism with which the Frankfurt School theorists were centrally concerned: the interpenetration of base and superstructure.

10 See, for example, Bronner (1994, 253). The view seems to be supported by Marcuse's opening admission in *The Aesthetic Dimension*: 'It would be senseless to deny the element of despair inherent in this concern [with aesthetics]: the retreat into a world of fiction where existing conditions are changed and overcome only in the realm of the imagination.' Immediately, however, Marcuse goes on to assert the explicitly *political* character of his aesthetic concerns: 'It seems that art as art expresses a truth, an experience,

a necessity which, although not in the domain of radical praxis, are nevertheless essential components of revolution' (Marcuse 1978, 1).

11 Horowitz, on the other hand, suggests that this is a misrepresentation of Freud's view. Marcuse's dichotomy seems to suggest the possibility of 'sexuality in its very essence' or 'the ideal-typical construct of the id' that can exist 'as such.' But such a thing can only exist in psychoanalytic theory, because the latter defines 'sexuality as such' as 'that which is restrained.' This does not mean, however, that restraint is strictly externally or socially imposed: 'restraint inevitably emerges, and not, in the first instance, out of society's need for work, but out of the biological nature of the organism in which "sexuality as such" is located. Civilization is indeed opposed to sexuality in the sense of the id's drive for total and immediate gratification, but it is so opposed from within, as well as from outside, the organism' (G. Horowitz 1977, 190–1).

7. Denaturalizing Ecological Politics

1 In spite of its title, Eckersley's *Environmentalism and Political Theory* considers only 'green political thought' – a stream that begins, again according to Eckersley, with 'the ecocentric challenge to Marxism.' The academic (sub)discipline of political theory, on the other hand, is generally conceptualized as the study of the history of political thought – a tradition that stretches back to Ancient Greece and often *ends* with Marx (and even where it is pressed into the twentieth century, those thinkers most often mentioned in political theory texts and courses – Arendt, Foucault, Rawls – barely rate a mention in Eckersley's study).

2 This should not be taken to suggest that Bookchin is insensitive to issues of gender domination. Indeed, he suggests that the sexual division of labour may be the first form of institutionalized social domination: 'long before man began to exploit man through the formation of social classes, he began to dominate women in patriarchal and hierarchical relationships' (1987, 67).

3 Plumwood previously went by the name Val Routley, whose ecocentric critique of Marx was discussed in chapter 4, above.

4 Davis's most recent work (2004) suggests the possibility of a study 'explor[ing] the ominous terrain of the interaction' between global climate change and 'the global catastrophe of urban poverty' (12).

Bibliography

Adorno, Theodor W. 1967. *Prisms*. Trans. Samuel and Shierry Weber. London: Neville Spearman.

– 1973. *Negative Dialectics*. Trans. E.B. Ashton. New York: Continuum.

– 1974. *Minima Moralia: Reflections from Damaged Life*. Trans. E.F.N. Jephcott. London: NLB.

– 1978. 'Subject and object.' In *The Essential Frankfurt School Reader*, ed. Andrew Arato and Eike Gebhardt, 497–511. Oxford: Basil Blackwell.

– 1980. 'Commitment.' Trans. Francis McDonagh. In *Aesthetics and Politics*, ed. Ronald Taylor, 177–95. London: Verso.

– 1984. 'The idea of natural history,' Trans. Bob Hullot-Kentor. *Telos* 60 (Summer): 111–24.

– 1991a. 'The essay as form.' Trans. Shierry Weber Nicholsen. In *Notes to Literature*, vol. 1, ed. Rolf Tiedemann, 3–23. New York: Columbia University Press.

– 1991b. 'Trying to understand *Endgame*.' Trans. Shierry Weber Nicholsen. In *Notes to Literature*, vol. 1, ed. Rolf Tiedemann, 241–75. New York: Columbia University Press.

– 1994. 'The stars down to earth: The Los Angeles *Times* astrology column.' In *The Stars Down to Earth and Other Essays on the Irrational in Culture*, ed. Stephen Crook, 34–127. London: Routledge.

– 1998. 'Television as ideology.' In *Critical Models: Interventions and Catchwords*, trans. Henry W. Pickford, 59–70. New York: Columbia University Press.

Agger, Ben. 1992. *The Discourse of Domination: From the Frankfurt School to Postmodernism*. Evanston, IL: Northwestern University Press.

– 1993. *Gender, Culture, and Power: Toward a Feminist Postmodern Critical Theory*. Westport, CT: Praeger.

Alford, C. Fred. 1994. 'Marx, Marcuse, and psychoanalysis: Do they still fit after all these years? In *Marcuse: From the New Left to the Next Left*, ed. John Bokina and Timothy J. Lukes, 131–46. Lawrence: University Press of Kansas.

Alley, Richard B. 2000. *The Two-Mile Time Machine: Ice Cores, Abrupt Climate Change, and Our Future*. Princeton, NJ: Princeton University Press.

Althusser, Louis. 1971. 'Preface to *Capital*, vol. 1.' Trans. Ben Brewster. In *Lenin and Philosophy and Other Essays*. London: NLB.

– 1977. *For Marx*, Trans. Ben Brewster. London: NLB.

– 1982. *Rousseau, Montesquieu, Marx: Politics and History*. Trans. Ben Brewster. London: Verso.

Alway, Joan. 1995. *Critical Theory and Political Possibilities: Conceptions of Emancipatory Politics in the Works of Horkheimer, Adorno, Marcuse, and Habermas*. Westport, CT: Greenwood Press.

Andrews, Jay. 1994. 'The withering away of Marx's inorganic body.' *Research & Society* 7: 69–79.

Aristotle. 1958. *Politics*. Trans. Ernest Barker. London: Oxford University Press.

Avineri, Shlomo. 1968. *The Social and Political Thought of Karl Marx*. Cambridge: Cambridge University Press.

Barthes, Roland. 1973. *Mythologies*. Trans. Annette Lavers. London: Paladin Grafton Books.

Bataille, Georges. 1988. *The Accursed Share: An Essay on General Economy*, vol. 1: *Consumption*. Trans. Robert Hurley. New York: Zone Books.

Baudrillard, Jean. 1981. *For a critique of the political economy of the Sign*. Trans. Charles Levin. St Louis, MO: Telos Press.

– 1983a. 'In the shadow of the silent majorities.' *In the Shadow of the Silent Majorities, or, The End of the Social and Other Essays*. Trans. Paul Foss, John Johnston, and Paul Patton. New York: Semiotext(e).

– 1983b. *Simulations*. Trans. Paul Foss, Paul Patton, and Philip Beitchman. New York: Semiotext(e).

– 1988. *America*. Trans. Chris Turner. London: Verso.

– 1993. *Symbolic Exchange and Death*. Trans. Iain Hamilton Grant. London: Sage.

– 1995. *The Gulf War Did not Take Place*. Trans. Paul Patton. Bloomington: Indiana University Press.

– 1996. *The Perfect Crime*. Trans. Chris Turner. London: Verso.

Becker, Carol. 1994. 'Surveying *The Aesthetic Dimension* at the death of postmodernism.' In *Marcuse: From the New Left to the Next Left*, ed. John Bokina and Timothy J. Lukes. Lawrence: University of Kansas Press.

Benhabib, Seyla. 1987. 'The generalized and the concrete other: The Kohlberg-Gilligan controversy and feminist theory.' In *Feminism as Critique: On the Pol-*

itics of Gender, ed. Seyla Benhabib and Drucilla Cornell. Minneapolis: University of Minnesota Press.

Benjamin, Walter. 1968. 'The image of Proust.' *Illuminations*, ed. Hannah Arendt and trans. Harry Zohn, 201–15. New York: Schocken Books.

Berman, Russell. 2002. 'Adorno's Politics.' In *Adorno: A Critical Reader*, ed. Nigel Gibson and Andrew Rubin, 110–31. Oxford: Basil Blackwell.

Biehl, Janet. 1991. *Rethinking Ecofeminist Politics*. Boston, MA: South End Press.

Bloom, Allan. 1997. 'Rousseau's critique of liberal constitutionalism.' In *The Legacy of Rousseau*, ed. Clifford Orwin and Nathan Tarcov, 143–67. Chicago: University of Chicago Press.

Boggs, Carl. 1997. 'The great retreat: Decline of the public sphere in late twentieth-century America.' *Theory and Society* 26, no. 6 (December): 741–80.

Bokina, John. 1994. 'Marcuse revisited: An introduction.' *Marcuse: From the New Left to the Next Left*, ed. John Bokina and Timothy J. Lukes, 1–24. Lawrence: University Press of Kansas.

Bookchin, Murray. 1987. *The Modern Crisis*. 2nd rev. ed. Montreal: Black Rose Press.

– 1990. *The Philosophy of Social Ecology: Essays on Dialectical Naturalism*. Montreal: Black Rose Press.

– 1991. *The Ecology of Freedom: The Emergence and Dissolution of Hierarchy*. Rev. ed. Montreal: Black Rose Press.

Booth, William James. 1989. 'Gone fishing: Making sense of Marx's concept of Communism.' *Political Theory* 17, no. 2 (May): 205–22.

Bronner, Stephen Eric. 1994. *Of Critical Theory and Its Theorists*. Cambridge, MA: Blackwell.

Buck-Morss, Susan. 1977. *The Origin of Negative Dialectics: Theodor W. Adorno, Walter Benjamin, and the Frankfurt Institute*. New York: The Free Press.

Bullard, Robert D. 1990. *Dumping in Dixie: Race, Class and Environmental Quality*. Boulder, CO: Westview.

– ed. 1993. *Confronting Environmental Racism: Voices from the Grassroots*. Boston, MA: South End Press.

Butler, Judith. 1990. *Gender Trouble: Feminism and the Subversion of Identity*. New York: Routledge.

– 1993. *Bodies That Matter: On the Discursive Limits of 'Sex.'* New York: Routledge.

Caputo, John D. 1993. *Demythologizing Heidegger*. Bloomington: Indiana University Press.

Cassirer, Ernst. 1954. *The Question of Jean-Jacques Rousseau*. Ed. and trans. Peter Gay. New York: Columbia University Press.

Chaloupka, William. 2000. 'Jagged Terrain: Cronon, Soulé, and the struggle over nature and deconstruction in environmental theory.' *Strategies: Journal of Theory, Culture & Politics* 13, no. 1 (May): 23–38.

Cheney, Jim. 1995. 'Postmodern environmental ethics: Ethics as bioregional narrative.' In *Postmodern Environmental Ethics*, ed. Max Oelschlaeger, 23–42. Albany: State University of New York Press.

Clark, John P. 1989. 'Marx's inorganic body.' *Environmental Ethics* 11, no. 3 (Fall): 243–58.

Cobban, Alfred. 1964. *Rousseau and the Modern State*. 2nd ed. London: George Allen & Unwin.

Cohen, Gerald A. 1978. *Karl Marx's Theory of History: A Defence*. Oxford: Oxford University Press.

Colletti, Lucio. 1972. *From Rousseau to Lenin: Studies in Ideology and Society*. Trans. John Merrington and Judith White. New York: Monthly Review Books.

Conley, Verena Andermatt. 1997. *Ecopolitics: The Environment in Poststructuralist Thought*. New York: Routledge.

Connolly, William E. 1988. *Political Theory and Modernity*. Oxford: Basil Blackwell.

Cronon, William. 1995. 'Introduction: In search of nature.' In *Uncommon Ground: Toward Reinventing Nature*, ed. William Cronon, 23–56. New York: W.W. Norton.

Darier, Éric. 1999. 'Foucault and the environment: An introduction.' In *Discourses of the Environment*, ed. Éric Darier, 1–33. Oxford: Blackwell.

Davis, Mike. 1998. *Ecology of Fear: Los Angeles and the Imagination of Disaster*. New York: Vintage Books.

– 2001. *Late Victorian Holocausts: El Nino Famines and the Making of the Third World*. London: Verso.

– 2002. *Dead Cities and Other Tales*. New York: W.W. Norton.

– 2004. 'Planet of slums: Urban involution and the informal proletariat.' *New Left Review* 26 (March–April): 5–34.

De Certeau, Michel. 1984. *The Practice of Everyday Life*. Trans. Steven Rendall. Berkeley: University of California Press.

de Man, Paul. 1979. *Allegories of Reading: Figural Language in Rousseau, Nietzsche, Rilke and Proust*. New Haven, CT: Yale University Press.

Debord, Guy. 1995. *The Society of the Spectacle*. Trans. Donald Nicholson-Smith. New York: Zone Books.

Deleuze, Gilles. 1984. *Kant's Critical Philosophy*. Trans. Hugh Tomlinson and Barbara Habberjam. Minneapolis: University of Minnesota Press.

– 1988. *Foucault*. Ed. and trans. Sean Hand. Minneapolis: University of Minnesota Press.

Dent, N.J.H. 1988. *Rousseau: An Introduction to His Psychological, Social and Political Theory*. Oxford: Basil Blackwell.

Derrida, Jacques. 1974. *Of Grammatology*. Trans. Gayatri Chakravorty Spivak. Baltimore, MD: Johns Hopkins University Press.

Devall, Bill, and George Sessions. 1985. *Deep Ecology: Living as if Nature Mattered*. Salt Lake City: Peregrine Smith Books.

Dings, John. 1994. 'Marx, nature, history: A reply to Jay Andrews.' *Research & Society* 7:80–3.

Dizard, Jan E. 1993. 'Going wild: The contested terrain of nature.' In *In the Nature of Things: Language, Politics, and the Environment*, ed. Jane Bennett and William Chaloupka, 111–35. Minneapolis: University of Minnesota Press.

Dobson, Andrew. 1998. *Justice and the Environment: Conceptions of Environmental Sustainability and Dimensions of Social Justice*. Oxford: Oxford University Press.

Dollimore, Jonathan. 1989. *Radical Tragedy*. 2nd ed. London: Harvester Wheatsheaf.

Dreyfus, Hubert L. 1991. *Being-in-the-World: A Commentary on Heidegger's Being and Time, Division I*. Cambridge, MA: MIT Press.

Eagleton, Terry. 1990. 'Art after Auschwitz: Adorno's political aesthetics.' In *The Significance of Theory*, 39–70. Oxford: Basil Blackwell.

Eckersley, Robyn. 1992. *Environmentalism and Political Theory: Toward an Ecocentric Approach*. Albany: State University of New York Press.

Evernden, Neil. 1992. *The Social Creation of Nature*. Baltimore, MD: Johns Hopkins University Press.

Fermon, Nicole. 1997. *Domesticating Passions: Rousseau, Woman and Nation*. Hanover, NH: Wesleyan University Press.

Foltz, Bruce V. 1995. *Inhabiting the Earth: Heidegger, Environmental Ethics, and the Metaphysics of Nature*. Atlantic Highlands, NJ: Humanities Press.

Foster, John Bellamy. 1998. 'The Communist Manifesto and the environment.' In *The Socialist Register 1998*, ed. Leo Panitch and Colin Leys, 169–89. Woodbridge, Suffolk, UK: Merlin Press.

Foucault, Michel. 1972. *The Archaeology of Knowledge and the Discourse on Language*. Trans. A.M. Sheridan Smith. New York: Pantheon Books.

– 1979. *Discipline and Punish: The Birth of the Prison*. Trans. Alan Sheridan. New York: Vintage.

– 1980. 'Truth and power.' In *Power/Knowledge: Selected Interviews and Other Writings 1972–1977*, ed. Colin Gordon, 109–33. New York: Pantheon Books.

– 1984a. 'Nietzsche, genealogy, history.' In *The Foucault Reader*, ed. Paul Rabinow, 76–100. New York: Pantheon Books.

– 1984b. 'What is an author?' In *The Foucault Reader*, ed. Paul Rabinow, 101–20. New York: Pantheon Books.

– 1989. 'The ethic of the case of the self as a practice of freedom.' In *The Final Foucault*, ed. James Bernauer and David Rasmussen. Cambridge, MA: MIT Press.

– 1990. *The History of Sexuality*, vol. 1: *An Introduction*. Trans. Robert Hurley. New York: Vintage Books.

Fox, Warwick. 1995. *Toward a Transpersonal Ecology: Developing New Foundations for Environmentalism*. Albany: State University of New York Press.

Fraser, Nancy. 1989. *Unruly Practices: Power, Discourse and Gender in Contemporary Social Theory*. Minneapolis: University of Minnesota Press.

Freud, Sigmund. 1976. *The Interpretation of Dreams*. Trans. James Strachey. London: Penguin Books.

– 1984. 'Two principles of mental functioning.' *On Metapsychology*, trans. James Strachey, 35–44. London: Penguin Books.

Freud, Sigmund, and Joseph Breuer. 1974. *Studies on Hysteria*. Trans. and ed. James and Alix Strachey. Harmondsworth, Middlesex, UK: Penguin Books.

Fromm, Erich H. 1969. *Escape from Freedom*. New York: Henry Holt.

Gane, Mike. 1991. *Baudrillard: Critical and Fatal Theory*. London: Routledge.

– 1993. 'Introduction.' In Jean Baudrillard, *Symbolic Exchange and Death*. London: Sage.

Gare, Arran E. 1995. *Postmodernism and the Environmental Crisis*. London: Routledge.

Gay, Peter. 1987. 'Introduction.' In Jean-Jacques Rousseau, *The Basic Political Writings*, vii–xvii. Indianapolis: Hackett.

Gibson, Nigel. 2002. 'Rethinking an old saw: Dialectical negativity, utopia, and *Negative Dialectics* in Adorno's Hegelian Marxism.' In *Adorno: A Critical Reader*, ed. Nigel Gibson and Andrew Rubin, 257–91. Oxford: Basil Blackwell.

Godzich, Wlad. 1994. 'The semiotics of semiotics.' *The Culture of Literacy*, 193–216. Cambridge, MA: Harvard University Press.

Goodin, Robert E. 1992. *Green Political Theory*. Cambridge, UK: Polity Press.

Gorz, Andre. 1980. *Ecology as Politics*. Trans. Patsy Vigderman and Jonathan Cloud. Montreal: Black Rose.

Gould, Stephen Jay. 1994. 'American polygeny and craniometry before Darwin: Blacks and Indians as separate, inferior species.' In *The Racial Economy of Science: Toward a Democratic Future*, ed. Sandra Harding, 84–115. Bloomington: Indiana University Press.

Grundmann, Reiner. 1991. *Marxism and Ecology*. Oxford: Clarendon.

Guha, Ramachandra. 1989. 'Radical American environmentalism and wilderness preservation: A Third-World critique.' *Environmental Ethics* 11, no. 1 (Spring): 71–80.

– 2000. *Environmentalism: A Global History*. New York: Longman.

Guha, Ramachandra, and Joan Martinez-Alier. 1997. *Varieties of Environmentalism: Essays North and South*. London: Earthscan.

Haraway, Donna J. 1991. 'A cyborg manifesto: Science, technology, and Socialist-feminism in the late twentieth century.' In *Simians, Cyborgs, and Women: The Reinvention of Nature*, 149–81. New York: Routledge.

Harvey, David. 1996. *Justice, Nature and the Geography of Difference*. Cambridge, MA: Blackwell.

Hay, Peter. 2002. *Main Currents in Western Environmental Thought*. Sydney: UNSW Press.

Heidegger, Martin. 1962. *Being and Time*, trans. John Macquarrie and Edward Robinson. London: SCM Press.

– 1977. 'The question concerning technology,' trans. William Lovitt. In *The Question concerning Technology and Other Essays*. New York: Harper and Row.

Hohendahl, Peter Uwe. 1995. *Prismatic Thought: Theodor W. Adorno*. Lincoln: University of Nebraska Press.

Horkheimer, Max, and Theodor W. Adorno. 1987. *Dialectic of Enlightenment*. Trans. John Cumming. New York: Continuum.

Horowitz, Asher. 1987. *Rousseau, Nature, and History*. Toronto: University of Toronto Press.

Horowitz, Gad. 1977. *Repression: Basic and Surplus Repression in Psychoanalytic Theory: Freud, Reich, and Marçuse*. Toronto: University of Toronto Press.

– 1987. 'The Foucaultian impasse: No sex, no self, no revolution.' *Political Theory* 15, no. 1 (February): 61–80.

Jameson, Fredric. 1971. *Marxism and Form: Twentieth-Century Dialectical Theories of Literature*. Princeton, NJ: Princeton University Press.

– 1980. 'Reflections in conclusion.' In *Aesthetics and Politics*, ed. Ronald Taylor. 196–213. London: Verso.

– 1988. 'Periodizing the 60s.' *The Ideologies of Theory*, vol. 2: *The Syntax of History*. Minneapolis: University of Minnesota Press.

– 1990. *Late Marxism: Adorno, or, The Persistence of the Dialectic*. London: Verso.

– 1991. *Postmodernism, or, the Cultural Logic of Late Capitalism*. Durham, NC: Duke University Press.

– 1992. *The Geopolitical Aesthetic: Cinema and Space in the World System*. Bloomington: Indiana University Press.

– 1994. 'The antinomies of postmodernity.' In *The Seeds of Time*, 1–71. New York: Columbia University Press.

Jarvis, Simon. 1998. *Adorno: A Critical Introduction*. New York: Routledge.

Jay, Martin. 1984. 'Adorno in America.' *New German Critique* 31 (Winter): 157–82.

Kant, Immanuel. 1950. *Critique of Pure Reason*. Trans. Norman Kemp Smith. London: Macmillan.

– 1988. 'What is Enlightenment?' In *Kant: Selections*, ed. Lewis White Beck, 459–67. New York: MacMillan.

Kellner, Douglas. 1984. *Herbert Marcuse and the Crisis of Marxism*. London: Macmillan.

– 1989. *Jean Baudrillard: From Marxism to Postmodernism and Beyond*. Stanford, CA: Stanford University Press.

Klinenberg, Eric. 1999. 'Denaturalizing disaster: A social autopsy of the 1995 Chicago heat wave.' *Theory and Society* 28, no. 2 (April): 239–95.

Kovel, Joel. 2002. *The Enemy of Nature: The End of Capitalism or the End of the World*. Halifax: Fernwood.

Lacan, Jacques. 1981. *The Four Fundamental Concepts of Psycho-Analysis*. Ed. Jacques-Alain Miller, trans. Alan Sheridan. New York: W.W. Norton.

Laclau, Ernesto, and Chantal Mouffe. 1985. *Hegemony and Socialist Strategy: Towards a Radical Democratic Politics*. New York: Verso.

Lears, Jackson. 1997. 'Reality matters.' *Social Text* 50 (15, 1): 143–5.

Lee, Donald C. 1980. 'On the Marxian view of the relationship between man and nature.' *Environmental Ethics* 2, no. 1 (Spring): 3–16.

Leiss, William. 1974. *The Domination of Nature*, paperback ed. Boston: Beacon Press.

Levin, Charles, and Arthur Kroker. 1984. 'Introduction: Baudrillard's challenge.' *Canadian Journal of Political and Social Theory* 8, nos. 1–2 (Winter/Spring): 5–16.

Lewis, C.S. 1990. 'Nature.' In *Studies in Words*. Cambridge, UK: Cambridge University Press.

Luke, Timothy W. 1991. 'Power and politics in hyperreality: The critical project of Jean Baudrillard.' *Social Science Journal* 28, no. 3. 347–67.

– 1994. 'Marcuse and ecology.' In *Marcuse: From the New Left to the Next Left*, ed. John Bokina and Timothy J. Lukes, 189–207. Lawrence: University Press of Kansas.

– 1997. 'Green consumerism: Ecology and the ruse of recycling.' In *Ecocritique: Contesting the Politics of Nature, Economy, and Culture*, 115–36. Minneapolis: University of Minnesota Press.

Lukes, Timothy J. 1985. *The Flight into Inwardness: An Exposition and Critique of Herbert Marcuse's Liberative Aesthetics*. Toronto: Associated University Presses.

Lyotard, Jean-Francois. 1984. *The Postmodern Condition: A Report on Knowledge*. Trans. Geoff Bennington and Brian Massumi. Minneapolis: University of Minnesota Press.

Macpherson, C.B. 1962. *The Political Theory of Possessive Individualism: Hobbes to Locke*. Oxford: Oxford University Press.

Marcuse, Herbert. 1964. *One-Dimensional Man: Studies in the Ideology of Advanced Industrial Society*. Boston: Beacon Press.

– 1968. *Negations: Essays in Critical Theory*. Trans. Jeremy J. Shapiro. Boston: Beacon Press.

– 1970. *Five Lectures: Psychoanalysis, Politics, and Utopia*. Trans. Jeremy J. Shapiro and Shierry M. Weber. Boston: Beacon Press.

– 1972a. *An Essay on Liberation*. London: Penguin Books.

– 1972b. *Counterrevolution and Revolt*. Boston: Beacon Press.

– 1978. *The Aesthetic Dimension: Toward a Critique of Marxist Aesthetics*. Boston: Beacon Press.

– 1987. *Eros and Civilization: A Philosophical Inquiry into Freud*. London: Ark Paperbacks.

Marx, Karl. 1975. *Karl Marx: Early Writings*. Trans. Rodney Livingstone and Gregor Benton. New York: Vintage.

– 1977a. *Capital: A Critique of Political Economy*, vol. 1, trans. Ben Fowkes. New York: Vintage.

– 1977b. *Karl Marx: Selected Writings*, ed. David McLellan. Oxford: Oxford University Press.

– 1978. *The Marx-Engels Reader*. 2nd ed. Ed. Robert C. Tucker. New York: W.W. Norton.

– 1981. *Capital: A Critique of Political Economy*, vol. 3. Trans. David Fernbach. London: Penguin Books.

Marx, Karl, and Friedrich Engels. 1947. *The German Ideology (Parts I & III)*. Ed. R. Pascal. New York: International Publishers.

McKibben, Bill. 1989. *The End of Nature*. Toronto: Anchor Books.

Merchant, Carolyn. 1995. 'Reinventing Eden: Western culture as a recovery narrative.' In *Uncommon Ground: Toward Reinventing Nature*, ed. William Cronon, 132–59. New York: W.W. Norton.

Meszaros, Istvan. 1970. *Marx's Theory of Alienation*. 2nd ed. London: Merlin Press.

Meyer, John M. 2001. *Political Nature: Environmentalism and the Interpretation of Western Thought*. Cambridge, MA: MIT Press.

Mitrany, David. 1961. *Marx against the Peasant: A Study in Social Dogmatism*. New York: Collier Books.

Morrison, Roy. 1994. 'Two questions for theory and practice: Can you be Marxist and Green? Can Marxism be Green?' *Rethinking Marxism* 7, no. 3 (Fall): 128–36.

Naess, Arne. 1973. 'The shallow and the deep, long-range ecology movement.' *Inquiry* 16: 95–100.

Nagele, Rainer. 1983. 'The scene of the other: Theodor W. Adorno's negative dialectic in the context of poststructuralism.' *Boundary* 2 11, nos. 1–2: 59–79.

Nietzsche, Friedrich. 1956. *The Birth of Tragedy and The Genealogy of Morals*. Trans. Francis Golffing. Garden City, NY: Doubleday.

O'Connor, James. 1998. *Natural Causes: Essays in Ecological Marxism*. New York: Guilford.

Ollman, Bertell. 1971. *Alienation: Marx's Concept of Man in Capitalist Society*. Cambridge: Cambridge University Press.

Phelan, Shane. 1993. 'Intimate distance: The dislocation of nature in modernity.' *In the Nature of Things: Language, Politics, and the Environment*, ed. Jane Bennett and William Chaloupka, 44–62. Minneapolis: University of Minnesota Press.

Plattner, Marc F. 1997. 'Rousseau and the origins of nationalism.' *The Legacy of Rousseau*, ed. Clifford Orwin and Nathan Tarcov, 183–99. Chicago: University of Chicago Press.

Plumwood, Val. 1993. 'Nature, self, and gender: Feminism, environmental philosophy, and the critique of rationalism.' In *Environmental Philosophy: From Animal Rights to Radical Ecology*, ed. Michael E. Zimmerman, 284–309. Englewood Cliffs, NJ: Prentice-Hall.

Postone, Moishe. 1993. *Time, Labor and Social Domination: A Reinterpretation of Marx's Critical Theory*. Cambridge, UK: Cambridge University Press.

Rattansi, Ali. 1982. *Marx and the Division of Labour*. London: Macmillan Press.

Rodman, John. 1993. 'Restoring nature: Natives and exotics.' In *In the Nature of Things: Language, Politics, and the Environment*, ed. Jane Bennett and William Chaloupka, 139–53. Minneapolis: University of Minnesota Press.

Rolston, Holmes, III. 1986. *Philosophy Gone Wild: Essays in Environmental Ethics*. Buffalo: Prometheus Books.

Rose, Gillian. 1978. *The Melancholy Science: An Introduction to the Thought of Theodor W. Adorno*. London: Macmillan Press.

Ross, Andrew. 1991. *Strange Weather: Culture, Science and Technology in the Age of Limits*. New York: Verso.

– 1994. *The Chicago Gangster Theory of Life: Nature's Debt to Society*. London: Verso.

Rothberg, Michael. 1997. 'After Adorno: Culture in the wake of catastrophe.' *New German Critique* 72 (Fall): 45–81.

Rousseau, Jean-Jacques. 1911. *Emile*. Trans. Barbara Foxley. London: J.M. Dent.

– 1964. *Oeuvres completes de Jean-Jacques Rousseau*, vol. 3. Dijon: Gallimard.

– 1966. 'Essay on the origin of languages.' Trans. John H. Moran. In *'On the Origin of Language' (Two Essays by Jean-Jacques Rousseau and Johann Gottfried Herder)*, 1–83. New York: Frederick Ungar.

– 1987. *Basic Political Writings of Jean-Jacques Rousseau*. Ed. and trans. Donald A. Cress. Indianapolis, IN: Hackett.

– 1997a. *The Discourses and Other Early Political Writings*. Ed. and trans. Victor Gourevitch. Cambridge, UK: Cambridge University Press.

– 1997b. *The Social Contract and Other Later Political Writings*. Ed. and trans. Victor Gourevitch. Cambridge, UK: Cambridge University Press.

Routley, Val. 1981. 'On Karl Marx as an environmental hero.' *Environmental Ethics* 3, no. 3 (Fall): 237–44.

Ruben, Matthew. 1998. '*12 Monkeys* and the failure of everything: For a new method.' *Rethinking Marxism* 10, no. 2 (Summer): 106–23.

Rushdie, Salman. 1992. *The Wizard of Oz*. London: British Film Institute Publishing.

Sahlins, Marshall. 1972. *Stone Age Economics*. New York: Aldine de Gruyter.

Salleh, Ariel Kay. 1988. 'Epistemology and the metaphors of production: An eco-Feminist reading of critical theory.' *Studies in the Humanities* 15, no. 2 (December): 130–9.

Sandilands, Catriona. 1995. 'From natural identity to radical democracy.' *Environmental Ethics* 17, no. 1 (Spring): 75–91.

– 1997. 'Mother Nature, the cyborg, and the queer: Ecofeminism and (more) questions of identity.' *NWSA Journal* 9, no. 3 (Fall): 18–40.

– 2002. 'Opinionated natures: Toward a Green public culture.' *Democracy and the Claims of Nature: Critical Perspectives for a New Century*, ed. Ben A. Minteer and Bob Pepperman Taylor, 117–32. Lanham, MD: Rowman & Littlefield.

Schmidt, Alfred. 1971. *The Concept of Nature in Marx*. Trans. Ben Fowkes. London: NLB.

Seers, Dudley. 1979. 'The congruence of Marxism and other neoclassical doctrines.' *Toward a New Strategy for Development*, ed. Albert O. Hirschman, 1–17. Toronto: Pergamon Press.

Shakespeare, William. 1988. *The Complete Works*. ed. Stanley Wells, Gary Taylor, John Jowett, and William Montgomery. Oxford: Clarendon Press.

Shaw, William H. 1978. *Marx's Theory of History*. Stanford, CA: Stanford University Press.

Smith, Mick. 1995. 'Cheney and the myth of postmodernism.' In *Postmodern Environmental Ethics*, ed. Max Oelschlaeger, 261–76. Albany: State University of New York Press.

Smith, Neil. 1990. *Uneven Development: Nature, Capital and the Production of Space*, 2nd ed. Cambridge, MA: Basil Blackwell.

Soja, Edward W. 1989. *Postmodern Geographies: The Reassertion of Space in Critical Social Theory*. London: Verso.

Soper, Kate. 1995. *What Is Nature? Culture, Politics and the Non-Human*. Cambridge, MA: Blackwell.

Starobinski, Jean. 1988. *Jean-Jacques Rousseau: Transparency and Obstruction*. Trans. Arthur Goldhammer. Chicago: University of Chicago Press.

Stein, Rebecca. 2002. 'Israeli leisure, "Palestinian terror," and the question of Palestine (again).' *Theory & Event* 6, no. 3 [http://muse.jhu.edu/journals/theory_and_event/v006/6.3stein.html]

Thiele, Leslie Paul. 1995. 'Nature and freedom: A Heideggerian critique of biocentric and sociocentric environmentalism.' *Environmental Ethics* 17, no. 2 (Summer): 171–90.

– 1999. *Environmentalism for a New Millennium: The Challenge of Coevolution*. New York: Oxford University Press.

Tolman, Charles. 1981. 'Karl Marx, alienation, and the mastery of nature.' *Environmental Ethics* 3, no. 1 (Spring): 63–74.

Turse, Nicholas. [n.d.]. 'New morning, changing weather: Radical youth of the millennial age.' *49th Parallel* 4 [http://artsweb.bham.ac.uk/49thparallel]

Vogel, Steven. 1996. *Against Nature: The Concept of Nature in Critical Theory*. Albany: State University of New York Press.

Warren, Bill. 1980. *Imperialism: Pioneer of Capitalism*. London: Verso.

Warren, Karen J. 1993. 'The power and the promise of ecological feminism.' In *Environmental Philosophy: From Animal Rights to Radical Ecology*, ed. Michael E. Zimmerman, 320–41. Englewood Cliffs, NJ: Prentice-Hall.

Wellmer, Albrecht. 1985. 'Reason, Utopia, and the *Dialectic of Enlightenment*.' In *Habermas and Modernity*, ed. Richard J. Bernstein. Cambridge, MA: MIT Press.

Whitebook, Joel. 1985. 'Reason and happiness: Some psychoanalytic themes in critical theory.' In *Habermas and Modernity*, ed. Richard J. Bernstein, 140–60. Cambridge, MA: MIT Press.

Witkin, Robert W. 2003. *Adorno on Popular Culture*. New York: Routledge.

Williams, Raymond. 1976. *Keywords: A Vocabulary of Culture and Society*. Glasgow: Fontana/Croom Helm.

– 1977. *Marxism and Literature*. Oxford: Oxford University Press.

– 1980. 'Ideas of Nature.' *Problems in Materialism and Culture (Selected Essays)*. London: Verso. 67–85.

Wolin, Richard. 1992. 'Mimesis, Utopia, and reconciliation: A redemptive critique of Adorno's *Aesthetic Theory*.' In *The Terms of Cultural Criticism: The Frankfurt School, Existentialism, Poststructuralism*, 62–79. New York: Columbia University Press.

World Commission on Environment and Development. 1987. *Our Common Future*. Oxford: Oxford University Press.

Xenos, Nicholas. 1989. *Scarcity and Modernity*. New York: Routledge.

Zimmerman, Michael. 1979. 'Marx and Heidegger on the technological domination of nature.' *Philosophy Today* 23 (Summer): 99–112.

– 1994. *Contesting Earth's Future: Radical Ecology and Postmodernity*. Berkeley: University of California Press.

– 2003. 'On reconciling progressivism and environmentalism.' In *Explorations in Environmental Political Theory: Thinking about What We Value*, ed. Joel Jay Kassiola, 149–77. Armonk, NY: M.E. Sharpe.

Žižek, Slavoj. 1989. 'How did Marx invent the symptom?' *The Sublime Object of Ideology*. 11–53. London: Verso.

– 1994. *The Metastases of Enjoyment: Six Essays on Woman and Causality*. London: Verso.

Index